AF478185

LYRIC TRADE

LYRIC TRADE

READING THE SUBJECT IN THE POSTWAR LONG POEM

Julia Bloch

UNIVERSITY OF IOWA PRESS | IOWA CITY

University of Iowa Press, Iowa City 52242
Copyright © 2024 by the University of Iowa Press
uipress.uiowa.edu

Printed in the United States of America

Design by April Leidig

Printed on acid-free paper

Library of Congress Cataloging-in-Publication Data
Names: Bloch, Julia (Julia Alexandra), author.
Title: Lyric Trade: Reading the Subject in the Postwar Long Poem /
Julia Bloch.
Description: Iowa City: University of Iowa Press, 2024. |
Series: Contemporary North American Poetry Series | Includes
bibliographical references and index.
Identifiers: LCCN 2023031428 (print) | LCCN 2023031429 (ebook) |
ISBN 9781609389437 (paperback; acid-free paper) |
ISBN 9781609389444 (ebook)
Subjects: LCSH: Lyric poetry—History and criticism. | Lyric poetry—
Philosophy. | Poetics. | LCGFT: Literary criticism.
Classification: LCC PN1356.B66 2024 (print) | LCC PN1356 (ebook) |
DDC 809.1/4—dc23/eng/20231018
LC record available at https://lccn.loc.gov/2023031428
LC ebook record available at https://lccn.loc.gov/2023031429

A portion of chapter 1 originally appeared as "'Shut Your Rhetorics
in a Box': Gwendolyn Brooks and Lyric Dilemma," in *Tulsa Studies
in Women's Literature* 35, no. 2 (Fall 2016): 439–62; a portion of
chapter 4 originally appeared as "Alice Notley's Descent: Modernist
Genealogies and Gendered Literary Inheritance," in *Journal of
Modern Literature* 35, no. 3 (Spring 2012): 1–24; and portions of
chapter 5 originally appeared as "Epic Silence: On Myung Mi Kim's
Under Flag," in *Jacket2* and *Syndicate*. Excerpts from *Civil Bound*
by Myung Mi Kim (2019) are reprinted by permission of
Omnidawn Publishing. Copyright © 2019 by Myung Mi Kim.
All rights reserved.

CONTENTS

ACKNOWLEDGMENTS

A scholarly book is an act of collective imagining, and I am grateful to the many people who fostered the conditions necessary to complete this work.

Thank you to Barbara Allen and Rich Keiser, who first introduced me to the thrilling practice of deep-dive research; to Chana Bloch, Stephen Ratcliffe, and Elizabeth Willis, my first models of the poet-critic; to Bob Perelman, an unfailingly supportive and perspicacious advisor; to Charles Bernstein, who showed me how to think beyond received ways of reading; and to Josephine Nock-Hee Park, who taught me how to write about what you love. I am also indebted to Rachel Blau DuPlessis, whose seminar on the long poem served as the origin point for this book (and who was the first person to entertain my puzzlement over lyric), and to Al Filreis, who has created so many different "third spaces" in which to be a poet, teacher, and thinker that I can't fathom them all.

My utmost gratitude to Dee Morris, Alan Golding, and Lynn Keller of the Contemporary North American Poetry Series at University of Iowa Press, who cheered on this project even when the dual interventions of a pandemic and a newborn slowed its pace considerably. Your patience and goodwill as editors are without parallel. I also want to thank Andrea Brady and Joseph Jonghyun Jeon for their incredibly constructive feedback on the manuscript, as well as Knar Gavin, Josh Rutner, and Kenna O'Rourke for sterling editorial assistance, and Meredith Stabel at the University of Iowa Press for her care throughout the stages of publishing.

I have been fortunate to find community with a number of brilliant interlocutors who in many cases double as running partners, poetic allies, and close friends. Huge thanks to the Philadelphia-based writing group that workshopped early drafts of this book with kindness and rigor: Megan Cook, Sarah Dowling, Emily Hyde, Greta LaFleur, Melanie Micir, Jessica Rosenberg, Poulomi Saha, and Emma Stapely. And to the Penn reading groups in poetics and modernism, where Aliki Caloyeras, Sarah Dowling, Jonathan Fedors, Jessica Lowenthal, Jane Malcolm, Melanie Micir, Amy Paeth, Katie Price, Kathy Lou Schultz, Joshua Schuster, and

Greg Steirer taught me how to keep a field of inquiry restlessly open. A cluster of astonishingly smart peers at UC Berkeley generously added me to their writing workshop when I relocated back to San Francisco: thank you to Natalia Cecire, Hillary Gravendyk, Charles Legere, and Katie Simon. Extra thanks to Janet Neigh and Divya Victor for adventures in feminist poetics, and boundless cups of coffee to Sarah Dowling, Matt Goldmark, Jane Malcolm, and Emily Weissbourd, who read way more drafts than I deserved with patience and enthusiasm.

When I was teaching in the Bard College MAT Program in Delano, California, talented colleagues taught me that the twin labors of writing and teaching really are beautifully intertwined: thank you to Susan Cridland-Hughes, Carla Finkelstein, Leticia Garza, Merry Pawlowski, Logan Robertson, Laura Salas, Adam Sawyer, Brett Schmoll, Adrienne Walser, and William Webb. Since returning to the University of Pennsylvania, I have been surrounded by colleagues who carve out radically kind ways of being in the academy, including Gwendolyn Beetham, R. J. Bernocco, Laynie Browne, Christy Davids, Brooke O'Harra, Sharon Hayes, J †Johnson, Jamie-Lee Josselyn, Alli Katz, Jessica Lowenthal, Brooke O'Harra, Mingo Reynolds, and many others at the Center for Programs in Contemporary Writing and Kelly Writers House.

Thanks to Susan E. Erickson for showing me how to do the often unrewarded work of paying attention to women artists (and for weighing in with her musicological expertise on my sometimes harebrained thinking on the cadence) and to Sarah, Jonathan, Isaac, and Dominic Modrow for the Sunday Zooms, cubing demos, Sonic trivia lessons, and always the delicious, delicious meals. Thank you to Ella Konefal, Sophia Durka, and the caring teachers at Children's Community School in West Philadelphia. And to Barbara Joan Tiger Bass for July applesauce, Friday poems, and more than twenty years of sustaining friendship.

To Syd and Rafa Zolf, thank you for "building a new road" with me.

Robert Samson Bloch taught me to read everything and teach what you love. He did not live to see this book in print, but he was happy it was on its way. I dedicate it to him.

LYRIC TRADE

INTRODUCTION

Lyric Trade

To begin: two contemporary poems. Both are a kind of elegy; both are a kind of protest poem. Both play with different kinds of language: one plays with meter and rhyme; the other, with caesura and fragment. Each poem makes an argument about how language makes meaning. Each poem makes an argument about how language can fall short of saying what it ought to be able to say.

Each poem makes this argument using something it calls lyric. Something the poem calls lyric is cast out, and then is invited back in. One meaning of lyric is exchanged for another. It is not immediately clear whether lyric is a way of speaking, or a sort of musicality, or a certain tone, or a metrical or rhythmic form, like a ballad or a sonnet. What is clear is that something called lyric is very important to these poems and to what they have to say about language's possibilities—and its failures.

The first poem, written in 2017 by Evie Shockley, begins with a refusal. Shockley's poem uses the word "lyric" in its title to denounce racist nationalism. The title is long, complexly punctuated, and set in lower case: "a-lyrical ballad (or, how america reminds us of the value of family)." This title conveys a lot, but at least two meanings are clear. First, the hyphen in the title refuses the putative populism of Wordsworth and Coleridge's 1798 collection *Lyrical Ballads*, a collection that purported to set the "real language of men" to "metrical arrangement": to reject ornament and instead to embrace a kind of truth. Second, the parenthetical in the title is a smirk, ironizing the notion of US family values. Shockley's poem opens with three stanzas about Emmett Till, the Black Chicago teenager whose murder galvanized the US civil rights movement. The stanzas alternate metrical and sonic regularity with proselike free verse, and they end on a rhyming couplet with an italicized refrain:

> he was a boy from chicago, in mississippi heat,
> being as bad as a good boy could be,
> whistling his eyeful of an off-limits she,
>
> > and her menfolk dragged him out of bed, beat him to death, tied
> > a cotton gin to his body, and sank him in the tallahatchie river.
>
> it was three days before the remains were retrieved.
> *and the family grieved ~ o ~ the black family grieved*[1]

After the alyrical stance of its title, the poem enacts a number of supposedly lyric constraints, excesses, and refusals: extra stresses, free-verse lines, unrhymed couplets—but also rhyme, balladic stresses, and narration. The rest of the poem repeats the three-stanza pattern six more times for six more victims, the "black family" each time grieving the recursive violence that, as the title posits, "reminds us" of the failures of "American" values. It becomes clear what "family values" really means: care, integrity, or life itself promised to some US citizens and not others. The poem forges a braid of contrasts: the patterned regularity of the first stanza serves as a foil for the free verse of the middle couplet, while the elegiac italicized refrain upends the frank narrative of the middle couplet. Shockley's poem both refuses and enacts something its title calls lyric. This alyrical ballad is an argument about how certain forms cannot fully reckon with race-based murder in the United States.

The second poem also enacts a refusal. "Wait," a 2004 poem by Adrienne Rich about the US invasion of Iraq, contrasts the sonic agitation of an expansive war with the diminutive scale of poetic compression. Gaps between words halt the poem's speech and fray the ligaments between ideas and images. Rich writes:

> sand screams against your government
> issued tent   hell's noise
> in your nostrils   crawl
> into your ear-shell
> wrap yourself in no-thought
> wait   no place for the little lyric[2]

From the din of a desert landscape, the soldier in a government-issued shelter is commanded to retreat: from sound, from thought, from war itself. The soldier is told: "wait," and the caesura that follows that command enacts wait's duration. Then the poem declares: this is "no place for the little lyric." No place for the minor, the incidental, the superfluous—perhaps even for the literary, or for the aesthetic. Or maybe the poem imagines that what is needed here, what would be adequate to this hellish situation, is something like a "big" lyric, rather than immediacy or narrow detail or compactly formed compounds, like the "ear-shell" that joins military projectiles to bodily senses. Or maybe the poem wants both to reject the little lyric and to invite the big one in its place, like a poem by Langston Hughes, who in 1942 used the phrase "little lyric" to contrast diminutive poetic form with the enormity of urban hardship. His two-line poem "Little Lyric (Of Great Importance)" reads in its entirety, "I wish the rent / Was heaven sent."[3] Like Shockley's lament, or even Hughes's wish, Rich's outcry both refuses and enacts for strategic ends something it calls lyric. Written in free verse, without regular rhyme or meter, "Wait" engages the constraints of a supposedly lyric form. Rich's poem uses stasis, apostrophe, immediacy, condensation, and the traditional fourteen-line architecture of the Petrarchan or Shakespearean sonnet. "Wait" trades in the brevity and stopped time of the sonnet, and it trades in an apostrophic address to the individual soldier. This alyrical sonnet is an argument about how certain forms cannot fully grasp the alienating effects of US militarization.

Shockley's and Rich's poems both take up a difficult topic and then traffic in something they call "lyric" to explore the limits and possibilities of language. If one poem calls itself "a-lyrical" and then deploys the musicality of the ballad, and another declares "no place for the little lyric" and then deploys the lineation of the sonnet, what does lyric mean in either case? Or, to ask a different question: when a poem disavows the formal, historical, or ideological entailments of something called lyric, why might it then still draw on some of those entailments in the fibers of the poem's structure? Does doing so mean the poem subverts or reproduces whatever lyric means? Or does the way the term lyric circulates in the poem actually reveal something else?

In this book, I coin the phrase "lyric trade" to explain how poems both disavow and draw on something they call lyric. This book does not offer a single, fixed definition of lyric, but instead considers what the poems themselves pose as lyric meter and rhyme; lyric condensations and apostrophes; lyric expressive tonalities; lyric musicalities; or lyric subjectivities. The qualifiers I have attached to the term "lyric" so far—"something called lyric" or "supposedly lyric"—signal the term's fundamental instability. Some of the words that describe literary form might be relatively easy to define: a sonnet has fourteen lines; a novel is a long piece of prose. (What happens in those fourteen lines, and what happens in that prose, and what their relevance is to literary genre or the politics of taxonomy, to say nothing of the ways in which writers have produced things called "sonnets" and "novels" that break these rules, are topics of endless unfolding.) Trickier to fix is a definition of lyric, which famously eludes critical or literary consensus.

Some of the basic confusion that plagues the use of "lyric" in twentieth- and twenty-first-century poetics tracks back to the muddled terms of form and genre. Is lyric a genre like epic? Does lyric describe a set of formal techniques that animate an expressive, private, emotive, or sonically rich poem? Is René Wellek right to counsel, "One must abandon attempts to define the general nature of the lyric or the lyrical. Nothing beyond generalities of the tritest kind can result from it"?[4] Wellek's counsel is often cited in scholarship that nevertheless strains rigorously to theorize lyric or scrupulously to historicize it. In this book I instead ask: What is lyric standing in for; what does it reveal? What sorts of contradictions and productively ambivalent effects does it surface in a poem? What does the idea of lyric reveal about what a poem is arguing about history, about the subject, about language and meaning? Could a monograph of literary analysis devoted to lyric, such as the present one, elude the pitfalls of trying to theorize lyric? Could it instead diagnose what's going on in poems that take on the thicket of contradictions that the term "lyric" invites?

These are lyric questions: as Denise Riley notes punningly in *The Words of Selves*, "The strains of describing the self are also acute within those literary genres reliant on a covert self-presentation; hence it is a liar who writes, and a liar who tries lyric."[5] Nathaniel Mackey likewise notes in his preface to *Blue Fasa* that the slipperiness of lyric cuts across historical periods: "for centuries poets in English have punned or played on *lyre*'s homophony with *liar*, suggesting an awareness of words' ability to mislead."[6] Or Charles Bernstein, in *Recalculating*: "THE POET IS A LIAR. / THE POET IS A LYRE. / THE POET'S TIRED. / (Poetry abhors a narrative.)"[7] *Lyric Trade* assumes a self-suspecting wariness in its posture toward the term lyric. This book does not attempt to define the term; to do so would be to forestall the more generative process of uncovering the cultural politics of lyric theory—and discovering what poems themselves have to say. The poems I read in this book are invested in questioning the terms of literary taxonomy for what they foreclose and what they make possible. The poems make their own attempts to define and redefine lyric, poetic form, and the subject. And the poems reveal what lyric theory has often gotten wrong about the subject.

The two poems I opened with, by Shockley and Rich, ask what gets foreclosed by lyric and what might be made possible by it. Both poems experiment with language, something built into the history of lyric invoked in Shockley's title—in his preface to *Lyrical Ballads*, Wordsworth calls his anthology an "experiment." But what if, unlike Shockley's alyrical ballad and Rich's alyrical sonnet, the poem in question is an experimental postwar long poem, one structured by epic ambition, historical critique, extended discursivity, reassembled fragments, serial self-modifying, or procedural constraint—all the sorts of elements that have historically positioned the modern and contemporary long poem against something poets and readers call lyric? When a long poem draws upon the musicality, compression, interiority, or subjective expression associated with something poets and readers call lyric, that poem might appear to reappropriate or reproduce the very kind of lyric it purports to reject. That ambivalent relationship to lyric has implications for how a poem expresses—or does not express—a voice, a self, or a subject. That ambivalence also has implications for the voices, selves, or subjects unaccounted for in language. And if a poem has a conflicted relationship to something poets and readers call lyric, that conflict can reveal something bigger, something more important, about the relationship between form and meaning, and between language and the self.

In *Lyric Trade*, I argue that experimental North American long poems written after 1945 inherit a modernist rejection of lyric only to exchange it, traffic in it, trade in it, for variegated, often contradictory, ends.[8] I argue that in doing so these poems reimagine the function of genre as well as a poem's capacities and limitations for grappling with expression, presence, identity, and the larger structures that shape these things, such as nation and empire. *Lyric Trade* examines works in which an ambitious, culturally wide, historically inflected long poem breaks or sweeps into supposedly lyric registers—moments at which the melodic, the personal, the interior, or the private are redeployed to interrogate notions about the subject. I look at long poems in which sonnets and ballads refigure sound's relationship to identity; soliloquies reemerge as formally paralleled subjective splits and fissures; the quotidian detail stages ambient subjective presence; quest instrumentalizes catharsis; or fragments reshape the civil self. *Lyric Trade* argues that these long poems use lyric to do more than register the ideological contradictions of modernism's insistence on new forms. They map spaces for formal reimaginings of the subject.

This book begins with a form that is supposedly antilyric—the postwar long poem—and reads the lyric inside it. The modern and contemporary long poem is typically read, if not also written, against lyric; many have been categorized as epics for this reason, while others have been called serial, procedural, or narrative, and yet others have been said to cross the boundaries between such categories.[9] Yet long poems so frequently enact supposedly lyric moments within their borders that a conflicted alyricism appears constitutive of the long form itself. Even among the most historically ambitious or critically capacious modernist long poems there appear supposedly lyric moments. Consider Ezra Pound's deeply subjective *Pisan Cantos* as an interlude in the midst of the epic *Cantos*; or William Carlos Williams's lapses into compressed bits of verse, including "The Red Wheelbarrow," among the philosophically meandering *Spring and All*; or the sung genres in Louis Zukofsky's fugal long poem *"A,"* which Lorine Niedecker described as a "tightening often into such forms as canzones or ballades the tonality of our speech"; or the metricality and musicality of Zukofsky's *Anew*, about which Williams wrote: "This poetry is lyric in a way we have hardly sensed at all for a century."[10] *Lyric Trade* uncovers how long poems written in the wake of modernist antilyricism turn back to lyric in diverse moments of refusal or embrace, and how in doing so they reveal something about form and history. Modernism's insistence on "making it new" has shaped an understanding of modern and contemporary form as something that is continually being reinvented and innovated, but as numerous scholars have shown, that insistence on the new has often resolved into a brand of formalism that camouflages historical thinking. For example, the material conditions of racial othering have often constructed the thematic grounds of modernist innovation.

Consider Pound's "In a Station of the Metro," the quintessential poem of the antilyric imagist movement, which draws on orientalist accounts of the ideograph to make a supposedly "new" form of poetry. The poem's formal argument was fueled by modernism's attachment to an imagined Asian past and by what Josephine Nock-Hee Park has described as the "rich strangeness" that Pound and other modernists associated with the Far East.[11] When I write about long poems that inherit the ambitions of modernism, I signal this thicket of contradictions by pointing to where radical new form often hinges on the othering of certain subjects. *Lyric Trade* situates its approach alongside recent work that draws on comparativist and historicist models to dislodge entrenched thinking about modernist form—and about the cultural imperialism of US high modernism. Against a vision of modernism as "formalist totality," as Cara L. Lewis puts it, recent moves in the fields of formalist studies and modernist studies seek to trouble assumptions about modernist innovation.[12] Like other works in those fields, *Lyric Trade* seeks to dislodge habits of reading that assign poetic form "a stable, coherent cultural politics," as Mara de Gennaro puts it.[13]

Lyric Trade does not theorize lyric, but investigates how poems use lyric to shore up histories and politics of the subject, as in the two poems I opened with. For Shockley, lyric's association with song enables the poem to recast anti-Black violence in the United States. For Rich, lyric's association with the still moment and with subjective interiority enables the poem to recast US imperialism. Both poems trade in lyric to stage a critique of the othering of certain subjects, whether those subjects are targets of race-based violence or of the relentless war machine. In her notes, Shockley writes that her poem "joins the tradition of elegies for unjustly slain black people in the United States," and she dedicates her poem "to Emmett Till, Sandra Bland, Amadou Diallo, Renisha McBride, Trayvon Martin, Rekia Boyd, Tamir Rice, and . . . ," an ellipsis suggesting more names to come.[14] Shockley's list recalls Claudia Rankine's *Citizen: An American Lyric*, a long poem whose subtitle summons lyric and whose pages include an elegiac dedication, titled "In Memory Of," followed by a list of names of Black victims of police violence—a list that keeps accumulating with each subsequent printing of the book.[15] The poem that immediately precedes Rich's "Wait" opens with lines that depict the buildup to the 2003 US invasion of Iraq in a kind of anticipatory elegy: "Tonight as cargoes of my young / fellow countrymen and women are being hauled / into positions aimed at death."[16] Shockley's and Rich's poems expose the links between lyric and overarching concepts of race, gender, nation, and empire—and they also lay bare the question of which subjects are accounted for, and which are not, by the state.

Lyric Trade is a book about lyric and subjects both accounted for and unaccounted for, but it is also a book about the difficulty lyric poses to genre theory. I argue that this difficulty reveals a number of things about the relationship between poetry and the self because lyric reveals something specific about genre. My analytical phrase "lyric trade" corresponds with the notion of genre not as the conveniently fixed organization of literary texts but rather as a kind of economy in which genres relate differentially—and in which they resist easy denotation. An elegy, for example, has often been defined by its relationship to other literary genres, such as the ode, but also by its relationship to specific occasions (such as a funeral) and to expressive functions (such as mourning).[17] And in poems like those I have been discussing, elegy genre might relate to, be understood by its relationship to, the ballad, the sonnet, and a number of historical phenomena that shape its operations. To extend the economic metaphor: genres are often sorted according to their cultural or historical value, high or low; poems are often described as having an "investment" in a genre; genres are often described as mixed or pure. Genres have structures, but this is not the same thing as saying they are structural: Steve McCaffery has contrasted the notion of writing as a structure with the notion of writing as an economy, drawing on Georges Bataille's definition of general economy to describe how texts move and circulate. McCaffery writes, "As an alternative to structure, economy is concerned with the distribution and circulation of the numerous forces and intensities that saturate a text. A textual economy would concern itself not with the order of forms and sites but with the order-disorder of circulations and distributions."[18] A poem's differential relations to genre might also be described according to how Jacques Derrida famously distinguishes between the notion that a text "belongs" to a genre and the notion that a text merely "participates" in one.[19] By foregrounding the trait of participation over the notion of belonging—belonging is the essence of what it means to categorize, divide, and distinguish among texts—Derrida decenters the question of what a genre is in favor of what it does.

In this book, I argue that the trait of participation in a genre can take the form of exchange, disavowal, critique, reproduction, or traffic: different operations I collate under the moveable term "trade." Lyric trade is both an instance of exchange in a poem and an ongoing formal operation I track across the poems I read in this book.[20] If genre operates differentially and variously as in an economy, "trade" extends the metaphor by invoking exchange, benefit, and loss. I argue that postwar long poems trade modernist rejection of lyric for its formal potential, or they traffic in lyric forms for what those forms can offer. Trade offers more breadth than some of the diminutizing terms scholars have used to describe lyric in the long poem, such as "haunting," "gesture," "mark," "residue," or "trace."[21] Instead, the term "trade" describes the relations that shift into gear when a long poem adopts registers that have typically been named lyric. The term "trade" conveys situated and differential lyric relations within and across poems: a fractured ballad in a late objectivist poem by Lorine Niedecker behaves differently than a torqued epiphany in a second-generation New York School poem by Alice Notley or an ambiently odic address in a post-Language poem by Myung Mi Kim. Trade is semantically capacious, both transitive and intransitive, both verb and noun, conveying transaction as well as vocation, manner, habit, or method. Poems use lyric trade to surrender their claims to, for example, historiography, materialist poetics, or documentary practice, in return for an ideology of the individual. In doing so, these poems trade their anti-institutional or avant-garde commitments for the powerful affinities of a supposedly transcendental subject, or they trade their investments in the materiality of language for the seductive affect of epiphany, or they trade their commitment to identity difference for majority privilege. To trade in this way does not necessarily entail the collapse of these poems' critical potential, although I argue that in some cases it does entail just this. In some cases, the trade enables othered subjects to take shape. And in other cases, the trade does both.

The subject of lyric

This book uses the analytical phrase "lyric trade" to argue that long poems can map spaces for formal reimaginings of the subject. Often these poems define and redefine what is meant by lyric in the first place. Lyric is a matter of craft, as in the poems I discuss above by Shockley and Rich: the meter and rhyme of the ballad; the condensation and apostrophe of the sonnet. Or lyric is a matter of expression: a collective lament for the dead; a first-person address to a soldier on the battlefield. One of these definitions is about patterns of language, and the other is about experience, interiority, memory, affect, or subjective presence. The slippage between these definitions is a kind of slippage between different ways of reading a poem. That slippage constellates the discourse of aesthetic form with the discourse of the subject: the subject's presence, its identity, or its relationship to, and divestment from, identificatory structures such as race and gender. From the standpoint of linguistic theory, that slippage is a conceptual necessity, since things like rhetorical devices, tropes, or prosody link to human nature. From the standpoint of historicism, that slippage is a methodological necessity since changing notions of the self give rise to certain kinds of poetry. In poetics and cultural studies, that slippage between language and the subject is not a slippage at all. As Denise Ferreira da Silva puts it, "The subject is a linguistic figure"; as Adorno puts it, form is nothing but sedimented content; as Robert Creeley puts it, form is never more than an extension of content; as Elizabeth Willis, writing about Fred Moten, puts it, "Poetic form—like the form of the body—is not immutable; it is in motion"; as Moten puts it, "sing a shattered self is just a shelf, young captain, / sea?"[22]

Lyric Trade is grounded in this basic orientation toward genre and the subject as socially constituted and historically sedimented. But this book also performs a diagnostic inquiry into what happens when poets and critics return the term lyric to a definition that effaces the historical and social contingencies of literary genre—even and especially when lyric is invoked in discourses alert to those contingencies. This book is not primarily an argument against dehistoricized formalism; that argument is already axiomatic for a good part of the field of poetry and poetics.[23] Rather, *Lyric Trade* is most interested in how poetry itself takes the uneasy status of lyric to be a moveable and productive problem. I argue that sometimes a dehistoricized lyric reemerges in order to make a claim about the transcendental subject, sometimes a reappropriated lyric forecloses certain forms of expression, and sometimes other kinds of lyric create spaces for reimagining the very notion of subjectivity.

Efforts to theorize lyric always involve the imbricated discourses of genre and the subject. When Denise Riley describes the "strains" of the self in literary genres, she draws on the question Jacques Rancière poses in *The Flesh of Words* about lyric expression and the subject: what is it, Rancière asks, that "links the modern stance of poetic utterance with that of political subjectivity?"[24] For Rancière, who often finds it quite productive to investigate the work that genres are doing—he asserts that the cliché of a solitary Wordsworthian lyric wandering actually camouflages epic (an "erased and reinterpreted odyssey")[25]—the question of lyric and the political subject is the question of genre itself. Rather than historicizing literary form, taxonomic genre, or poetic utterance, Rancière makes it quite clear that the very division of genres sediments the historical features of poetic speech. What is more, the division of genres that ubiquitously counts lyric as one in a tripartition traditionally attributed to Aristotle and Plato—lyric, epic, drama—is itself a historical error.

This is the claim so carefully laid out by Gérard Genette in *The Architext*: neither Aristotle nor Plato assigned a definitive place in the system of genres to lyric. The misattributed tripartition, and the status of lyric in particular, is an anachronistic projection of expressive theories that are associated with eighteenth-century thought; pre-Romantic theories of lyric as spontaneous expression themselves complicate the idea that Romanticism behaves as a decisive break in thinking about poetry and the self.[26] Plato sought to expel poets from the republic, but, as Genette points out, Plato's generic schema specifically excludes nonrepresentational poetry, or what would go on to be called expressive lyric poetry. Aristotle briefly differentiates between the forms of the dithyramb, or choral song; the epic; and the dramatic dialogue. But, Genette argues, when Charles Batteux in the eighteenth century describes the dithyramb as the "lyric" of the three Aristotelian genres, he establishes a longstanding equivalence between a poetic form and an enunciative style. Genette adds that the dithyramb does not appear elsewhere in the *Poetics* except as a forerunner of tragedy, and that neither Aristotle nor Plato uses the dithyramb to illustrate lyric genre. Genette declares forcefully: "The passage Batteux cites is the only one in all the *Poetics* he could have invoked to give Aristotle's sanction to the illustrious triad. The distortion is flagrant."[27] Genette is far from being the only literary scholar to point out that the misattributed system of genres categorizes lyric as a genre, when lyric might be more properly understood—beginning with Plato and Aristotle—as a style. It is indeed the case that Plato put the system in place, Aristotle further developed it, and the system went on to be cited as the definitive tripartite of genres. And yet, Genette's apparent moral passion around this historical error notwithstanding, it is not clear why this error matters.

Genette's corrective illuminates some of the problems with lyric as a category, but the circulation of this error and its corrective must reveal something about the use of taxonomy in literary studies. When poets and critics return the term "lyric" to a definition that effaces its historical and social contingencies (including the tripartite error or the Wordsworthian cliché), or when they use terms like lyric and poem interchangeably, or when they link lyric to transhistorical elements of musicality or expression as well as to historicized forms of address or meter, those poets and critics recirculate those contingencies, that error, and that cliché. Those poets and critics recirculate the notion that the lyric error is also somehow its exemplarity. They recirculate the notion that lyric is both of and beyond genre; they recirculate the notion that its slipperiness is the point. Its moveability and multivalence allow lyric to stand in for a number of submerged and unacknowledged assumptions about literary language.

To write an entire book about lyric is to risk animating the very same recirculation of exemplarity, which is why it is so difficult to define lyric in these opening pages. Rather than trying to pin down whether lyric is best understood as a genre, a style, a mode, or something else, I focus instead on poems' machinations around lyric—what I call lyric trade—in order to shift the focus from what a lyric might be to what the poems themselves do. This book does not construct a new typology, genre study, or method to classify poetic forms as lyric. Instead, it reads poems that negotiate their own ideas of lyric. The poems I discuss in *Lyric Trade* approach lyric as incurably mixed, as a semantic, tonal, and structural marker of ideologies of subjectivity, and they redeploy that lyric in differential ways, in circuits of critique and reinvention. By subject I mean both the self that speaks in the poem, and the philosophical discourse of the subject that follows both epistemological and ontological lines of inquiry into knowledge, identity, and the nature of being. While subjectivity and self are often used interchangeably, the former term typically encompasses the larger political and historical contexts that shape identity, including textuality, or what Michel Foucault introduced as the paradigm-shifting notion of discourse as a structure of identity.[28] Lyric's seeming untheorizability is not some essential quality of its status as a genre; rather, its constant retheorization is its ontological condition. Its status as a moving target signals its relationship to conceptions of the subject in literary studies. It may indeed be now a critical commonplace that "The identity of a social subject—this construct of ideology displaced into the world—is essentially, then, a function of language," as Ben Friedlander writes, or "I may feel linguistic unease as I am necessarily and constantly displaced from my centrality to my own utterance," as Denise Riley writes.[29] And yet lyric is often understood as a glyph for the status of the supposedly socially unmarked literary as against cultural studies and avant-garde poetics. Lyric often functions as shorthand for the walling off of literary studies against the concerns of race and gender that came to the forefront during the rise of cultural studies and since, or it functions as shorthand for the walling off of literary studies against the political imperatives of modernist and postmodernist studies.[30]

Lyric trade might even describe some attempts to theorize the lyric. For example, the theory of "lyric reading" that has come to prominence at times reinstalls supposedly discarded notions of the subject. When Virginia Jackson first described "how poems become lyrics in history,"[31] she established lyric not as a transhistorical literary category but as an act of reading that creates both an abstract genre and an abstract personification of its author.[32] The turn toward the "new lyric studies" activated by Jackson's book *Dickinson's Misery* and subsequent anthologies, PMLA special issues, and the like signaled both a return to genre critique in literary studies and a renewal of debates over identity and the literary.[33] As it was during the wars over New Criticism, the status of the literary in literary studies was identified as a "lyric" problem, a problem *of the lyric*. Subjectivity is at the heart of Jackson's study of what she calls—using a term that fixes genre as something observed, rather than as something naturalized—the "phenomenology" of lyric. Jackson's central claim in *Dickinson's Misery* is that the genre called lyric is actually a structure of address that came to be naturalized as a generic distinction in the nineteenth century: a lyric that activates the fallacy of poetic speech as a private address made available to the reader. Jackson argues that lyric reading produces the equation of the private with the transcendent: "the voice that speaks to no one and therefore to all of us."[34] Lyric reading also effaces what Jackson refers to as the more complicated "economy" of poetic address, installing instead a syllogistic logic of address that converts any particular "I" or "you" of poetic discourse into a universal "we," denying the poem "any intersubjective economy of its own."[35] Finally, lyric reading entails the collapse of verse genres like the ballad, ode, elegy, epistle, or epitaph into "an idealized version of poetry as lyric," as Jackson puts it in another essay, in which "economies of circulation begin to blend together to form one big idea of Poetry."[36] Not the fact of lyric but its circulation; not a fixed genre called lyric, but a structure of reading.

"Lyric trade" shares critical grounds with "lyric reading": both phrases are meant to analyze the histories and theories of the self that are projected onto poems—and the histories and theories of the self that are removed from them. Yet the phrases differ in their critical motives. For example, Jackson looks closely at what Emily Dickinson does with apostrophe in Poem 706, which begins (in the Franklin edition), "I cannot live with You—." Jackson reads Poem 706 as "a pathos of literal seclusion" that comes to be lyrically read by scholars as "a pathos of figurative seclusion—that is, with Dickinson's lyric self-address."[37] Dickinson's concluding lines read:

And that White Sustenance—
Despair[38]

Jackson punctures prevailing interpretations of Dickinson's poem that would "mistake the performative dimension of apostrophe for a statement of historical presence." She argues against lyric readings that project both the historical presence of Dickinson's voice and the idealization of that presence as ahistorical, transcendent subjectivity.[39] Jackson reads "White Sustenance" instead as the page that materializes the complex operations of address—"at once a comforting material presence and as blank as the figure of a figure."[40] Jackson shows how lyric reading displaces the "complex discursive field" that makes up the conditions of address in Dickinson's poem.[41]

But what of the phrase "White Sustenance"? When Jackson delves into the significance of that white page, she implicates a whiteness whose claims to universality and ahistoricism resemble those she has been tracing for lyric reading. Jackson writes: "Not I, not you, not here, not there, not this, but 'that,' if [']White Sustenance' is a figure for the page then it is a figure without a face. It is the historical, as opposed to the fictive, material of address."[42] If we are to take subjectivity seriously in lyric studies, ought we not to disabuse ourselves of the notion that a "white" page is blank—or that its ambition is, either? Jackson's reading risks trading a historical critique of the transcendental subject for an unacknowledged whiteness. There is no "lyric" prior to literary studies, possibly also no such thing as a "poem."[43] But isn't the same to be said of the "I" and "you" of a poem—and of its "White Sustenance"? Jackson's book describes a poem's capacity to anticipate and correct the readings we make of it, and *Dickinson's Misery* posits a critique of female embodiment. Yet *Dickinson's Misery*, as much of lyric studies, does not always extend the same faith to a poem's capacity to reckon with whiteness.[44]

Critiques of lyric can rehearse the very habits they mean to dismantle. And critiques poised to question the white universal subject of lyric reading are capable of keeping that subject position intact, in turn leaving open the possibility that lyric theory cannot actually account for whiteness—or for the othering of the nonwhite subject. Rather, critiques often recapitulate the lacuna of identity, in its place installing an unacknowledged whiteness. John Keene has used Harryette Mullen's phrase "aesthetic apartheid" to characterize the whiteness of *The Lyric Theory Reader*, the major critical anthology that followed *Dickinson's Misery*, suggesting that the problem is not just in the material conditions of the critical text but in the premise behind the field of study: "consider the future generations of students and scholars who, in the absence of more broadminded doctoral exam lists and committees, are internalizing the premise that the study of the lyric," Keene writes, "by its very nature brackets off questions and issues of race."[45] *Lyric Trade* enters this conversation by considering how genres constellate certain ideological motives and interests and how genres activate certain interests in poetry and literary studies, where an "interest" is an affiliative investment and a type of labor—a trade. This book joins works in poetics, ethnic studies, and gender and sexuality studies that treat subjectivity and literary texts as always already imbricated discourses.

To employ the critical terms of this book—lyric, the long poem, and the subject—comes with some risk. One analytical risk manifests in the book's archival grounds, a selection of long poems written mostly by modern and contemporary women poets. I do not rationalize or theorize this curatorial choice as something that is necessarily crucial to the book's argument: indexing women poets according to aesthetic or formal categories would risk enforcing the arbitrariness of essentialist criticism. Jennifer Ashton, in a critique of anthologies of women's poetry that could easily extend to critical monographs on women's poetry such as the present one, writes that essentialist collections insinuate the limitations of essentialism itself. Ashton writes: "once the relation between form and identity is indexical, we have as many forms, however similar they might be, as there are subjects, however similar they might be."[46] Ashton's formulation shows that women's writing as a concept betrays plurality rather than essential sameness. To think otherwise is to perform the operation that this book works against vis-à-vis lyric: it would suggest that there is a stable category of women's poetry that can be classified and known. On the other hand, my choice to read long poems written mostly by modern and contemporary women poets aligns with the notion that curatorial choices do political work by their very enactment: Jennifer Scappettone speaks to the artful politics of anthologies of avant-garde women's writing that have done the essential work of bringing poems to readers. In a response to Ashton, Scappettone traces the historical contours of the gendered avant-garde, centering—of all things—the lyric in her argument: "Is there really a contradiction between the critical imperative to exceed the constrictions of gendered subjectivities imposed by the lyric tradition and the critical desire to insist on the socially imposed difference of women's experience? Or is there a dialectic at play in contemporary women's constructions of authorship, aimed at producing a collective that still has work to do, even if the forms of subjugation it addresses are not identical to those of decades past?"[47] The selection of poems by women in *Lyric Trade* keeps aloft such a dialectic.

Another analytical risk of this book's critical terms manifests in a tendency to focus on how poems themselves theorize lyric, to propose not a new theory of lyric but instead a way of reading how poems' self-conscious, overt, and subtle references to lyric's terms and modalities usefully problematize the term lyric. Take Claudia Rankine's long poems *Don't Let Me Be Lonely* and *Citizen*, which are both subtitled *An American Lyric*. Rankine's own descriptions of lyric do not at first sound particularly dissimilar from a common cliché of lyric: she has said that the lyric is "the private language of the self," a self that "feels a gap between itself and the external world."[48] But what distinguishes her works, particularly *Citizen*, in their efforts to problematize that cliché is the way in which they recalibrate lyric privacy as a failed social exchange. One passage in *Citizen* is placed opposite an iconic 1930 image in which lynched African American bodies have been digitally removed, leaving only the white spectators visible in the image. Rankine's text describes the injured or ruptured throat, absent from the photograph, as internal to the racial subject, and to the book itself:

> inside our lives where we are all caught hanging, the rope
> inside us, the tree inside us, its roots our limbs, a throat
> sliced through and when we open our mouth to speak,
> blossoms, o blossoms, no place coming out, brother, dear
> brother, that kind of blue. The sky is the silence of brothers
> all the days leading up to my call.[49]

"All living is listening for a throat to open— / The length of its silence shaping lives," Rankine writes later.[50] Even against the image of a throat cut by the history of US racial violence, her poem suggests, there might yet be a possible poetic speech. Rankine's passage metatextually confronts the limits of—here, a specifically "American"—lyric to make subjects legible.[51]

Lyric and/or formalism

Lyric Trade opens up new possibilities for historicizing the relationship between the literary avant-garde and subjectivity by asking what it means to challenge, subvert, or otherwise refuse a genre called lyric within the antilyric long poem.[52] To take subjectivity and literature as imbricated discourses means to confront both the possibilities and the violences of formations of the self; it also means to break down a conceptual and disciplinary stalemate between cultural studies and poetics, or between a view of literature as ideological and the concretely textual methods of close reading. I read a number of postwar long poems that carry within their structures the antilyricism of modernism and then redeploy lyric in order to reimagine the subject.

One of the notions that *Lyric Trade* investigates is subversion as a literary-political goal. The aura of subversion hovers around scholarship on the kinds of poems I discuss in this book: the assumption that one of the chief tasks of formally divergent, experimental, innovative, or otherwise avant-garde poetry is to subvert the fixed categories of genre. This assumption, I contend, has structured—and limited—theoretical approaches to the lyric subject. As such, it is worth returning to Derrida's examination of literature and the law. Across two key essays—"Before the Law" and "The Law of Genre"—Derrida insists that the question of genre immediately and always carries with it the juridical questions of the lawful operations of and obedience to norms. In the first place, Derrida takes up the question of the literary as a question of the law: texts may be classified as literary or nonliterary, they may "stage and suspend" their own laws of categorization, and they may even find their identity as literary texts "guaranteed by law": still, he insists, law can never exclude its own historicity.[53] Genre carries within it an "authoritarian summons" to its lawful operation: "As soon as the word *genre* is sounded, as soon as it is heard, as soon as one attempts to conceive it, a limit is drawn. And when a limit is established, norms and interdictions are not far behind: 'Do,' 'Do not,' says 'genre,' the word *genre*, the figure, the voice, or the law of genre."[54] The law of genre also guarantees mixing and excess, a lack of purity: there is no subversion if the law of genre inheres in genre itself.[55] Playing upon the connotations of the French word *genre*—which can be rendered in English as genre, genus, or gender—Derrida collapses the distinction between nature (*phusis*) and the arts (*techne*). There might be something distinctive about literature, but it is not genre.[56]

Some scholars have argued that identificatory categories such as race and gender share fundamental epistemological and hermeneutic norms with genre. Yet some of this scholarship reproduces a notion of subversion as a generalizable goal rather than treating subversion as a juridical question written into the categories of race or gender.[57] An argument that something called "feminist lyric" subverts the norms of "patriarchal epic" often leaves lyric untheorized and unhistoricized, unlike the categories of gender that are scrutinized. As scholars in queer theory have shown, identificatory categories must be understood as epistemic models—effects of institutions, practices, and discourses—rather than as stable sources of agency or as sites of subversion.[58] And the same can be said for genres. In fact, queer theory and avant-garde poetics share some of the same risks that attend a vague claim to being postgender and postgenre. Those risks include the universalization of dominant modes of experience, further marginalization of expressions of identity that are already excluded from literary study, and the reification of supposedly transhistorical and transcendental identity categories—whiteness perhaps most perniciously. Therein lies the irony: when subversion is posited as a primary and generalized goal, something that can supersede something like a gender or a genre, subversion assumes the conceit of an epistemological model outside cultural specificity—and risks reproducing forms of universality.[59]

As scholars in critical race studies have made clear, genre norms can embed the very norms of difference that accord universality to a white subject. Take for example Sylvia Wynter's philosophical work on prevailing notions of the human as a series of "genres of the human" that hew to differences of race, gender, and sexuality. Wynter writes that she uses the word genre "to denote the fictively constructed and performatively enacted different *kinds* of *being human*, of which *gender coherence* is itself always and everywhere a function."[60] Extrapolating from Derrida's notion that the historical, cultural, or linguistic limits of the concept of "Man" are rarely examined, Wynter argues that "in extending Derrida, the history of the concept of secular Western *Man*'s discursively invented and objectively institutionalized series of *Human Others* is never examined as well"—among those others Wynter includes the categories of the enslaved person, the neo-serf laborer, and a number of other "embodied signifiers" of otherness.[61] Wynter's thinking unveils the ways certain kinds of literary formalism can reinscribe narratives of the human, of belonging and non-belonging, and of difference, enabling the "systemic non-recognition of the humanly invented nature" of concepts of the human.[62] As Denise Ferreira da Silva puts it, "it is important to recall that humanity is a racial signifier."[63] Approaching cultural and historical taxonomical principles and hierarchies in a way that attends to the constructedness and performative enactedness of literary genres can begin to articulate a cultural poetics whose refusals are as productive and generative as they are subversive.

Such a method of reading can expand the capacity of late-twentieth-century materialist poetics to account more acutely for race and gender. The long poems I read in this book enact complicated mixtures and refusals of the expectation of genres in order to think about the subject. In one of the foundational essays of materialist poetics and the subject, written in 1983, Lyn Hejinian appears to describe the lyric inside the long poem. Hejinian's essay "The Rejection of Closure" describes the limits of a closed text, a text in which "all the elements of the work are directed toward a single reading of it." The closed text is directive, rather than generative; emphasizes product over process; and values commodification, authority, and hierarchy in reading and writing.[64] One example of the closed text is what Hejinian describes as the "coercive, epiphanic mode in some contemporary lyric poetry," a lyric poetry characterized by "its smug pretension to universality and its tendency to cast the poet as guardian to Truth."[65] The open text, on the other hand, eschews epiphany and universality. The open text "invites participation, rejects the authority of the writer over the reader and thus, by analogy, the authority implicit in other (social, economic, cultural) hierarchies."[66] The open text imagines a different kind of poet and reader. Setting aside for the moment the tremendous optimism of this declaration—surely there are materially open texts that nonetheless trade in social, economic, or cultural hierarchies; one thinks of the contested cultural politics of Conceptualism, to take an obvious example[67]—I read Hejinian's description of the open text as an instance of lyric trade.

"The Rejection of Closure" contains a discussion of Hejinian's own poem "Resistance," which was at that time in progress (it would later be published in Hejinian's book *The Cold of Poetry*). Hejinian describes how "Resistance" combines lyric with the long poem. Her description uses strikingly geometric, spatial, and physical vocabulary:

> My intention (I don't mean to suggest that I succeeded) in a subsequent work, "Resistance," was to write a lyric poem in a long form—that is, to achieve maximum vertical intensity (the single moment into which the idea rushes) and maximum horizontal extensivity (ideas cross the landscape and become the horizon and weather). To myself I proposed the paragraph as a unit representing a single moment of time, a single moment in the mind, its content all the thoughts, thought particles, impressions, impulses—all the diverse, particular, and contradictory elements—that are included in an active and emotional mind at any given instant. For the moment, for the writer, the poem *is* a mind.[68]

Hejinian characterizes the lyric as vertical, the long poem as horizontal; lyric as the single moment, long poem as landscape, horizon, ambient weather; lyric as the active, emotional mind at a given instant, long poem as multiple thoughts, impressions, impulses. To conceive of the "poem" as a "mind" is to foreground the text itself as the source of thought and to dissipate the aura of the author. Yet Hejinian's materialist poetics—a poetics that foregrounds the practice of making, or *poiesis*, rather than foregrounding the supposed consciousness of its maker—still opens with the declaration that "The essential question here concerns the writer's subject position."[69]

This is lyric trade: a subject broken open and rewritten in the long form. In order to write horizontal and vertical intensity, Hejinian writes, she turns to the poetic form most associated with subjectivity: the lyric. "The Rejection of Closure" describes a poem that uses lyric trade to theorize a subject whose single moment-oriented consciousness takes hold inside a long form. A subject rewritten in this way figures an alternative to the hierarchies of what Hejinian describes as lyric's epiphanies (again, setting aside for the moment the skepticism this proposition invites). Hejinian cites the long poem as that specific form whose extensivity invites something it calls lyric subjectivity and then torques it, opening the text. Hejinian's discussion of "Resistance" invokes a history of twentieth-century antilyricism, a history in which the lyric is both problematized and deployed as a site to reimagine the subject.

I realize that in order to define materialist poetics I am describing an essay about a poem and not the poem itself; that is because theorizing happens across categorical boundaries of "essay" and "poem." The long poem that Hejinian describes in "The Rejection of Closure" joins two discourses: the text-oriented discourse of materialist poetics and the self-oriented discourse of lyric theory. The common reading of these two discourses' meeting focuses on all the ways in which late-twentieth-century materialist poetics is conceived of as antilyric, as postlyric, or as otherwise alyric in its rejection of a transcendental self. Take Language writing, for example. Marjorie Perloff offers a handy catalog of terms that this movement of poets (among whom Hejinian is counted) reject as lyric: voice, ego, the human as a unified persona, personal subject matter, personal communication, authenticity, experience, and self-presence.[70] Perloff generates her catalog by reading a 1988 *Social Text* essay, "Aesthetic Tendency and the Politics of Poetry," by Ron Silliman, Carla Harryman, Lyn Hejinian, Steve Benson, Bob Perelman, and Barrett Watten, an essay that positions Language writing against a poetic mainstream in which "the personal, 'expressive' lyric has been held up as the canonical poetic form" and in which "The elevation of the lyric of fetishized personal 'experience' into a canon of taste has been ubiquitous and unquestioned."[71] Against this fetishization of personal experience, "Aesthetic Tendency" posits the conceptual-material openness found in Hejinian's "The Rejection of Closure": a poetic I that would instead generate "an openness to the implications of experience, associated with the *I* here that is more generative of insight than the transcendent elevation of carefully scripted incidents."[72] "Aesthetic Tendency" traces this I not just back to twentieth-century modernism but further back in time: to Whitman, to Coleridge. This is not a new I, ready to be fixed in place of lyric, but an open I already present, yet occluded by the tastes of the latter half of the twentieth century that would efface the aesthetic inheritance of the modernist avant-garde.[73] The "Aesthetic Tendency" essay actually uses the word "lyric" fairly sparingly: more at stake for its authors is the self "as the central and final term of creative practice" and Language writing as a critique of that self.[74] When Hejinian cites the "subject position" of her lyric inside the long poem, she alludes to Language writing's critique, a critique that inherits "openness of self in the present"[75] from the formal interventions of US modernism.

Lyric Trade is indebted to many of these ideas from materialist poetics. But it takes a posture of curiosity toward how open texts can end up shaping narratives of identity and the subject in conflicting ways. For example, H.D.'s 1955 long poem *Helen in Egypt* uses lyric trade to question the gendered and raced cultural narratives of poetic form. H.D.'s speaker, Helen, reflects on the apparent demand to choose between "the lyre and the sword"—lyric and epic, genres burdened by the ideologies of a Poundian modernism as well as by earlier ideologies of colonial expansion—and imbricates them in a poem that seeks to rewrite the dominant Western cultural narrative of the female form. Helen asks:

> The lyre or the sword?
> Theseus has both together,
> this is Athens, he said;
>
> this is Athens or was or will be,
> but O the ecstasy—familiar fragrance,
> late roses, bruised apples[76]

Helen invokes the lyre and the sword as classically drawn opposites that stand for opposites of other sorts: art and politics; song and narrative; music and war; fertility and the ramparts of war. The putatively classical icons of the lyre and the sword stand for H.D.'s midcentury modernism: in combining lyric with epic, she draws a contrast between Helen, whose emotional quest seeks to mend the broken cultural memory of war, and Theseus, who already "has both together." In its turn from cultural narrative to singular remembrance, a form of expression driven by sense-memory, H.D.'s long poem enacts the expressive turn associated with something called lyric at the same time that it calls attention to the modernist conflation of the female subject with expression.[77] Yet the poem's equivalence also foregrounds the instability, and thus the critical potential, of the term lyric. Lyric is described in *Helen in Egypt* as a song but also a heroic voice, as the hallmark of classical lyrical poetry as well as that of tragedy, as an allegory for gendered midcentury poetics. And, as I show in this book's chapter on *Helen in Egypt*, the whiteness that figures Helen's body constrains the feminist critique otherwise leveraged by the poem. This is *Helen in Egypt*'s lyric trade: the poem invokes whiteness in order to interrogate the gendered cultural burdens of its female subject position, sacrificing the interrogation of whiteness for feminist critique. The analytical phrase lyric trade works to uncover the ideological biases present in texts that interrogate or install certain subject positions at the same time that they obscure others. *Lyric Trade* looks out from a supposedly postgenre avant-garde moment in poetry and wonders how readers come to understand generic categories as things that ought to be subverted. In the process, this book considers how correspondent subversions of the self render other selves invisible.

Claims to radical new form often disavow their own histories of power. So do claims about formalism. Literary criticism is fond of devising schemas to rationalize and organize meaning, then using those schemas to read and decode texts, or then using the texts to decode the schemas, while often overlooking the work those texts themselves do to rationalize and organize meaning, to identify and describe, to theorize abstract concepts and lived reality. Writing a book about a particular concept such as lyric necessarily invites categorical thinking: these works deal with lyric, while others do not. Or: these works deal with lyric differently, while others deal with lyric in a way germane to certain concerns and not to others. Writing a book about any particular term presents impossible and seemingly arbitrary choices that are endemic to the act of criticism. At the same time, *Lyric Trade* argues that there is something distinctive about the categorical term lyric: its relationship to subjectivity; its circulation in conversations about aesthetics, history, and politics. Dwelling in the complex ways this categorical term is deployed by the texts themselves can both uncover and begin to undo ideologies of the subject and instead to do what Kandice Chuh describes as the work to "elicit subjects and social structures disinvested" in the "entangled histories" that inscribe the othering of certain subjects.[78]

This book examines how poems themselves use lyric to do this work. This book could just as well trace the so-called new lyric studies, which has been populated by a number of theories about what the lyric is and what it does: a theory of lyric reading; a theory of apostrophic address; a theory of lyric shame; and a resurgence of critical discourse around what constitutes form, from the defense of form as a useful abstraction for thinking about history and politics, to an application of mathematical formalism to literary form, to the study of particular iterations of form such as rhythm and meter. Some of the implications of this discourse include: the opposition of form and culture; the question of what distinguishes art from other forms; the question of what distinguishes literary form from history, politics, sociology, or culture; and the relationship between an aesthetic form and the formation of the self.[79] Recent studies like Anna Kornbluh's *The Order of Forms* puzzle over whether a literary form derives from social conditions, or whether a literary form is an abstract category unfettered of history. "The value of what forms build recedes," writes Kornbluh (employing the language of economy with the word "value"), when literary criticism privileges certain kinds of making over others: specifically, modernism over realism, or fragmentation over synthesis.[80] To take another recent example: Caroline Levine writes in her book *Forms* that "forms are not outgrowths of social conditions; they do not belong to certain times and places."[81] Often the critical rebuttal is: "yes, they are, and yes, they do: here are some examples." But claims such as Kornbluh's and Levine's present an opportunity to reassess form for materialist poetics.

When I write that the trait of participation in a genre takes the form of trade, exchange, or even traffic, I mean that trade, exchange, and traffic are formal operations whether they apply to objects and bodies or whether they function as generative metaphorical terms to describe what is happening in poems. To understand terms such as "trade," "exchange," and "traffic" as formal, and to invite the distinction between a metaphorical term about a poem and a historical term at work within a poem to fray and collapse, is to set aside a longstanding opposition of form versus culture, or aesthetics versus politics, or literature versus ideology.[82] To set aside those oppositions is to align instead with claims such as one made by Walt Hunter in his recent book on poetry and globalization: "the terms that we use to think about poems are just as much products and producers of the liberal discursive frameworks of subjectivity, freedom, humanity, and intimacy."[83] Or to align with this declaration by Dorothy Wang: "Poems are never divorced from contexts and from history, even as they are, among other things, modes of thinking philosophically through an engagement with formal constraints."[84] Or to align with this observation by Myung Mi Kim in an interview about form: "Form is the body for speculation."[85] Or to align with this question posed by Nathaniel Mackey in a lecture on breath and precarity: "Is radical pneumaticism as much a holding action as an elegiac lament?"[86] In a thrilling rebuttal to "Projective Verse," Charles Olson's now canonical essay on the poetics of breath, Mackey historicizes the turn toward breath in 1950s and 1960s US experimental poetry alongside what he describes as "a history of black necks and black windpipes broken, whether by ropes or by cop strangleholds," against which "Transmutation or alchemization, the digestion and sublimation of antiblack violence, harassment, and predation, has been one of the jobs of black music, black art, black cultural and social life in general."[87] Mackey refuses to unsuture a form such as elegy from its embeddedness in the social history of precarious breath, and what is more, he theorizes social history itself as literary formal history—my word "embeddedness" doesn't adequately capture the profound way text and history relate to one another.

The forms taken up by Anglophone poetry—its genres, its subgenres, its modes, or any number of taxonomic names given to its textures— track constructions of subjectivity throughout Western thought. The word "track" invokes metaphors of trail, pursuit, mark, or what Mackey calls the "pull" of lyric and the self: "Pull is disjunctive sensibility's call, a dynamic in which undular and corpuscular senses of self meet and unravel."[88] Mackey's description of the long poem as an extended lyric illuminates a dense imbrication of subjectivity and form in which contrasting modes of expression coalesce: "The long song, the long poem, particularly the serial poem, the extended lyric, is one in which carol and qualm, carol and qualification, carol and caveat run as one."[89] When Mackey describes how Black cultural and social life does the work of transmutation or alchemization of anti-Black violence, the question of whether forms are or are not "outgrowths of social conditions" falls away. Mackey does not ask whether form is the outgrowth of a social condition but poses a different question about the interplay of literary and musical forms and the expressive shapes of the subject.[90] The poems I read across the chapters of this book deploy lyric to meet the demands of their historical moment.

Reading lyric trade

The postwar long poems I read in this book both denounce and employ something called lyric. Each poem casts out lyric, and then invites it back in. I argue that competing formal impulses within texts written in the wake of modernism stage a critique of the subject not just by means of collage and mixture but by means of trade, and that they use trade to reveal how language forms the subject: its representation, its suppression, and its foreclosure—the subjects who take form and the subjects who remain othered. In many cases, the poems I discuss in *Lyric Trade* foreground the intersubjectivity modernists considered antithetical to the singularity and expressivity of lyric. In other cases those poems foreground historicity rather than expression, or ambience rather than delineated speech tones. In all the cases that I examine, long poems use lyric trade to stage an argument about the subject: its formation in language, its foreclosure by literary inheritance, its ambivalent indebtedness to a complicated nexus of literary histories and writerly genealogies, and its relationship to power, expression, and presence.

The book's first three chapters look at midcentury long poems that use lyric to navigate competing narratives of modernism. These chapters discuss three poets—Gwendolyn Brooks, H.D., and Lorine Niedecker—whose work crosses over decades in which modernist and postmodernist poetic revolts struggle in variegated ways to articulate a materialist poetics that can account for representational and political failures. These poets shift their creative practice to confront what they see as the social imperatives of their time. For Brooks, the focus of chapter 1, lyric trade in the 1949 long poem *Annie Allen* negotiates the differential relationships between Anglo American modernism, avant-garde form, and radical Black poetics. I argue that in stitching sonnet and ballad forms into the long form, Brooks articulates a subject position between the margins of putatively abstracted innovation and instrumentalized social poetry. For H.D., the focus of chapter 2, the 1955 long poem *Helen in Egypt* trades in classically lyric tropes of white femininity. I argue that lyric trade yokes Helen's subjectivity to whiteness. For H.D. and Brooks, lyric trade splits the poetic speaker between opposed narratives and political claims. In chapter 3, I read the polyphonic musical cadences of Lorine Niedecker's 1968 poem "Paean to Place." The association of lyric with feminized birdsong is a familiar one, but I argue that Niedecker is doing something different: by reading the poem against the musical concepts of cadence and polyphony, I find that Niedecker's key intervention is not into the figure of the bird but into its sound. What I call Niedecker's cadential lyric shifts the book's focus from the subjectivity of the poetic speaker to the subjective implications of sound.

The book's fourth and fifth chapters take up lyric trade and the entailments of empire. In chapter 4, I argue that Alice Notley's 1992 long poem *The Descent of Alette* uses lyric trade to stage a critique of patriarchal form. I read *Alette*'s distinctive formal intervention—a complex structure of quotation marks that cite and displace its subjects—as expressive feminist lyric textures that interrogate male modernism, only to reproduce the modernist practice of using racialized subjects to forge new poetic forms. I follow my discussion of *The Descent of Alette* with a discussion in chapter 5 on civil lyric in the work of Myung Mi Kim. I take up Kim's own description of lyric in her 2002 book *Commons*: "The lyric undertakes the task of deciphering and embodying a 'particularizable' prosody of one's living."[91] While this statement would seem to reify lyric as something that can necessarily attend to the particularizable elements of individual life, I argue that Kim's lyric trade instead stages a critique of the civil subject. I analyze how the appropriated and fragmented textures of Kim's 2019 long poem *Civil Bound* trouble civil subjectivity and questions of empire as social forms.

In a coda, I return *Lyric Trade* to its diagnostic contribution to genre theory. I argue that one of the things that happens when poets and critics either deploy or problematize lyric as transhistorical or universal, particularly when they assume a postgenre standpoint, is that they actually do so in the service of defending a white Western literary tradition—sometimes coded as "the literary" or "the poetic"—as against the identification of its own ideological bias. I speculate how reading an alternative lyric genealogy might give rise to a theory of the lyric distinct from the possessive individualism that dominates Western aesthetic theory. And I suggest that this kind of reading meets the urgency of being able to imagine—and recognize—radically different, more inclusive, more expansive ways of being in the world.

1

"Shut Your Rhetorics in a Box"

Annie Allen's Lyric Dilemma

In the poem that opens this book, Evie Shockley uses lyric trade to make an argument for a language adequate to the demands of historical experience. Her poem first casts out and then invites back in the structures of the ballad to confront the conundrum of writing about Emmett Till, whose death galvanized the US civil rights movement.[1] Shockley includes an epigraph from another poem about Till and the ballad—this one by Gwendolyn Brooks, writing in 1960:

> From the first it had been like a
> Ballad. It had the beat inevitable. It had the blood.[2]

Fifty-seven years before Shockley published her book *Semiautomatic*, Brooks published two poems about Till in her book *The Bean Eaters*. Both poems refer explicitly to the ballad's capacity to reckon with history. One of these poems is titled "The Last Quatrain of the Ballad of Emmett Till" and is prefaced by Brooks's own epigraph: "After the murder, / After the burial."[3] (Till's open-casket funeral on September 3, 1955, was followed three days later by the Montgomery bus boycott.) "The Last Quatrain," written from the perspective of Till's mother, Mamie Till, draws on the formal structures of the ballad in its stresses and rhymes, but it also exceeds those constraints—Brooks calls it a quatrain, but the poem consists of eight lines that may or may not be four lines split each in two, their irregular stresses glancing against neat rhymes. It's also the last quatrain of a ballad not seen or heard; Brooks writes the ending of a poem that that does not appear on this page. Until its last quatrain, the poem eludes composition, as if not just the ballad but poetry itself fell short of the task of history.

Brooks's other Emmett Till poem, titled "A Bronzeville Mother Loiters in Mississippi. Meanwhile, a Mississippi Mother Burns Bacon," comes before "Last Quatrain" in *The Bean Eaters*. "Bronzeville Mother" is the poem Shockley uses for her epigraph. It stretches for seven pages and is written from the perspective of the white cashier Carolyn Bryant, who testified against Emmett Till and whose husband and half-brother murdered Till in Mississippi (the kinship of Till's killers another cynical reference to what US "family values" might mean in Shockley's title). "Bronzeville Mother" opens with a five-line stanza that, like Shockley's "a-lyrical ballad," self-consciously invokes the limits of supposedly lyric form to reckon with historical experience. These opening lines are the ones from which Shockley selects for her epigraph:

> From the first it had been like a
> Ballad. It had the beat inevitable. It had the blood.
> A wildness cut up, and tied in little bunches,
> Like the four-line stanzas of the ballads she had never quite
> Understood—the ballads they had set her to, in school. (333)

Rather than the formal constraint in "Last Quatrain," here Brooks's ballad behaves as a simile whose formal inevitability—the last stanza of the poem refers to "The last bleak news of the ballad" (339)—mirrors the scripted fate of a poetic subject grappling with the brutality of Jim Crow–era race relations as she moves between the small violences of her own kitchen. Brooks calls the ballad "inevitable" presumably for its rhythm, its stanzaic patterns, its segmented and lineated constraints. Brooks's ballad behaves as a simile for "it," that indeterminate pronoun referring to the historical situation of the South; the Till investigation; the burgeoning struggle for civil rights; or the allegorized and objectified figure of the white woman who "never quite / Understood" the ballad she herself had been "set to." The next stanza opens by confirming that Bryant herself is "set to" the raced and gendered narrative inevitabilities of received form:

> Herself: the milk-white maid, the "maid mild"
> Of the ballad. Pursued
> By the Dark Villain. Rescued by the Fine Prince.
> The Happiness-Ever-After. (333)

Brooks's poem imagines a speaker so embedded in the tropes of white supremacy that she becomes abstracted by ballad form. That the Carolyn

Bryant of Brooks's poem does not actually understand the ballad but knows enough to liken it to her own subjectification is Brooks's larger discursive argument about complicity. When Brooks first published this poem, Till's murderers were newly acquitted; nearly half a century later, Bryant confirmed that she had falsified her testimony.[4] Brooks's poem, then, anticipates even more chillingly the inevitability of white supremacy's capacity to submerge divergent narratives within literary and juridical structures.

Although it bears some elements of the form—including narrative, incremental repetition, and the occasional four-stress and three-stress line—"A Bronzeville Mother Loiters in Mississippi. Meanwhile, a Mississippi Mother Burns Bacon" is not a ballad. It is a free-verse poem that uses ballad as a simile as well as a hinge to the poem that follows it in *The Bean Eaters*: its final line reads, "The last quatrain" (339), the same phrase Brooks uses for the title of "The Last Quatrain of the Ballad of Emmett Till." In "Bronzeville Mother," Brooks explicates the ballad's constraints in theory to confront the historical subject at the same time that she animates those same constraints to tell the story. This reflexive posture toward form is characteristic of Brooks's practice: "Bronzeville Mother" belongs to a moment midway between two major periods in Brooks's poetic career that are distinguished by their uses of formal constraint and free verse, and that are distinguished by their variant approaches to the link between audience and poetic form. The first period, beginning with the 1945 publication of her book *A Street in Bronzeville*, comprises a body of work that Haki R. Madhubuti (writing in 1972 as Don L. Lee) described as "strained" in its use of European sonnets and English ballads.[5] The second period, shaped by Brooks's 1967 encounter with the Black Arts Movement, encompasses the range of work that Brooks hoped would "somehow successfully 'call' (see Imamu Baraka's 'SOS') all black people: black people in taverns, black people in alleys, black people in gutters, schools, offices, factories, prisons, the consulate; I wish to reach black people in pulpits, black people in mines, on farms, on thrones."[6] In emphasizing the capacity of poetry to "call" African American readers from all quarters, Brooks borrows a crucial term from Amiri Baraka's "SOS," a poem that inaugurated the specifically diasporic aims of the Black Arts Movement: "Calling black people / Calling all black people, man woman child."[7] The contrast between the European forms of Brooks's pre-1967 output and the diasporic commitments of her post-1967 work has situated Brooks within the wider critical discourse surrounding African American poetic reception as well as the cultural politics of poetic form, politics she calls readers' attention to in work like "Bronzeville Mother" that scrutinizes the histories of forms like the ballad. Scholarly emphasis on two distinct periods of Brooks's work suggests a clean break between, for example, the wrought ballad-sonnets of 1949's *Annie Allen* and the free verse of 1968's *In the Mecca*, aligning each side of the break with differently situated audiences and lineages. However, focus on this break has also served to circumscribe the heterogeneity of Brooks's body of work—including long poems such as *Annie Allen*—and overlook how it negotiates competing narratives of experimentalism, politics, and the subject.

In this chapter, I argue that Brooks's long poem *Annie Allen* uses lyric trade to negotiate the differential relationships between modernism, avant-garde form, and radical Black poetics. I first consider the dilemma of influence that manifests in Brooks's work as a major factor in her lyric trade, reading that dilemma against that of an African American poet negotiating modernism in the long poem twenty years after *Annie Allen*: Melvin B. Tolson, whose long poem *Harlem Gallery* invokes the rhetorical operations of historical subjective interpellation as a problem of poetic form. I then read Brooks's uses of ballad and sonnet forms in *Annie Allen* in order to consider how the dilemma of influence manifests in formal heterogeneity for African American poetics, for US modernism, and for what it means to write poetry as social critique. I argue that by reflexively combining received poetic forms with the gestures of the high modernist long poem, *Annie Allen* confronts a fundamental dilemma of subjectivity.

"Definitionless in this strict atmosphere": The dilemma of influence

Brooks's sonnets and ballads frequently encode sociohistorical particulars in the textures of subjective expression. In "Bronzeville Mother," Brooks treats ballad constraints as a simile for white female subjectivity. Eleven years earlier, in her 1949 long poem *Annie Allen*, Brooks uses the rhyme and meter scheme of the Petrarchan sonnet to probe the confining qualities of motherhood. In iambic lines that sound vaguely scriptural even as they offer a discomfiting view of motherhood, the poem's speaker asks how to provide for children in a landscape of scarcity. In "the children of the poor," which appears in the third section of *Annie Allen*, Brooks writes:

> What shall I give my children? who are poor,
> Who are adjudged the leastwise of the land,
> Who are my sweetest lepers, who demand
> No velvet and no velvety velour (116)

These lines offer a thicket of compressions, redundancies, and abstractions. The children in the poem are described as "sweetest lepers," as figures who demand the speaker's endearment even as they might be regarded as outcast and maladjusted by the public. The children also appear doubly diminutive; they are described several lines later as "little halves," objects that are insufficiently able to make up a whole person. A half is a fraction of a whole, not a diminutive quality at all, except by comparison to some other object. These children, then, may even be the other halves of the speaker herself; they are not, strictly speaking, fifty percent of anything.

The next few lines of Brooks's sonnet further articulate not just the essential insufficiency of the children but their very dehumanization, suggesting that whatever they do possess is offset by a profound, even metaphysical, sense of sociopolitical lack. The scarcity here is a poverty of circumstance, but Brooks draws on another meaning of scarcity, one attached to the very notion of personhood. Brooks's speaker tells us that the children "have begged me for a brisk contour," as if they were begging the speaker to give them shape:

> Crying that they are quasi, contraband
> Because unfinished, graven by a hand
> Less than angelic, admirable or sure. (116)

Brooks describes the children using the prefix "quasi," which instead of modifying an adjective stands alone, followed by a comma. Calling the children "quasi" reinforces their virtuality, while ascribing their creation to a hand "Less than angelic, admirable or sure" assigns a genealogical inevitability to their condition. These are the children of the poor, but they are also poor at being children: "contraband," prohibited, smuggled into view—and into the poem.

By combining abstracted thematics with the patterned constraints of Petrarchan meter and rhyme, "the children of the poor" navigates two formal tensions. The first is a binary that distinguishes received forms such as the sonnet and ballad from the free-verse techniques of modernism: "To break the pentameter, that was the first heave," notes Pound parenthetically in Canto 81.[8] I have indexed Brooks's uses of ballads and sonnets as her chief materials of lyric, but the association of ballads and sonnets with something called lyric is not necessarily straightforward. Jonathan Culler in his sweeping *Theory of the Lyric* holds that the sonnet is best understood as a "subgenre" of the general category of the lyric.[9] And Brooks's deeply perspectival sonnet might also bear out Paul de Man's claim that "The principle of intelligibility, in lyric poetry, depends on the phenomenalization of the poetic voice."[10] To draw either conclusion about Brooks's poem—that a sonnet is a subgenre of lyric, or that a sonnet's perspectivalism is a lyric principle—is complicated by Genette's reminder that the historical relationship between "sonnet," which he distinguishes as a genre, and "lyric," which he distinguishes as a mode, is a kind of error produced by the Romantic reinterpretation of modes as genres.[11] To draw either conclusion is further complicated by critical studies of the sonnet and ballad as forms culturally associated with African American history and poetics and formally associated with forms such as spirituals, folk, and blues, in addition to European lyric.[12]

The preceding sentences only begin to gesture toward the spuriousness of the taxonomic imperative. And my own reading of Brooks's sonnets and ballads so far risks rehearsing a critical tendency to index instances of "lyric" as the version of poetry into which "stipulative" verse genres such as sonnets and ballads collapse.[13] But, as I asked in this book's introduction, what if, instead, the historical lyric error, or the phenomenon of lyric reading, or the taxonomic imperative, all reveal something else? *Lyric Trade* is interested more in the cultural politics of lyric than in chasing its classification. This is the second tension navigated by "the children of the poor": Brooks's sonnet marks the intersection of competing narratives of experimentalism and politics in African American poetics and, more broadly, the formal and thematic intersection of poetry as social critique. Writing between the periodic and aesthetic margins of formal innovation and a more instrumentalized social poetry, Brooks uses lyric trade to dramatize the dilemma of poetic influence as a problem of subjectivity.

Like a number of midcentury long poems, Brooks's 1949 work *Annie Allen* experiments with collage and fragmentation; it favors inductive assemblage over linear narrative; it plays with chronology and recursive time. Brooks structures her poem's three main sections—"Notes from the Childhood and the Girlhood," "The Anniad," and "The Womanhood"—around the biographical progression of its central figure, Annie, putting the poem in dialogue both with a philosophical-biographical long poem tradition that might loosely be charted from William Wordsworth in the nineteenth century to William Carlos Williams in the twentieth, and with the influence of both classical epic and modern seriality in twentieth-century long works. Particularly in the case of the poem's middle section, "The Anniad," whose title puns both on Homer's *Iliad* and on Virgil's *Aeneid*, *Annie Allen*—like H.D.'s *Helen in Egypt*, which I discuss in my next chapter—evinces a modernist engagement with classical form. Even though *Annie Allen* draws on the sonnet and ballad constraints other modernists rejected, Brooks's poem also draws on the densely allusive practices the modernists championed. In a 1967 interview with Paul Angle, Brooks says both that "There are certain hard specifics that can be taught. Sonnet rules. Guards against free verse" and that when she joined a writing group with Inez Cunningham Stark in 1941 on the South Side of Chicago, Stark "introduced me to many of the moderns" at a time in which she felt she "was subscribing too obediently to the older poets."[14] In its moments of cultural critique—including, particularly in the third section, polyphonic representations of a city beset by racial and economic tension—*Annie Allen* links Brooks to the "moderns" she cites who take treatise or argument as their major ambition.[15] Although *Annie Allen* shares the critical mode of other US long poems, the "hard specifics" of its sonnet and ballad forms both enact and trouble lyric expression. For Brooks, the influence of modernist and divergent forms was a generative lyric dilemma.

Brooks encountered the dilemma of poetic influence early on. Born in 1917 in Topeka, Kansas, Brooks spent most of her life on the South Side of Chicago, which was home to the second largest population of African Americans (after Harlem) who left the South during the Great Migration. As she writes in *Report from Part One* (1972), young Gwendolyn Brooks, who had just been furnished by her proud parents with her first writing desk, was told by her mother that she would soon be "the *lady* Paul Laurence Dunbar*"; Brooks's mother refers to the poet whose uses of African American dialect in his 1896 collection *Lyrics of Lowly Life* were popularly received but also criticized by readers who suggested they reinforced negative racial stereotypes.[16] Brooks's mother's remark is frequently cited by scholars as an early acknowledgement of Brooks's artistic skill, but it also signals the fraught position in which many US writers have found themselves as their work negotiates the culturally burdened spaces of literary heritage. Dunbar and Brooks write at different points in US literary history when the mastery of European forms was a test of literacy as well as a measure of literary authority.[17] Tensions surrounding the uses of European forms, free verse, and nonstandard English also characterized the literary movements with which Brooks has been associated. By the time of Brooks's death, in 2000, she had come to be identified with the modernism of the 1910s and 1920s, the Harlem Renaissance of the 1920s and 1930s, and the Black Arts Movement of the 1960s and 1970s.[18] When Brooks won the Pulitzer Prize for *Annie Allen*, in 1950, she became the first African American to be awarded a Pulitzer in any category. Critics such as Madhubuti suggested that the prize assimilated Brooks for a white audience. Madhubuti wrote in 1972: "In the eyes of white poetry lovers and white book promoters, the publicity was to read 'she is a poet who happens to be black'; in other words, we can't completely forget her 'negroness,' so let's make it secondary."[19] While the prize, Madhubuti wrote, "aided her in the pursuit of other avenues of expression and gave her a foothold into earning desperately needed money by writing reviews and articles for major white publications," it also furthered Brooks's self-definition according to "Euro-American" logic. Madhubuti's comments summarize the legitimizing power of the literary prize economy but also the dilemma surrounding what it meant for an African American poet to write "legitimate" poetry for both white and Black audiences.[20]

Brooks's dilemma resembles that of Melvin B. Tolson, whose 1965 work *Harlem Gallery* spans twenty-four cantos, each named after a letter of the Greek alphabet, in an extended meditation on the relationship of the African American artist to the community—and who, like Brooks, inherited what Kathy Lou Schultz calls "proto-modernist Paul Laurence Dunbar's attempts to synthesize modern black identity."[21] Also like Brooks, Tolson does not fit chronologically into one particular literary movement, instead dwelling (like Brooks) in the midcentury gap between the Harlem Renaissance and the Black Arts Movement. This chronological slippage is one characteristic of *Harlem Gallery*'s own capacity to wrestle with impulses both aesthetic and historical. Tolson's extant work, subtitled *Book I, The Curator*, summarizes the distinctive landscape of his epic poem using both typographical and rhetorical ellipses: "The Harlem Gallery / . . . the creek that connects the island and the mainland . . . / . . . a *q* in Old Anglo-Saxon . . . "[22] The gallery is as much a no-man's land as it is a staging ground for the Black artist's dialectic. The Curator, Tolson's "Afroirishjewish" storyteller, summarizes the artist's situation using one of the book's many Hamlet references:

> Poor Boy Blue,
> the Great White World
> and the Black Bourgeoisie
> have shoved the Negro artist into
> the white and not-white dichotomy,
> the Afroamerican dilemma in the Arts—
> the dialectic of
> to be or not to be
> a Negro. (336)[23]

Whereas Hamlet's soliloquy dramatizes a life-or-death choice between action or inaction, the Curator's recapitulation posits an absurd choice "to be or not to be / a Negro." Hideho Heights, *Harlem Gallery*'s "vagabond bard of Lenox Avenue" (258), sees his "Negro artist" identity divided between public and private, ballad and modern:

> He didn't know
> I knew
> about the split identity
> of the People's Poet—
> the bifacial nature of his poetry:
> the racial ballad in the public domain
> and the private poem in the modern vein. (335)

Tolson may be positing, as many critics have concluded, that one must write in "the modern vein" to survive ("with no poems of Hideho's in World Lit— / he'd be a statistic!"). Yet, crucially, Tolson's verse also refuses to posit Anglo American modernism as a solution to the African American writer's dilemma, instead using the poem to dramatize the racial nature of subject formation in the third and fourth stanzas of the poem's opening canto:

> As a Hambletonian gathers his legs for a leap,
> dead wool and fleece wool
> I have mustered up from hands
> now warm or cold: a full
> rich Indies' cargo;
> but often I hear a dry husk-of-locust blues
> descend the tone ladder of a laughing goose,
> syncopating between
> the faggot and the noose:
> "Black Boy, O Black Boy,
> is the port worth the cruise?"
>
> Like the lice and maggots of the apples of Cain
> on a strawberry tree,
> the myth of the Afroamerican past
> exacts the parasite's fee. (209–10)

In addition to these two stanzas' employment of oppositions—the speaker's identification with a Hambletonian, a trotting horse descended from a (nobler) stallion; hands warm and cold; another impoverished choice between the lit faggot and the noose; rotting apples on a mock apple tree—the passage reads as a description of interpellation.

Louis Althusser's description of the constitutive process of interpellation foregrounds the disciplinary quality of a scene like Tolson's, in which the voice of power calls to the subject using the slur "Black Boy."[24] Althusser's familiar scene dramatizes the phenomenon in which ideology "recruits" the subject by the operation he calls *interpellation* or hailing, and which can be imagined along the lines of the most commonplace everyday police (or other) hailing: 'Hey, you there!'" In Althusser's iconic scene, the hailed individual pivots to recognizes the address, in turn becoming an ideological subject.[25] In *Black Skin, White Masks*, Frantz Fanon describes a scene of hailing that—despite having been written a few years earlier—usefully modifies Althusser's formulation to account for race. Early in his development as a racialized subject, Fanon writes, "I found that I was an object in the midst of other objects," and this basic fact of humanity was further transformed by a scene of racial hailing:

"Look, a Negro!" he heard a child cry.[26] Fanon later argues that the traditional dialectic of race cannot articulate Black consciousness: "Without a Negro past, without a Negro future, it was impossible for me to live my Negrohood. Not yet white, no longer wholly black, I was damned."[27] Quite different in content from the moment of hailing in *Harlem Gallery* (and quite different from the presence of children in Brooks's poem), Fanon's scene helps make clear how "Black Boy" functions in Tolson's text as a continuously dialectical refrain that can never be closed or transcended. The subject is left occupying three places that lie disparate. In Tolson's *Harlem Gallery*, the text pivots to answer the call. Of course, as in Fanon, the hailing in *Harlem Gallery* is not just a hail but a taunt: "is the port worth the cruise?" Coming as it does just before a description of the "fee" Cain's insufficient offering of apples exacts upon the African American artist, "cruise" acts as a cruel provocation, implying a reference to the Middle Passage for a subject caught between the false divide of subject and object, the "the white and not-white dichotomy, / the Afroamerican dilemma in the Arts."

For Tolson as for Brooks, the tension between public and private, ballad and modern, was a question of audience: whether to write for an African American diaspora or a narrowly Anglo modernist readership. And for both poets, that tension manifested in forgings of blues, ballad, and sonnet forms within modernist epic structures. The question of Tolson's modernism emerged in one of the first critical appraisals of Tolson's work. In his introduction to the 1965 edition of *Harlem Gallery*, Karl Shapiro revealed perhaps more about racial tensions in American literary modernism than he might have intended: "It is not enough to equate Tolson, as his best critics have done, with [T. S.] Eliot or Hart Crane" because "Tolson writes and thinks in Negro, which is to say, a possible American language."[28] *Harlem Gallery*, Shapiro continues, performs

> the primary poetic rite for our literature. Instead of purifying the tongue, which is the business of the Academy, he is complicating it, giving it the gift of tongues. Pound, Eliot, and [James] Joyce did this, but with a pernicious nostalgia that all but killed the patient. Tolson does it naturally and to the manner born.[29]

Seventeen years earlier, while serving on the committee for the Bollingen Prize, Shapiro had voted not to award the prize to Pound for *Pisan Cantos*. It is difficult not to interpret Shapiro's introduction to *Harlem Gallery* in the context of Pound's anti-Semitic fixation upon racial purity. Shapiro might be trying to read Tolson's embrace of complication over purity as a recuperative act for American poetry.[30] Shapiro's use of race in his introduction makes his own essay an artifact of white literary culture's romanticization of the African American artistic imagination (Shapiro writes that Tolson is "naturally" suited to his project because of his race), as it also indexes tensions between the critical reception of twentieth-century African American poetics and the institutional power of white Anglo modernism. In a 1967 interview, Brooks invoked Shapiro's introduction to Tolson when she suggested that the issue of reception was crucial to the shaping of her own poetic career: "I can't say that I have been hindered, because of my race, in the field of writing," she told Paul Angle; but, she added, "I do believe that it is true, as Karl Shapiro says, that many white anthologists will not admit black writers to their pages."[31]

For Tolson and for Brooks, the ballad figures, variously, populist aesthetic, narrative inevitability, and subjectification; ballad functions as a simile for larger rhetorics of literary-institutional power within modernism. Brooks, writing twenty years before *Harlem Gallery*, used the very same structures of the ballad and the sonnet to dramatize the dilemma of interpellation under modernist influence. For early critics of *Annie Allen*, its mixture of ballad, sonnet, and free-verse modernist forms elicited a dismissal of Brooks's overly specialized modernist "abstraction."[32] Descriptions of the book's competing lyricism and experimentalism range from praise for the poem's formal ambition to disdain for the poem's rhetorical qualities as cold and psychological. *Annie Allen* was assailed for two kinds of abstraction—formal and theoretical—that foreclosed political critique. In a 1949 piece in the *Saturday Review of Literature*, for example, J. Saunders Redding approvingly compares Brooks's "liquid lyricism, momentarily held in delicate static poise" to a "silver figure" of the sixteenth-century Italian artist Benvenuto Cellini.[33] But Redding also suggests that *Annie Allen* "devotes itself to setting forth an experience even more special and particularized than the usual poetic experience" in a way that "puts itself under unnecessary strain." The review launches a polemic against what Redding considers the specious abstractions of modernism put to the task of representing African American subjects and experience: "No one wants to read a psychological treatise or any treatise whatever, for that matter, in order to get at the true meaning of a poem."[34] Redding suggests not that Brooks's compressed lines are so modernist as to be generally alienating; rather, he considers the poetry to have been written only for an African American audience: "Who but another Negro can get the intimate feeling, the racially particular acceptance and rejection, and the oblique bitterness of this?" In its use of "the highly special feeling derived from an even more special experience," *Annie Allen*, Redding suggests, evinces a central "flaw." The poem raises the essential question, Redding says, of "whether Miss Brooks or any poet (now when so many people find modern poetry obscure and unrewarding) can afford to be a coterie poet." Redding criticizes Brooks for using the modernist tools of obscurity to convey specifically African American experience, setting "coterie" against craft. The book in his view is ultimately "artistically sure" and "esthetically complete" but, Redding famously adds, "I do not want to see Miss Brooks's fine talents dribble away in the obscure and the too oblique."

Redding's remarks suggest the extent to which Brooks was increasingly held accountable for creating poetry that could be heard in what Tolson would later call both the "public domain" and the "private vein"—an interpretation governed by the putative neutrality of a white public audience. For Brooks, the "public domain" also came to signal her changing relationship to cultural poetic vernaculars in the decades that followed the publication of *Annie Allen*. Brooks's move toward socially engaged poetry is documented most extensively as her 1967 radicalization after attending the Black Writers' Conference at Fisk University, where Brooks encountered writers and activists of the Black Arts Movement. Brooks describes meeting Amiri Baraka as a pivotal moment, her signature wordplay punning on the notions of respect, expectation, and jubilation:

> Coming from white white white South Dakota State College I arrived in Nashville, Tennessee, to give one more "reading." But blood-boiling surprise was in store for me. First, I was aware of a general energy, an electricity, in look, walk, speech, *gesture* of the young blackness I saw all about me. I had been "loved" at South Dakota State College. Here, I was coldly Respected. [. . .] Imamu Amiri Baraka, then "LeRoi Jones," was expected. He arrived in the middle of my own offering, and when I called attention to his presence there was jubilee in Jubilee Hall.[35]

That jubilee spurred Brooks to adopt Baraka's aim to "call all black people" by stretching the bounds of her longstanding practice: "My newish voice," she later wrote, "will not be an imitation of the contemporary young black voice, which I so admire, but an extending adaptation of today's G. B. voice."[36] Houston A. Baker locates her "newish voice" in the tonal shifts between *Annie Allen* and Brooks's later work, in particular her 1968 collection *In the Mecca*, which was nominated for the National Book Award, as a matter of audience.[37] "The ironies that Brooks directed at supercilious whites and the detached, subtle amusement with which she approached some black subjects in earlier work," Baker suggests, are absent in later works that affirm Black nationalism.[38] Baker cites Brooks among Black writers of the 1950s who changed their practices to meet political demands. The vocabulary of his criticism, in light of the reading by Redding, recapitulates the notion of modernist abstraction:

> In sum, black writers of the 1950s were not certain they had a country. They worked, perhaps too often, in a world of abstractions that included not only their most esteemed values, but also their hypothetical or implied Western audience. In the 1960s and 1970s, on the other hand, black spokesmen were convinced that their real audience, like the nation to come, was black, and their values and canons were designed to accord with this conviction.[39]

In the Mecca formally and thematically marks Brooks's radicalization after the Fisk conference as well as her break with mainstream publishing; it was the last book she would publish with Harper and Row before partnering with African American small presses, including Broadside Press and Third World Press.[40] Baker confirms the subtext of Redding's review: the problem with *Annie Allen* is not that it addresses a specialized audience, but that it refuses to be circumscribed by a presumed white audience.

While Baker identifies Brooks's aesthetic shift as a matter of tone, others, including Brooks herself, locate the shift in terms of meter: the sonnets and ballads that were also taken to be a form of abstraction. In 1973, Madhubuti described *Annie Allen* as "conditioned" (a word Madhubuti lifts from Brooks's own characterization) by European and English forms, too wedded to the stylistic textures of received form at the expense of historical urgency:

> The early years reaped with self-awareness—there is no denying this—
> even though at times the force of her poetic song is strained in iambic

pentameter, European sonnets and English ballads. Conditioned! There is a stronger sense of self-awareness than most of her contemporaries with the possible exception of Margaret Walker. She was able to pull through the old leftism of the 1930s and 1940s and concentrate on herself, her people and most of all her "writing." Conditioned! Her definitions of the world as represented in the early poetry are often limited to accommodating her work and her person to definitions that were imposed on her from the outside; and she becomes the reactor rather than the actor.[41]

In Brooks's later work, Madhubuti concludes, history frees her poetry from metrical confinement; *In the Mecca* (1968), *Riot* (1969), and *Family Pictures* (1970) are directed "to her people"; free verse and blank verse resemble "a man getting off meat, turning to a vegetarian diet."[42] Madhubuti points to "the children of the poor" as an exception to the two poles in Brooks's work: because it combines the strains of European style with situated, historical urgency, "we begin to sense the feel of home again."[43] Madhubuti associates European forms with excess and fatty meat, and Brooks's post-1967 output with trim cuts and streamlined craft; Madhubuti does not suggest that Brooks fully abandons European forms, but rather that she infuses them with a newfound sense of "greatness"[44] as she confronts the poet's dilemma: "How does a black poet (or any black person working creatively) define himself and his work: is he a poet who happens to be black or is he a black man or woman who happens to write?"[45]

The way Brooks's work articulates and confronts the racial dilemma of US modernism can be traced to these two thematic strands in the reception of *Annie Allen*, as articulated by Baker and Madhubuti—tonal ironies that are said to keep African American readers at a distance, and European metrical styles that are said to overly condition otherwise urgent historical Black content. Critics have often described Brooks's competing formal gestures as a manifestation of W. E. B. Du Bois's trope of double consciousness, or what he defined as the internal conflict faced by a subject carrying multiple strands of identity: African and American heritage, or, in the case of Brooks's poetics, European and African American poetic forms. Du Bois wrote most extensively about double consciousness in his 1903 book *The Souls of Black Folk*, in which he writes of having been "born with a veil" to a world that thwarts him access to self-consciousness, "but only lets him see himself through the revelation of the other world."[46] Du Bois describes the "peculiar sensation" of "always looking at one's self through the eyes of others, of measuring one's soul by the tape of a world that looks on in amused contempt and pity. One ever feels his two-ness,—an American, a Negro; [. . .] two warring ideals in one dark body." For Brooks, critics have often claimed, those "two warring ideals" can be understood as her uses of white style and Black content, or her uses of European form and Black sociohistorical critique.

But comparing Brooks to Du Bois is a highly complex operation. I have been arguing that for Brooks, literary influence manifested as a dilemma of subjectivity: when it is read against Du Bois's articulation of Black subjective experience, this dilemma comes into relief as one acutely sociohistorical. In *The Souls of Black Folk*, Du Bois summons the language of craft and occupation when he identifies the individual in double consciousness as a "black artisan" who, having sought to escape "white contempt," suffers a poverty of "trade."[47] Du Bois's artisan is both exemplar and metonym for his exegesis of double consciousness and for the text of *Souls of Black Folk* itself. In an essay published a year and a half after *Souls*, Du Bois writes of his own ambivalence toward the book, suggesting that its fourteen essays might suffer from "rather abrupt transitions of style, tone and viewpoint," for "It is difficult, strangely difficult, to translate the finer feelings of men into words."[48] In the end Du Bois finds his own book, if lacking in trade, full of deep feeling and unified by a "personal and intimate tone of self-revelation"; he declares, "In its larger aspects the style is tropical—African. This needs no apology. The blood of my fathers spoke through me and cast off the English restraint of my training and surroundings."

Reading Brooks's work against the notion of double consciousness, then, demands a great deal of nuance, particularly given the metatextual element of Du Bois's own reflections upon how *Souls of Black Folk* might lack what Du Bois calls "trade," even if it is unified in its "feeling." As Brooks became more invested in how the vernacular poetics of the Black Arts Movement could advance and strengthen group identity, she herself came to describe *Annie Allen* as overly "poetic" in its engagement with lyric—and she distanced herself from what she characterized as her early formal ambition.[49] Still, Brooks also dismisses the notion of a clear break between her lyric earlier work and her politicized later work. For example, in a 1969 interview she rejects the idea that lyricism belongs to the domain of received form: "I have not abandoned beauty, or lyricism, and I don't consider myself a polemical poet. I'm a black poet, and I write about what I see."[50] And in 1967, asked if poets are affected by social unrest, she appears to reject the conventional encoding of lyric privacy and interiority at the expense of social relevance: "The poet, first and foremost an individual with *a* personal vision, is also a member of society. What affects society affects a poet. So I, starting out, *usually* in the grip of a high and private suffusion, may find by the time I have arrived at a last line that there is quite some public clamor in my product."[51] Brooks's second remark suggests especially that this "high and private suffusion" does not preclude public-oriented poetics; rather, she suggests poetic speech, whatever its form, is always social in its "public clamor." For both Brooks and Du Bois, the terms of subjectivity continually call the terms of craft, expression, and history into question.[52] I have pointed to Du Bois's later writing on *Souls*, but as Anthony Reed points out, scenes of writing and revision in *Souls of Black Folk* also negotiate language and writing in the course of the book's exposition. Double consciousness is as much an allegory for textuality as it is for subjectivity. Du Bois, in Reed's words, "submits in his book to the implicit interpellative demand that he *narrate* his having come to racial consciousness, of having recognized the veil."[53]

Textuality, form, and poetry as social practice—the conceptual and historical borders between these things are fully contested. Modernism sought to "make it new," but the very idea of experiment and innovation is often attached less to a broad idea of tradition itself and more to the cultural politics of inclusion and exclusion, to say nothing of what many studies of modernist literature have identified as its cultural imperialism.[54] Attending to the cultural work of innovation and poetic form in the Harlem Renaissance and Black Arts movements deterritorializes US modernism, opening up its chronological and cultural borders.[55] The marker of literary innovation, encoded with race, ethnicity, and gender norms, is not sufficient to redraw those borders. Poets like Brooks and Tolson, writing at midcentury, particularly dramatize the contradictions of modernism precisely because of how their works illuminate the fluidity of movements and the ways in which certain poets circulate between and outside them. "It is brave to be involved," Brooks writes in *Annie Allen*;

"To be not fearful to be unresolved" (93). *Annie Allen* has often been viewed primarily as a symptom of the dilemma of modernist influence, but Brooks's poem confronts that dilemma and makes legible the broader politics of innovation at midcentury. A sonnet in Brooks's 1960 book *The Bean Eaters* concludes: "People are coming. They must not catch us here / Definitionless in this strict atmosphere" (363). Brooks tests the limits of expressive form to reckon with histories of the subject.

"wrought bedevilling":
Lyric trade in *Annie Allen*

"My last defense / Is the present tense," Brooks writes in "Old Mary," from *The Bean Eaters* (332). Before Brooks appeared to distance her poetry from what she saw as the overly technical approaches of modernism in favor of free verse, *Annie Allen* used idioms, rhyme schemes, and metrical patterns to construct a poetic speaker whose lyric trade embodies the dilemma of how to reconcile the lineage of poetic form with the social and political demands of the contemporary moment. Tolson's scene of interpellation in *Harlem Gallery* encapsulates poetry's capacity to reflect, and reflect on, subject formation and racial difference. *Annie Allen* draws on the productive instability of lyric in order to dramatize the difficulty of poetic speech.

In his study of avant-garde Asian American poetry and racial objectification, Joseph Jonghyun Jeon contrasts the resistant nature of self-definition with the critique of representational power, a contrast typically associated with activist or representational poetry on the one hand and experimental, avant-garde, or modernist poetry on the other hand. While I do not want uncritically to transpose Jeon's specific argument about Asian American poetry to the present discussion of African American poetry, I cite his study because his work begins by questioning "the widely regarded incompatibility between avant-garde artistic forms and racial politics," an incompatibility indexed in Brooks reception.[56] Jeon's insights into identity and representation offer terms that shed light on the reception of Brooks's work as articulating African American subjectivity "conditioned" (as Madhubuti puts it, taking the term from Brooks) by both modernist abstraction and the "European American logic" of received form. Jeon argues that the contested term of representation is what sets two discourses in conflict: "whereas in the activist mode, self-definition becomes a resistant gesture aimed at wresting away representational power from hegemonic forces that determine stereotypes, avant-garde poetry tends to place a greater degree of emphasis on metacritical examinations of the formation of representational power itself."[57] Jeon's formulation torques the binary of representation and experiment; it also suggests the ways in which poems use lyric trade to negotiate representational power.

Brooks shapes the voice as precisely metatextual in the way Jeon suggests. The second poem in *Annie Allen*, "Maxie Allen," locates in Annie's mother a "voice" caught somewhere between first-person interiority and dialogic relationality. Brooks writes that "Sweet Annie tried to teach her mother / There was somewhat of something other" (84). In rhyming couplets Maxie's daughter seeks to elucidate for her mother what possibilities lie outside their "narrow room":

> Her mother thought at her full well,
> In inner voice not like a bell
> (Which though not social has a ring
> Akin to wrought bedevilling)
> But like an oceanic thing:
>> What do you guess I am? (84–85)

This "inner voice," which is "not like a bell"—not merely melodic—but also "not social"—not universalizable or otherwise relational—is, instead, "oceanic," the word Freud used to describe the "residue" of being bonded with the outside world.[58] In Freud's formulation, oceanic feeling subtends limitlessness; here, that feeling subtends a question about the limits of the self as perceived by the other: "What do you guess I am?" Subjective representation lies at the heart of the lyric cliché, a lyric whose speech emits from and articulates a discrete body. Brooks's poem invites that cliché before the voice goes silent. The poem's metatextuality entails a rethinking not only of the binary of representation and metacriticism—where poetry that follows received forms is interested in representation, whereas poetry that is formally innovative performs metacriticism—but also of the usefulness of the term "lyric." Brooks's poem exfoliates what the lyric cliché does to render sociohistorical subjects as phenomenological entities. In this way, Brooks's work invites a larger philosophical discussion about voice. Lyric theory often fixates upon how poetic speech both resists and embodies the essential conflict between the individual and the social; Genette's corrective reinscribes lyric presence as having to do with the enunciating situation of the poem rather than its preexisting subject formation; theorists such as Adriana Cavarero and Fred Moten have argued for a conception of the voice as something related to but not reducible to speech, something social and multiple, and something that originates in material, physical, historical reality, such as the urban poverty of postwar Chicago.[59] Read metatextually, the Petrarchan sonnet in Brooks's *Annie Allen* contests each of these terms of voice and presence.

In "the children of the poor," child figures appear not as ghostly presences who might have access or stature beyond that of being human but as "Less than angelic," "unfinished" by a hand that has left them "graven," formed as if sculpted or carved in stone (116). If form is sedimented content (pace Adorno), it here is made form again in Brooks's lines. The notion of children of the poor being carved in stone further suggests the inevitability of poverty, diminutive figures racing toward mortality. Later, when the children die, they appear "granitely discreet"; their deaths manifest as a non-organic event (119). The children are not the only figures who are abstracted by Brooks's terse diction: the speaker, too, appears to be charged with creating a form of contested viability. Brooks writes:

> My hand is stuffed with mode, design, device.
> But I lack access to my proper stone.
> And plenitude of plan shall not suffice
> Nor grief nor love shall be enough alone
> To ratify my little halves who bear
> Across an autumn freezing everywhere. (116)

The speaker pictures a hand that holds "mode, design, device," all terms to describe something that can take form and shape and yet resist its own thingness; here, they remain abstract concepts whose actual forms are diffuse to a speaker who "lack[s] access" to her "proper stone." The phrase "proper stone" indicates the mythical philosopher's stone that has the power to turn base metal to gold or to heal illness—or, in this case, possibly, to ease poverty. The speaker is unable to "ratify" her "little halves." Brooks's lines invoke the legalistic rhetoric of property, injunction, or sanction to describe lack. "Plenitude" or fullness of plan or intent cannot suffice to validate these children. Brooks's lines suggest a poetic speaker with certain formal tools at her disposal who lacks the one tool that would be most immediately useful: a poetic voice that can adequately respond to her children's dehumanization.

In the sequence's fifth sonnet, Brooks uses another surprising compound to constellate motherhood, poverty, and abstract form, one that launches a critique of the specifically pedagogical function of adequate form:

> May not they in the crisp encounter see
> Something to recognize and read as rightness?
> I say they may, so granitely discreet,
> The little crooked questionings inbound,
> Concede themselves on most familiar ground,
> Cold an old predicament of the breath:
> Adroit, the shapely prefaces complete,
> Accept the university of death. (119)

The children of the poor are described as "shapely prefaces," precisely paratextual rather than central to the poem itself despite the significance they are given by Brooks's title. When these "shapely prefaces complete," Brooks writes, they "Accept the university of death." Their deaths are a historical dilemma, an "old predicament," their demise inevitable. The word "university" derives from a series of Anglo-Norman and Old French terms including "corporation," "community," "totality," and "universality," terms that indicate not just comprehensive and totalizing bodies of knowledge but also the process of transmitting that knowledge—through a "social" voice, perhaps. Here, with the phrase "university of death," Brooks ironizes the notion of knowledge to suggest that the children of the poor are being primed for an early demise by an institution that otherwise promises social mobility.

The speaker's hand as well as her maternal capabilities, then, are unable to effect her children's social mobility, and Brooks depicts this situation using mathematical, alchemical, and aesthetic values that navigate the experiences of urban poverty not by greater specificity of image, as in the more documentary-inflected poetics of some of her contemporaries, but by greater abstraction. The poem suggests a speaker unable to realize her full poetic powers, a subject caught between modes of action. "Halves," "quasi," "mode," "design," "device," "stone": all these terms resist specificity at the same time that they anchor a poem that calls forth a scene of social and domestic discord. Brooks's emphasis on a speaker whose voice and abilities appear stunted, frustrated, or halted within the sonnet frame in a certain sense remains faithful to the early modern sonnet's capacity to convey intensities of emotion and vivid temporality. One thinks, for example, of Shakespeare's tendencies toward condensed phrasing and obscure imagery, or of the Petrarchan sonnet's tendency to stall and distort time.[60] The poem uses its formal critique to situate the stalled creativity of motherhood within the more far-reaching problem of social inequity.

Annie Allen's metatextual voice invites comparison to a lyric novel Brooks published just a few years later, which likewise metaphorizes the notion of form for subjectivity. When Brooks's novel *Maud Martha* appeared in 1953, it was described in the *New Yorker* as "a hopeful piling up of small details"[61]—this fixation on Brooks's "small details" as a sort of "style" in her novel betrays an assumption about the "smallness" that characterizes Brooks's uses of poetic language, particularly its allusive detail, as well as its domesticity. Both *Annie Allen* and *Maud Martha* use intricately numbered sequences to follow their heroines from early childhood to later adulthood; both assemble titles and segmented structures that range from the descriptive to the elliptical; both cultivate "small details" that among other things collate into a portrait of postwar Chicago. Both texts also construct a central figure who foregrounds her own competing impulses toward singular self-expression and outward-directed cultural critique.

Maud Martha appears at times herself as a kind of detail. In the sixth vignette of the novel, Maud Martha, at sixteen, attends a concert at Chicago's Regal Theatre and reflects on fame. The performance having left her feeling cold, Maud Martha articulates an alternative vision for what her own creative efforts might entail:

> To create—a role, a poem, picture, music, a rapture in stone: great. But not for her.
>
> What she wanted was to donate to the world a good Maud Martha. That was the offering, the bit of art, that could not come from any other.
>
> She would polish and hone that.[62]

Maud Martha imagines herself as a "bit of art," "good" rather than "great," rendering herself literally into diegetic detail. As these details of self-description accumulate, the novel starts to forge implicit parallels between the racist norms Maud Martha encounters outside the home and the misogynist norms inside it. In "tradition and Maud Martha," the disconnect grows between her desire for intimacy and permanence and the drudgery of the routine of housewifely service:

> What she had wanted was a solid. She had wanted shimmering form; warm, but hard as stone and as difficult to break. She had wanted to found— tradition. She had wanted to shape, for their use, for hers, for his, for little Paulette's, a set of falterless customs. She had wanted stone[.] (102)

"Solid," "form," "stone," "found," "shape": Maud Martha's desire has gone from art to monumental experience. In *Annie Allen*, adequate or proper form is absent from the speaker's hands as an impossible chunk of stone; in *Maud Martha*, stone is figurative flesh. Maud Martha both makes a claim to the singularity of her subjectivity—"that could not come from any other"—and suggests the way her estranged subjectivity comes to be polished in craft.

Detail enlarges *Maud Martha* beyond story; the novel becomes a critique of the forces that would otherwise shape and hone its central figure. Note, for example, Brooks's penetrating invocation of intersectionality when Maud Martha observes that while World War II combat may have ceased, race and gender norms live on. Her brother Harry has come home from the war, the spring light is coming into the kitchenette, and the spring air coming through the window figure as possibility: "What, *what*, am I to do with all of this life?" (178, italics in the original). Maud Martha's "sharp exhilaration" is interrupted by thoughts of the war's dead and wounded and of the US racial climate:

> And the Negro press (on whose front pages beamed the usual representations of womanly Beauty, pale and pompadoured) carried the stories of the latest of the Georgia and Mississippi lynchings. (179)

Maud Martha turns away from these thoughts, choosing to focus on the living. "And, in the meantime," she thinks, "while people did live they would be grand, would be glorious and brave." This is where Brooks's novel ends, with survival hinging on the style of the details that make up all of a life.[63]

Annie Allen likewise offers a central figure circulating between abstraction and social ties. The link between this complicated presence and the contradictions of speech is clarified in "do not be afraid of no," in which ten rhyming couplets disaggregate the link between intense sound patterning and subjective action. The first four couplets are characterized by abstract lines of action grounded in a finely regular sound pattern with no established metrical regularity:

> "Do not be afraid of no,
> Who has so far so very far to go":
>
> New caution to occur
> To one whose inner scream set her to cede, for softer lapping and
>   smooth fur!
>
> Whose esoteric need
> Was merely to avoid the nettle, to not-bleed.
>
> Stupid, like a street
> That beats into a dead end and dies there, with nothing left to
>   reprimand or meet.
>
> And like a candle fixed
> Against dismay and countershine of mixed
>
> Wild moon and sun. And like
> A flying furniture, or bird with lattice wing; or gaunt thing, a-stammer
>   down a nightmare neon peopled with condor, hawk and shrike.
>
> To say yes is to die
> A lot or a little. The dead wear capably their wry
>
> Enameled emblems. They smell.
> But that and that they do not altogether yell is all that we know well.
>
> It is brave to be involved,
> To be not fearful to be unresolved.
>
> Her new wish was to smile
> When answers took no airships, walked a while. (92–93)

Ostensibly these couplets introduce two figures, one with a heard voice indicated by quotation marks and one with an unheard thought pattern. It is not obvious to whom the first couplet, surrounded by quotation marks, belongs (it could belong to Annie Allen's mother, who appears in "Maxie Allen" and elsewhere). "Do not be afraid of no" begins with an address to the long poem's central figure, whose status as a subject remains uncertain: Annie is figured in this poem as an apostrophe whose presence is ambivalent.[64] Annie's own perspective, as the locus of the "caution" and "inner scream" and "new wish," is characterized by convoluted syntax and syntactical deferral. Her perspective is also problematized by the repetition of "who" throughout the first two couplets, which has the effect of insistent sonic referral at the same time that it forms a question, as if the poem were asking, *Who* has so far to go? The third couplet's dependent clauses resist identifying this "who" with any certainty: "Whose esoteric need / Was merely to avoid the nettle, to not-bleed." These are actions of safety and self-protection phrased in the negative, in the "mere" and "esoteric" register of stasis. Annie's need remains unresolved: there is no triumph of *no* and no obvious indication of a conceding *yes*, either. Annie's bravery is identified with fearless, unthinking inaction. The poem oscillates between the consenting affirmative and the protesting negative as the consequences of assent emerge in the seventh and eighth couplets, which indicate the vexed position of a central figure who navigates the ideologies of familial and romantic attachments but remains static in her moves. In their uses of internal, eye, and end rhymes, these lines anticipate Brooks's later participation in the musically inflected revolutionary African American avant-garde.

Brooks's poem questions the way subjects are represented by poetic speech as it also suggests the difficulty of speaking in opposition to dominant power structures, to opposing what she calls the "enameled emblems" of assent and complicity. In calling the need *not* to say no "esoteric," the poem suggests that to remain in a space of "yes" is itself esoteric, is narrow and specialized. One of the cognitive effects of rhyme is to cause a reader to perceive disparate words as if they were conceptually fused; here, the reader is invited to read "die" with "wry."[65] The end-word "die" also appears to be stacked above the word "little," which appears midway through the line that follows, suggesting a second pairing that inflects the poem's approach to death and contraction. To pair "die" with "little" is to thwart the temporality of life and death: to think of death in degrees is to suggest an emotional or psychic—and slow—death as a result of social forces. Brooks positions heroism—the act of saying yes—as a wry gesture of self-sabotage.

The working title of "The Anniad" bears this instrumentalizing of heroic form out even further. Brooks originally set out to title this section "The Hesteriad," after the central figure she originally named Hester Allen: "Well, the girl's name was Annie, and it was my little pompous pleasure to raise her to a height that she probably did not have," Brooks said in an interview. "I thought of the *Iliad* and said, I'll call this 'The Anniad.'"[66] The original title would, like "The Anniad," have punned on Homer's *Iliad* or Virgil's *Aeneid* but also would have invoked the longer discursive history of hysteria, the form in which the female body and emotional excess coalesce. Titling the section "The Hesteriad" would have reappropriated the cultural narrative of hysteria as a circumscribed feminine malady and redeployed it instead as heroic narrative. Eventually titled "The Anniad," the central section of *Annie Allen* draws upon the formal encodings of the heroic genre while remaining grounded in the ambivalent singularity of its speaker, who voices the blunted effects of interior and domestic speech. Rather than grounding the dilemma of poetic influence in a narrative about triumphant femininity, "The Anniad" figures the dilemma as one of lyric. "Shut your rhetorics in a box," Brooks writes; "Pack compunction and go home" (108). Brooks signals how words' failures as well as the affective response to those failures might all be set aside in the interests of resisting the imperative to resolve the elusive qualities of rhetorical protest into coherence.

2

"O Voice Prompting My Strophies"

Helen in Egypt's Lyric Whiteness

I have argued that when one meaning of lyric is exchanged for another, this trade can show how poetry converts sociohistorical particulars into phenomenological abstractions. In addition to the ways in which it uses lyric trade to negotiate the differential relationships between modernism, avant-garde form, and radical Black poetics, Gwendolyn Brooks's *Annie Allen* invokes a long discursive history of female subjects in classicism in its central section, which Brooks says she "pompously" titled "The Anniad." Six years after the publication of Brooks's long poem, H.D. published a long poem that in its critique of modernism also draws on classical ideologies of gender. Though in H.D.'s case, the alignment of lyric trade with allusions to classicism effects a very different type of exchange.

The first section of H.D.'s 1955 long poem *Helen in Egypt* begins with a scene of blackface. H.D.'s eponymous speaker solicits her lover's affections by purporting to blacken her white face and arms so that she might resemble "Isis, the Egyptian Aphrodite, the primal cause of all the madness."[1] Helen plans to take a burnt stick out of the fire and disguise her skin so that she might no longer be apparent to Achilles as white-skinned Helen of Troy, catalyst of the Trojan War and of his death by Paris. Instead, she contemplates assuming the face of Isis, the "cursèd" deity, "femme noire" to Achilles (17, 15). If Helen can exchange one problem—one face—for another, she might win Achilles's love. She might then also wrest control of the recursive narrative of this accretive three-hundred-page poem into which they are both locked.

"But," H.D. writes, "it doesn't work." Before Helen manages to blacken her skin with ash, Achilles intervenes:

I drew out a blackened stick,
but he snatched it,
he flung it back,

"what sort of enchantment is this?
what art will you wield with a fagot?
are you Hecate? are you a witch?

a vulture, a hieroglyph,
the sign or the name of a goddess?
what sort of goddess is this?

where are we? who are you?
where is this desolate coast?
who am I? am I a ghost?" (16)

Achilles's interrogatives indict the "enchantment" of Helen's dissembling art. He pivots to Helen's questionable subjectivity as witch, vulture, hieroglyph, or sign before finally evincing his own shaky claims on embodiment, as if Helen's indeterminacy were contagious. A few pages later, Helen remarks that Achilles's angry speech in effect blackens her: "in the dark, I must have looked / an inked-in shadow; but with his anger, / that ember, I became // what his accusation made me" (23).

Helen's blackening is figured as a series of problems around aesthetic making. "What art" is this, Achilles wonders; Helen describes Isis as "the primal cause of all the madness"; "I became // what his accusation made me," Helen conjectures; Helen compares her own body to divine creation as well as to discursivity itself, "as if God made the picture / and matched it / with a living hieroglyph" (16, 15, 23, 23). These problems around aesthetic making are problems of the subject and its presence, its identity, and its difference—all problems associated with lyric. H.D.'s Helen seeks to assume a dark-skinned visage—Isis—as an Egyptian figure of "racial inheritance" (13). When Achilles accuses Helen of embodying Isis, he anticipates the moment in *Helen in Egypt* when a so-called "lyric voice" intervenes to mend violent narratives both geopolitical and interpersonal, both classical and modern. That lyric voice merges the figure of Isis with her "opposites," resolving those opposites using the iconography of whiteness. The white face Helen initially seeks to camouflage with a burnt stick is recuperated as the poem's mediating, revisionary feminist trope.

Lyric in *Helen in Egypt* trades feminist critique for whiteness. Among all the poets I discuss in *Lyric Trade*, H.D. is most frequently characterized in literary scholarship as the poet whose feminist lyric intervenes into modernist epic: her lyric, it is said, torques epic's masculine narrative of heroic deeds, its commitment to the public and universal, its discursive authority. H.D.'s work nurtures a literary-critical account of lyric as subversive in its feminization, its interiority, and its expressive resistance to narrative.[2] This critical commonplace is an artifact of the work's own self-conscious reflection on genre — "I tell and re-tell the story / to find the answer" (84) — and of H.D.'s long engagement with the choral I of Euripides; it is also a product of 1970s and 1980s feminist and psychoanalytic criticism's tendency to align H.D.'s practice with the goals of a cultural poetics invested in tracing the gendered contours of literary form. *Helen in Egypt*'s lyric countermeasure — a countermeasure H.D. had been cultivating since her earliest writings — modernizes its classical origins: *Helen in Egypt* adapts Euripides's play *Helen*, itself based on a fragment by Stesichorus in which Helen never sailed to Troy but was hidden in Egypt during a war fought for her *eidolon*, or illusion. If Helen of Troy can be considered the centerpiece of the Western epic tradition, Helen the eidolon figures a white lyric countermeasure for the modernist long poem.[3]

H.D.'s lyric elsewhere manifests as a deliberation around making, but also as a meditation on aesthetic taste. In her 1921 roman à clef *Paint It Today*, for example, H.D. figures lyric song against epic violence in describing the proclivities of her alter ego, Midget:

> Large, epic pictures bored her, though she struggled through them. She wanted the songs that cut like a swallow wing the high, untainted ether, not the tragic legions of set lines that fell like black armies with terrific force and mechanical set action, paralyzing, or broke like a black sea to baffle and to crush.[4]

Against epic H.D. positions the song of clarity, purity, and delicacy, all of which she metaphorizes as the beat of a small wing. The "swallow wing" in *Paint It Today* takes shape as a delicate, feminine poetics set against heavy, historically inflected, masculine epic. The "swallow wing" also emerges as a psychoanalytically inflected personal form of reasoning that intervenes in a wrecked modernist world, a form of reasoning that trades not in the rhythms of historically burdened epic but in the semantic compressions, tonal intensities, and subjective expressivities of song. Against the masculinity, nationalism, and imperialism of epic, H.D. positions the indeterminacy, interiority, and feminine knowledge of something called lyric. H.D.'s feminist lyric functions as a critique of epic, of making, and of taste—and of the early modernist poetics of H.D. herself. Her lyric both extends and turns away from the work of "H.D. Imagiste," the label Pound affixed to H.D. when he edited her poems in 1912 and which continues to attach to her allegiance to sparse, concrete detail.[5] Pound himself distinguishes "lyric" from both imagism and vorticism in his 1916 catalog of verse, positing imagism as a kind of poetry in which the visual image crosses over into speech.[6] And H.D. eventually disavows imagist doctrine in favor of myth-based examinations of female agency. Yet the association of song with lyric poetry in *Paint It Today* echoes how the long poem accommodates and even resists the compressions of the single image. Later, in *Helen in Egypt*, H.D. animates the image—the specter known as an eidolon—to speak a lyric countermeasure to her modern moment.

Drawing on an enthralled classicism to counter modern poetic ideologies, H.D.'s lyric countermeasure also positions whiteness as the site at which conflict, contradiction, and subjective fragmentation will be resolved. Lyric trade installs an ideology of the racial subject in place of the gender problematic it seeks to supersede. Midget's "legions of set lines" dramatize the problem of the mechanical, paralyzing, baffling, crushing modernist long poem against which *Helen in Egypt* positions itself—and they also allude to the constellation of gender, nation, and race that undergirds H.D.'s feminist critique. This chapter uses the phrase "lyric whiteness" to describe H.D.'s racial appropriation. I begin by discussing H.D.'s short 1924 poem "Helen," which imagines Western female subjectivity as impossibly split. I then turn to how the lyric countermeasures of H.D.'s 1955 long poem, *Helen in Egypt*, mend that split. I argue that the racial othering of an appropriated Egypt mobilizes the figures of Isis and Thetis to resolve the fractured female subject into a putatively neutral and mediating form of whiteness.

Dead Helens

One of the implications of imagining poetic genre as a kind of economy is that a text's participation in a genre can lay bare the differential relations between subjects and speech, or between image and power, or between critique and assent. When Helen purports to blacken her white face and arms, H.D.'s poem participates in a longstanding modernist habit of appropriating and caricaturing Blackness, as well as reinstalling whiteness. Aldon Nielsen summarizes things this way: "When white American poets such as Gertrude Stein, Vachel Lindsay, T. S. Eliot, e. e. cummings, William Carlos Williams, and H.D. take the blackness that they have constructed back into themselves, like the product of the paint factory in Ralph Ellison's *Invisible Man*, they become still whiter."[7] Sara Ahmed uses the language of trade to describe how the political and affective economics of whiteness mean "it is distributed between bodies and things without itself being something, as a distribution that gives bodies and things 'affect' and 'value.'"[8] To describe race not in terms of its own "being something" but in terms of what it activates clarifies the scene of racial othering in *Helen in Egypt*. Isis, the other, is a face that is desired, mimicked, camouflaged, and then attacked as profoundly destabilizing. This scene recalls the way Ahmed describes othering as a phenomenology of the self:

> The otherness of things is what allows me to do things "with" them. What is other than me is also what allows me to extend the reach of my body. Rather than othering being simply a form of negation, it can also be described *as a form of extension*. The body extends its reach by taking in that which is "not" it, where the "not" involves the acquisition of new capacities and directions—becoming, in other words, "not" simply what I am "not" but what I can "have" and "do." The "not me" is incorporated into the body, extending its reach.[9]

H.D.'s poem figures Isis as an other who will eventually come to be incorporated into Helen's subjectivity, but only after activating a crisis of self that, as Ahmed suggests, incorporates the other.

This crisis activates the poem's feminist critique of gendered classicism as well as of the modernism that draws on classical gender ideologies.

When William Carlos Williams contemplates the modernist inheritance of Helen of Troy, he thinks of "the *Iliad* / and Helen's public fault / that bred it"; then he suggests: "Were it not for that / there would have been / no poem but the world."[10] Williams takes up the world-creating origins written into Helen's fault—a fault of the female figure: "All women are not Helen, / I know that, / but have Helen in their hearts."[11] Williams's modernism cites an impossible subject position for Helen: a female subject whose fault and fracture is both psychic and temporal. *Helen in Egypt* revises modernist terms of gender by creating a new body for Helen, one split between worlds, grieving the chaos pinned to the cultural memory of her visage.

In order to forge Helen's new body, H.D. turns to a classicism beholden to both European and Anglo American norms of intellectual and aesthetic authority. Early in her career, H.D. began to think of Greece—Helen's destination in *Helen in Egypt*—as a blank canvas. The metaphor is both aesthetic and cultural. In "Notes on Euripides," H.D. describes Greece as a "leaf hanging a pendant to the whole of Europe," Greece's supplemental cultural powers as inherent to its seductive mysteries:

> Look at the map of Greece. Then go away and come back and look and look and look at it. The jagged contours stir and inflame the imagination, time-riddled banner of freedom and fiery independence, a rag of a country, all irregular, with little torn-off bits, petals drifting, those islands, "lily on lily that o'er lace the sea." Look at the map of Greece. It is a hieroglyph. You will be unable to read it and go away and come back after years and just begin to spell out the meaning of its outline. Then you will realize that you know nothing at all about it and begin all over, learning a cryptic language. I am never tired of speculating on the power of that outline, just the mysterious line of it, apart from the thing it stands for. That leaf hanging a pendant to the whole of Europe seems to indicate the living strength and sap of the thing it derives from. Greece is indeed the tree-of-life, the ever-present stream, the spring of living water.[12]

H.D. depicts Greece as a "tree-of-life" with endlessly generative potential for meaning. In emphasizing its inscrutability as well as its relationship to Europe—supplemental, perhaps decorative, yet also somehow foundational—the passage figures Greece's cryptic universality using the orientalist vocabulary of the East, or what Edward Said describes as both "underground" to and "surrogate" for the West.[13] H.D. cites Europe as the governing element of her map of Greece, evincing what Eileen Gregory calls the modern revival of classicism as "a purification of style" as well as an "effort to return to western origins, to revitalize a sense of the literary past."[14] H.D.'s classicism further draws on a particularly white American notion of the West. As Annette Debo has shown, H.D. conceived of American identity as fragmented, amalgamated, and multiple, rather than monolithic—yet H.D.'s attempts to divest herself of monolithic whiteness in favor of an American identity that would somehow stretch past the color line left the tropes of dominant whiteness intact.[15]

H.D.'s invocations of classical knowledge take shape in the forms that characterize her modernist principles of the concrete, the visual, and the spare. Many of H.D.'s earliest works turned to ancient Greece for what she took to be a realm of knowledge both more accurate and more adaptable than that offered by her present moment. Classicism also made it possible to confront the urgencies of her moment, offering the kind of unknowability that was adequate to the task of writing through two world wars. H.D.'s best known early sequence, 1916's "Sea Garden," combines the harsh loveliness of a bleak cliffside landscape with the intensity of mythological figures who seem to burst into the modern moment only to be stayed by a minimally constructed line. In "Hermes of the Ways," H.D. marks the boundaries of the marginal world in a gnarled scene: "The boughs of the trees / are twisted / by many bafflings; / twisted are / the small-leafed boughs."[16] "Hermes" calls to the god whose role as messenger and whose changeability H.D. frequently found generative, and the poem ends resoundingly on its scenic imagery: "Hermes, Hermes, / the great sea foamed, / gnashed its teeth about me; / but you have waited, / where sea-grass tangles with / shore-grass" (39). The poem declines exposition or discursive expansion, instead sticking close to its hard objects. H.D. followed "Sea Garden" with a number of works in poetry, fiction, and translations of Greek literature, many of which drew on classical iconography to experiment with modernist collage and narrative, particularly in her semiautobiographical novels and romans à clef. *Helen in Egypt* is in a way all of these forms: poem, semiautobiographical novel, roman à clef. It is as much a poem of classical knowledge as it is a feminist critique of modernism.

But reading that critique for its ideological entailments reveals the cultural work that genres do when those genres are mobilized to speak back to dominant discourses. One central thesis of *Helen in Egypt* is that lyric is uniquely able to subvert the ideological narratives of masculine epic quest and mend the fractured female self. That thesis is formally and thematically anticipated by a short poem H.D. published in 1924. In "Helen," which appears in H.D.'s collection *Heliodora*, H.D. dramatizes the ancient cultural hatred of Helen of Troy as a public body excoriating a lifeless body—a statue—before the public's fury reduces it to ashes. H.D. builds into her 1924 poem's syntax a figure whose instability confronts the female abjection cited in Williams's modernism. That Helen, figured first as a surface projection for the burdens of culture, becomes a syntactical embodiment of the central Western cultural narrative that Helen seeks to overcome. And like the Helen of *Helen in Egypt*, this earlier Helen trades female abjection for whiteness.

In H.D.'s 1924 "Helen," the whiteness of Helen's body appears as a canvas—like Greece—onto which Western culture projects its failures, a point made clear by the stark depiction of Helen in the poem's first five lines. The poem opens with Helen as a still, white, statuelike figure framed by Greece's hatred:

> All Greece hates
> the still eyes in the white face,
> the lustre as of olives
> where she stands,
> and the white hands. (154)

The poem flatly casts Helen in the third person, equating Helen's "white" and "wan" face and hands. Helen's dull body appears practically as dead weight, a ghoulish figure whose pale, lifeless color activates public, undifferentiated emotion. Her body also appears undifferentiated, her "white hands" stacked visually underneath "where she stands." Helen's standing feet form a pedestal, and the hands extend from it, as if the statue were already toppled over. Helen is not a living body converted into stone, a flesh woman converted into deadened aesthetic; she is already a deathly statue that is growing more statuelike, or, as Diana Collecott has suggested, dismembered by culture into its disparate parts: eyes, face, hands, and feet.[17]

The stanza that follows reproduces Helen's faults. Equivocating grammatical patterns figure Helen's statue as both cultural projection and feeling subject:

> All Greece reviles
> the wan face when she smiles,
> hating it deeper still
> when it grows wan and white,
> remembering past enchantments
> and past ills. (155)

Lines one through four follow an alternating pattern of subjects and objects: Greece, Helen's face; Helen as statue, Helen as smiling, living flesh. Rather than reiterating its differentiated tropes, this alternating pattern gives way to a deep equivocation that both animates and deadens its subjects. The comma between lines two and three links Greece as the subject of the active verb "reviles" with the participle "hating," and the comma that divides lines four and five links the pronoun "it" of the inanimate statue with the animate act of "remembering." And the patterns equivocate the other way around: the inanimate "it" refers to Greek culture; the animate "she" does the remembering. Commas shift syntactic units: the action of remembering follows the action of growing wan and white, as if both the face and Greece were remembering. To be both the surface onto which cultural memory is projected and the figure who remembers means that the poem's Helen is divided in the precise way Euripides divides her in his play *Helen*, on which H.D.'s later poem is based. Euripides's Helen says, "I am dead from my troubles though not in fact."[18] Euripides merges the traumatic memory of his phantom Helen at Troy with that of his Helen in Egypt. Helen's flesh faces no imminent risk, but has the felt experience of trauma.[19]

In the third and final stanza of H.D.'s 1924 poem, Helen, unable to distinguish between the effects and the fact of her death, transforms from lifeless statue to a pile of white ashes:

> Greece sees unmoved,
> God's daughter, born of love,
> the beauty of cool feet
> and slenderest knees,
> could love indeed the maid,
> only if she were laid,
> white ash amid funereal cypresses. (155)

Sound pairs Helen's body with hatred: "hates" chimes with "face," "reviles" with "smiles," "unmoved" with "love," "maid" with the funereal "laid." Even "love" is undercut by the eye rhyme "unmoved," rather close in spelling to the word "unloved." There is very little palpable difference between the effects and the fact of death. H.D. instead positions a poetic speaker whose equivocating lifelessness circulates without either mortal or moral closure. Helen stands as the object of Greece's hatred, but she assumes ownership over her deeds. She cannot subvert the cultural narrative, despite H.D.'s poetic intervention.

In "Helen" and other works, H.D. draws on classical statuary to explore the body as ideal and impassive surface even as she foregrounds subjective indeterminacy. The subject formation in "Helen" recalls H.D.'s 1917 poem "Pygmalion," in which the mythic sculptor undergoes a crisis of identity upon forging an affective attachment to the art object. "Pygmalion" foregrounds the statue's flesh as a question of materiality: the sculptor says, "I made image upon image for my use, / I made image upon image, for the grace / of Pallas was my flint," but then laments, "fire has shaken my hand, / my strivings are dust" (49).[20] Affective attachment to the statue leads H.D.'s sculptor to crisis, and the poem is swarmed by a series of indeterminate questions:

> Which am I,
> the stone or the power
> that lifts the rock from this earth?
> am I the master of this fire,
> is this fire my own strength? (49)

The distinction between artmaking and art object starts to blur, with H.D.'s speaker at the mercy of a threatening god. The poem questions not only the materiality of its own speaker, but also the very materials of art: fire, rock, marble, light. This crisis of material subjectivity leads the poem, finally, to an epistemic quandary:

> am I the god?
> or does this fire carve me
> for its use? (50)

H.D. does not explicitly figure the art object of "Pygmalion" as one of female beauty, instead spotlighting how the myth of Pygmalion confronts the problem of aesthetic materiality. "Helen," on the other hand, portrays an idealized female figure crafted and animated by an unforgiving culture who likewise undergoes epistemic crisis. Feminist criticism has tended to focus on how "Helen" contravenes the deadening effects of masculine mythmaking, as if the poem were a portrait inverse to that drawn by Edgar Allan Poe, whose 1831 poem "To Helen" likens Helen to an inanimate and doubly allegorical object: "How statue-like I see thee stand, / The agate lamp within thy hand! / Ah, Psyche, from the regions which / Are Holy Land!"[21] Whereas Poe's statue of Helen is spotlit by the private imagination of her admirer, H.D., it is said, turns the story of Helen's legendary beauty into an indictment of the Western eye: she reverses the private apprehension of Helen that was prominent in late nineteenth- and early twentieth-century poems, particularly Poe's "To Helen" and Yeats's "No Second Troy."[22] Poe, who famously remarked that "the death, then, of a beautiful woman is, unquestionably, the most poetical topic in the world,"[23] suggests a Helen whose lifelessness is a measure of her beauty.

H.D.'s poem aestheticizes Helen's body before the statue's perspectival subversion of it.[24] The poem transliterates the myth of Helen into a version that shuttles between ancient and modern, in effect using the poem to annotate the myth. H.D. wrote "Helen" on the back leaves of her copy of Theodore Buckley's edition of Euripides, in which H.D. underlined Teucer's line to Helen: "For all Greece hates the daughter of Jove."[25] H.D. instrumentalizes Helen to foreground the deadening effects of the aesthetic gaze, but just as important is the way in which H.D. builds into the poem a divided Helen who is not primarily poised to resist that aestheticization. "Helen" constructs a female subject of irresolvable contradiction. The poem's divided and equivocating syntax draws a Helen who cannot be reconciled, and who anticipates the gendered fracture to be mended by lyric trade in *Helen in Egypt*.

After *Heliodora*, H.D.'s works become increasingly palimpsestic, a word that typically refers to thematic and narrative repetition as well as porous and competing narratives, voices, and themes that represent what H.D. saw as the spiraling motion of thought.[26] A material palimpsest is writing on a surface that betrays the writing underneath that surface—such as parchment or wax—creating competing discursive meanings. The notion of palimpsest captures both the discrete textuality of H.D.'s ambiguities and the poem's competing meanings. Palimpsest is best understood as a function of narrative, but extends to syntactical tactics as well. Across H.D.'s work, punctuation invokes competing actions between words within a single stanza often by torquing grammatical structures, using parataxis to obscure and conflate meaning. For example, the following lines appear frequently throughout *Helen in Egypt*, first spoken by Achilles:

> Helena, which was the dream,
> which was the veil of Cytheraea? (36)

By using a comma both to enjamb the spoken line and to convert the syntax of the two clauses into parataxis, H.D. opens the refrain to at least two readings. Achilles may be asking Helen to differentiate between the "dream" and the "veil of Cytheraea." Or, he may be asking her to identify the specific dream "which was the veil of Cytheraea." And the poem confirms both readings elsewhere: speakers in *Helen in Egypt* contrast the dream with the veil, and speakers also refer to the veil as a dream or a memory; the lines repeat and get collaged into other segments; key words from these lines reappear alongside other anchors.[27]

The syntactical structures of "Helen" both deaden her and invest her with agency, but they also collapse whiteness into femaleness. When the verbs in the 1924 "Helen" cross over between Helen and Greece, the poem both reverses their roles and reveals Helen to be multiply embodied: woman, Helen, Greek. Helen's equivocations contravene a number of dominant values: of temporality, of morality, of materiality. Helen is "unmoved"—physically cemented and affectively impassive as well as already dead, even as she supposedly smiles or remembers Troy. Her whiteness—face, hands, ash—reproduces what Nell Irvin Painter has shown to be an ongoing "fetishization of ancient Greek beauty" born in large part of Johann Joachim Winckelmann's fundamental misreading of polychromatic statuary: Painter describes how Winckelmann "saw only Roman versions of beautiful young men carved of hard Italian marble that shone a gleaming white. Thus, Winckelmann elevated Rome's white marble copies of Greek statuary into emblems of beauty and created a new white aesthetic."[28]

The white statuary of "Helen" generates a thesis of woman as impassive idealization, positioning white female subjectivity as the generic female self. This is the heart of the poem's feminist critique of classical and modernist ideologies of Helen. In Euripides's play, Helen, grieving over the destruction at Troy, laments: "Would that I might be rubbed away, like a statue, and given a more disgraceful body."[29] Another translation renders the lines this way: "If only I could have been erased, like a picture, and then have taken a meaner form in place of this beautiful one, and the Greeks had forgotten the bad that has been my lot and were keeping in mind the good."[30] Classics scholars have interpreted these lines in a number of different ways: Helen could be referring to a statue stripped of its polychrome features, unfinished and unsatisfactory in appearance, or to the rubbing away of a cult idol by devotees, or to a sponge destroying a picture.[31] Helen is not converted into a lifeless statue by Western aesthetic but stands dead from the beginning. Whether translated as "disgraceful," "mean," or otherwise, the source text for H.D.'s Helen statue suggests how the putatively blank surface of H.D.'s 1924 portrait of Helen is excoriated—a word that means both to decry and to flay—by "All Greece" before it resurfaces in *Helen in Egypt*. In English translations of Euripides, "meaner" can mean a few different things: disgraceful, so that Helen's body would repel, rather than seduce, the male warriors (a translation that gives Helen more reason to disparage her beauty). Mediocre, so that her body would make little impact in the first place. Common, so that she would resemble all other women, would appear to be unremarkably female. Etymologically, "mean" derives from any number of Anglo-Norman, classical Latin, or Old English terms meaning "middle," "held jointly," or "intermediary." In *Helen in Egypt*, Achilles recognizes in Helen "some power other than her legendary beauty": as H.D. writes, "it was not that she was beautiful, / [. . .] but he stared and stared / across the charred wood" (251, 252). A mean is a middle; it is also an ideal.

H.D.'s imaginative map of Greece as cryptic mystery hinges on the fantasy of another map: that of Egypt, which Helen seeks to decipher "from the depth of her racial inheritance" (13). As a number of scholars have shown, H.D.'s classicism overlaps with the emergence of the American discipline of Egyptology, a colonial project that detached Egypt from Africa and associated it instead with the Ancient Near East, in turn orienting the United States as the cultural inheritor of a sentimentalized, occupied Egypt.[32] The white ash to which Helen is reduced in H.D.'s 1924 poem is replaced by the black ash Helen seeks in her 1955 poem, in which Helen calls on the Egyptian Isis to mend the wounds of war. Both of H.D.'s poems about Helen of Troy formalize the affective identification with war by leveraging a supposedly mediating lyric voice—both the first-person introspective speech of "Helen" and the lyric song of *Helen in Egypt*. These two dead Helens—one excoriated in Greece, the other carried away to Egypt—confront the problem of a fractured female subjectivity by lyric countermeasures that reproduce the notion of universalizing whiteness.

"whiter than bone":
Lyric whiteness in *Helen in Egypt*

When H.D. sent her longtime editor and friend Norman Holmes Pearson the first draft of *Helen in Egypt* in 1952, she emphasized less its engagements with classicism or Egyptology and more its posture toward modernism. H.D. told Pearson that her new long poem set the trauma of World War II, which she had also depicted in 1944–1946's *Trilogy*, in concert with the esoteric spiritualism of her 1946–1947 novel *The Sword Went Out to Sea*. After having taken a five-year hiatus from writing poetry, H.D. turned from the autobiographical *Sword* to the myth of *Helen*. "It is the 'phantasmagora' or unreality of war as against the reality of the eternal and of Love," H.D. tells Pearson, using a variant spelling of the term for a fantastic series of images.[33] In another letter eight months later, she mimicked the title of Pound's masterwork: "It is refreshing to review my Greeks & the Euripides; it makes me happy, whether I do any more of the so-called Cantos, or not."[34] In resurrecting the segmented formal architecture of her 1946 war poem *Trilogy*—three-line stanzas and frequent end-line punctuation—for her new cantos, H.D. also turned to the female position as divided at its root. Doing so enabled H.D. to confront the masculinization inherent in the Poundian long form. In 1924, syntax divides Helen into contradiction; in 1955, Helen's split persona generates a "lyric voice" to mend the personal and public memory of war. Fashioning this voice as lyric in order to stage a critique of both classical genre and modernist epic, *Helen in Egypt* integrates the culturally fractured female subject only to foreclose its racial others. Lyric is produced by the poem's economies of whiteness, or what Ahmed calls the phenomenological relation of otherness.

Sedimented in this feminist work's imaginative reach is the equation of whiteness with beauty, purity, and mastery—an equation made possible precisely via the transmission of antiquity along dominant intellectual and aesthetic channels. Scholars such as Eileen Gregory have acknowledged the extent to which H.D. conceived of her longstanding practice of Greek translation—she began translating Euripides in 1913—as it both reproduced and complicated imperial forms of appropriation and transmission.[35] Works such as *Helen in Egypt* are often celebrated for the ways in which they break the rules of conventional translation and homage: rather than standing as a work of masterful reproduction, H.D.'s long poem foregrounds Helen as "a text constantly subject to translation by others" who "becomes herself a reader and translator" of the Euripides play, as Gregory puts it.[36] That H.D. turned to classicism to promulgate open form is not at issue—neither is classicism's whiteness. Rather, the way H.D.'s open form, frequently identified as lyric, reproduces that whiteness reveals how lyric often goes untheorized along lines of race. To complicate an understanding of classicism, open form, and lyric in this way is a task complementary to that undertaken by scholars such as Tsitsi Jaji, who writes that the point is not to arbitrate the definition of the classic but instead to analyze the ways in which Black artists took up its reinventions in order to complicate its cultural capital.[37] The task I undertake here is something of the inverse: to complicate H.D.'s reinventions of the classic—and the lyric—by making sense of how those reinventions reinvest in lyric's supposed value. Such reinvestments can be understood as a form of lyric trade.

Helen in Egypt uses classicism as an interpretive method to reckon with H.D.'s own century. In a 1953 letter, H.D. calls the story behind *Helen in Egypt* "authentic myth, Euripides refers to it."[38] She characterizes this "authenticity" in "Notes on Euripides," in which she writes that Euripides's lines are as vivid as any text of the modern age. "Euripides lived through almost a modern great-war period," she writes, after all: "How would 1917 London have acclaimed such anti-war propaganda?"[39] Alongside her description of Greece as a pendant hanging off Europe, H.D. describes ancient Greek literature using another supplemental metaphor:

> For we are too apt to pigeon-hole the Attic poets and dramatists, put
> them B.C. this or that, forget them in our survey of modern life and

> literature, not realizing that the whole spring of literature (even of all life) is that one small plane-leaf of an almost-island, that tiny rock among the countries of a world, Hellas.

H.D. imagines Greece as a decorative pendant dangling from Europe and its literature as a leaf dangling from London's native plane tree. H.D. metaphorizes London and centers Anglo culture, but her metaphor also serves an interpretive function. Greek drama and lyric offer not just vivid textual representations of a differently modern moment but "portals" and "windows" to "our world, our restricted lives."

This metaphorization of expansive ancient Greece and constrained midcentury modernism, separated by a permeable geographical and temporal boundary, informs H.D.'s depiction of Helen as psychically and materially split by psychic, historical, and moral faults—a figuring she borrows from Euripides and Stesichorus, for whom Helen represented not only a thwarted character of heroic culture but a lyric voice intervening into prevailing epic genre.[40] *Helen in Egypt* takes up the basic premise of Euripides's play: the war at Troy was fought not for Helen herself, who is hidden physically in Egypt, but for her eidolon, or image. The notion of Helen of Troy as a phantom originates in an earlier fragment by the Greek poet Stesichorus, who as H.D. notes in her introduction to *Helen in Egypt* wrote an apology, or palinode, for Helen after being struck blind for slandering her in his odes. After writing the palinode, Stesichorus had his sight returned, his text supposedly redeeming both his faults and Helen's. Phantom Helens appear across other works by Euripides; in Plato's *Republic*, as an example of false pleasures; in a parody of Euripides by Aristophanes.[41] In Plato's *Phaedrus*, Socrates describes "an ancient tradition governing how those who commit an offence in the domain of story-telling have to purify themselves, which Homer may have failed to recognize, but Stesichorus didn't. After losing his sight as a result of slandering Helen, Stesichorus didn't fail to recognize his fault, as Homer had."[42] *Helen in Egypt* likewise engages the classical gesture of storytelling in order to purify Helen's narrative, recursive and nonlinear as its storytelling might be. H.D.'s long poem inherits the equivocating syntax of the 1924 "Helen" and locates the poeisis of culturally normative practices in Helen herself, in split structures of the subject's own making. Euripides parallels Helen's divided subjectivity with the play's mixed genre: his *Helen* uses choral lyric to torque and interrupt the dramatic dialogue that governs the play's main action. Unlike Euripides, who subordinates lyric to dialogue, H.D.'s poem centers first-person lyric.

That lyric has been frequently read as the speech of a traumatized analysand whose interior, segmented speech contravenes both the modernist doctrine of the image and the epic long poems of H.D.'s modernist contemporaries.[43] H.D. herself read *Helen in Egypt* as a coded psychotherapy session structured by palimpsestic and hieroglyphic forms: in her letters she describes *Helen in Egypt* as a roman à clef in which Theseus stands in for her own analyst, Sigmund Freud. H.D., who sat for many sessions with Freud, describes her "intense, dynamic interest in the unfolding of the unconscious or the subconscious patterns," or what she frequently represented as the hieroglyph.[44] In *Helen in Egypt*, Theseus/Freud guides Helen/H.D. to "re-integrate" and recall the trauma of war. Walking the ramparts of Troy over and over, Helen attempts to decode cultural memory. Helen revisits events in an effort to mend her fractured psyche, coming to privilege the emotional "acceptance" of knowledge over rationality. *Helen in Egypt*'s lyric modifies H.D.'s own early imagism, furnishing a poetics of reflective and expansive knowledge rather than the single point of perception. In *The Cantos*, Pound transitions from the brief image of "In a Station of the Metro" to loosely connected sequences of ideograms; in *Tribute to Freud* and *Helen in Egypt*, H.D. shifts from the image to the hieroglyph.

Like the palimpsest, which H.D. conceived of as transmission of transhistorical meaning, the hieroglyph could supposedly cross boundaries of time, a notion that participates in the archeological sensibility that characterizes what Marsha Bryant and Mary Ann Eaverly call "Egypto-modernism." Egypto-modernism posited an ancient Egypt that provided the West with a "usable past": while previous Western archaeology posited Egypt in terms of its supposed primitivism or evolutionary scheme, Egypt came to be foregrounded in the New Past theory, which held Egypt as the source of Western civilization. H.D.'s "archeological sensibility" in *Helen in Egypt* and other works takes the shape of the hieroglyph, a form of epigraphy that emerges as a modernist fascination with material artifacts.[45] H.D. draws on the culturally burdened hieroglyph and palimpsest to intervene into Western modernism, but the biggest intervention that appears in *Helen in Egypt* is a lyric voice to mend Helen's faults.

Helen in Egypt conceives of lyric as song, as speech accompanied by lyre, as counterindication to war, as singular remembrance, as sense-memory. *Helen in Egypt* conceives of lyric as intervention, mediation, narrativization, and genealogical revision. But first of all, *Helen in Egypt* conceives of lyric as a plot twist. In the second section of H.D.'s poem, Thetis has called Helen from Egypt to Leuké, "l'isle blanche" where in yet another alternative version of her story Helen married Achilles and gave birth to Euphorion. In the present action of the poem, Theseus, authoritative "hero-king" of Leuké (and the figure standing in for Freud in this roman à clef), guides Helen to "re-integrate" the trauma of Troy. He tells her she need not fear "the shock of the iron-Ram, / the break in the Wall, / the flaming Towers" (170); he narrates his own version of "the story," reminding Helen that Chryseis, Deidamia, Briseis, and Polyxena "were all sacrificed in one way or another" (173). The fall of Troy becomes the story of any number of dead women; Theseus generalizes Helen to a female condition. Helen's voice splits:

> do you hear me? do I whisper?
> there is a voice within me,
> listen—let it speak for me. (175)

This "heroic voice, the voice of Helen of Sparta" (176), questions the production of her own selfhood through war:

> O, the rage of the sea,
>
> the thunder of battle,
> shouting and the Walls
> and the arrows; O, the beauty of arrows,
>
> each bringing surcease, release;
> do I love War?
> is this Helena? (177)

A newly lyric voice replaces Helen's heroic one. This lyric voice does a lot of different things, but its most telling action is discursively to shuttle Helen back to Egypt along what H.D. describes as the "Greek mode" of its form. In an italicized passage (one of the "captions" that preface each poem throughout *Helen in Egypt*), H.D. summarizes how the Greek mode of this lyric—its rhythms, alliterations, strophes—as well as its elusive denotations—"We can not altogether understand this evocation"—activate differential genealogies and merge Helen's opposites:

> *Again, the "voice" seems to speak for Helen. It is a lyric voice this time, a song rather than a challenge. It takes us back to Egypt but in a Greek mode. Isis is Cypris (Cytheraea) and Isis is Thetis. Amen-Zeus is the father of Isis-Thetis-Aphrodite (Cypris). We can not altogether understand this evocation, the rhythms must speak for themselves and the alliterations, Cypris, Thetis, Nephthys, Isis, Paris. Proteus, the legendary King of Egypt, as we have learned before, takes many shapes. Could he "manifest as Achilles"? If so, (the question is not asked but implied), could he manifest as Paris? Then, could the two opposites (the slayer and the slain) merge into one, and that One, the Absolute?* (178, italics in the original)

In the tercets that follow, Helen's lyric voice enables her to think outside Troy: "O voice prompting my strophies" (180), she says reflexively with a variant spelling of "strophe," as if lyric were somehow both inside and apart from verse—or as if the poem's voice shuttled between a Euripidean choral lyric and a modern individual one. By the end of "Leuké," Helen has wrested control of narrative time—"I will encompass the infinite / in time, in the crystal, / in my thought here" (201)—and become altogether "free from time-restrictions" (206). Lyric propels Helen into the third and final section of the book, "Eidolon," in which she returns to Egypt newly capable to "superimpose" her newfound "Greek thought and fantasy" upon the "old pictures" of Egypt (264).

The insistent whiteness of "l'isle blanche" that makes it possible for Helen to subsume Egyptian hieroglyphs beneath Greek thought collates with any number of other references to white beauty and purity in the objects, places, and figures throughout "Leuké." Helen's hands "whiter than bone" (125); l'isle blanche as itself "the most beautiful woman in the world" (136), "immaculate purity" (194), "her island, her egg-shell" (197); "the white fire of unnumbered stars" of Helen's room in Priam's palace (142); a flower whiter than nenuphar or cyclamen (160); the flash of Troy's destruction "whiter than frost, / whiter than snow, / whiter than the white drift of sand / that lies like ground shells, / dust of shells— // —dust of skulls" (160–61);[46] Elysian asphodels (173); a "snow-palace" where "marble and snow / were one" (174); Helen lying "quietly as the snow" (174). Whiteness characterizes the purity and iconicity of mythological figures throughout H.D.'s oeuvre, whether the statuary of "Helen" and "Pygmalion" or the more vaporously described figure of Narcissus or the "snowy head" of the asphodel.[47] Whiteness characterizes the harshness of seaside cliffs and landscapes in "Sea Garden" and the narcotic flower of incense in *Bid Me to Live*.[48] H.D. links whiteness with erotic desire in 1921's *Hymen*: "For her head is covered over / With her mantle / White on white, / Snow on whiter amaranth, / Snow on hoar-frost, / Snow on snow, / Snow on whitest buds of myrrh."[49] All these references to whiteness's purity, loveliness, or desire are of a piece with Anglo modernist presumptions of whiteness as the defining feature of classical iconography. They also install whiteness as a form of female universality.

Female universality depends on a complicated appropriation of Egypt as ultimately supplemental to the synthesis Helen seeks. Helen uses the "Greek mode" of her lyric to return to Egypt without risking the mystical threat Egypt supposedly poses. Theseus describes how Greece's Egyptian "inheritance" leaves it vulnerable to being "dissolved or washed away" by the Nile:

Crete would seduce Greece,
Crete inherited the Labyrinth from Egypt,
the ancient Nile would undermine

the fabric of Parnassus;
was this true? (169)

In Euripides's play, Egypt itself is depicted as a kind of underworld with its connections to the watery mouth of the Nile. Confinement in Egypt serves as a living death for Helen, as Euripides writes: "And for all purposes I am dead, yet live in fact."[50] Yet for H.D. in 1955 to acknowledge Greece's Egyptian debt is in fact to speak back to versions of Egyptology that would detach it from presumptively Anglo versions of Greek heritage. The "Greek mode" of Helen's lyric can also be said to adapt Euripides's choral I, which circulates between collective incantation and private expression.[51] However, lyric's "Greek mode" also positions the poem as a form of discursive mastery—signaling the Egyptian debt without succumbing to its threat of fragmentation or dissolve. What unfolds is genealogical indebtedness interwoven with the cultural narrative of white European mastery, absorption, and dominance. "Isis is Cypris (Cytheraea) and Isis is Thetis" (178): H.D.'s poem situates Helen's potency not in her beauty but in her Black heritage, or what the poem refers to as Helen's "racial inheritance" (13). In the beginning of the poem, H.D. writes that Helen has "lost caste" (15), a loss apparently equivalent to the loss of materiality itself: "Then, what is this Helen?" This loss of racial inheritance overlaps with the loss of Troy: it is precisely because Helen in Egypt carries the burden of her own phantom that she then decides to blacken her face to camouflage it from Achilles. As several critics have noted, the poem's suggestion that Egyptian identity equips Helen to accept both the nonrational and her Greek identity, to master intellectual modes of knowing, rehearses the notion of whiteness as that site that can incorporate otherness.

This genealogical imaginary is anticipated by H.D.'s portrayal of Thetis, Achilles's mother, as a female figure whose unstable materiality the poem links to her inscrutable racial identity. Near the end of the third section of *Helen in Egypt*, "Eidolon," Thetis is dedicated with her son to the sea. Fixed in the form of a wooden carving at the prow of a ship, Thetis is already sea-worn, abstracted: "an image, an idol // or eidolon, not much more than a doll, / old, old—for ship-rigging and beam / can be changed, a mast renewed, // a rudder re-set but never the hull" (244). The poem struggles to pin down her origins based on the features of her face in a tercet H.D. repeats (with variation) twice more after this passage:

> Did her eyes slant in the old way?
> was she Greek or Egyptian?
> had some Phoenician sailor wrought her? (245)

Helen's musings on the eidolon's origins invoke both maritime Phoenician expansion and the colonial usurpation of Egypt. A few pages later, Thetis's eidolon is determined to be an import: "it was not his own ship // but a foreign keel / that had brought him here" (253). But when H.D.'s poem links the figure's "foreign" origins with Helen herself—asking who built the ship, what kind of ship it is that ferries Achilles back to Troy, what brings Achilles in catastrophic relation with Helen—the poem's critique of the instability of the female image comes to assume racial instability as a threat to self. H.D. links Thetis's foreignness with her failures, as well as with Achilles's fateful encounter with "hated Helen."

Thetis's ship is "a foreign keel," in which the eidolon's eyes "slant in the old way." The poem locates Thetis's threat in her indeterminately "foreign" face:

> O Thetis . . .
> so she failed at last,
> and worse than failure,
>
> the mockery, after-death,
> to stumble across a stretch
> of shell and the scattered weed,
>
> to encounter another
> whose eyes slant in the old way;
> is she Greek or Egyptian? (254, ellipsis in the original)

The poem fixates on Thetis's otherness and, by extension, the otherness of all women in Western epic:

> Briseis, Chryseis, Polyxena; name again
> Deidamia, the king's daughter,
> he married in Scyros;
>
> did any of them matter?
> did they count at all,
> or were they mere members of a chorus
>
> in a drama that had but one other player? (241)

The chorus, drama, and player cited in H.D.'s tercets enact a racial fantasy in which Helen forges a revised archive of female subjects by performing an othering that reifies the white female self. Later, the poem describes how Achilles as a child carved a figure of Thetis from red cedar and "set her upon a plinth / like the curved prow of a ship" (292); the poem, moving backward in time, suggests the Trojan War as both childhood fantasy and family drama. The poem offers a temporal slide in which Thetis's "slanting eyes" evoke classicism as well as a contemporary lexicon of orientalism; Achilles's trip cannot help but invoke a contemporary geopolitical exoticism. British Egyptology is unthinkable without its ties to colonial ventures, orientalism, and hierarchies of civilization that privilege a supposedly civilized past over the present.

The poem's claim is a formal one and a subjective one. In seeming agreement with Williams's suggestion that without Helen's public fault there would be "no poem but the world," Helen wonders if her legend was merely created by the gods for the sake of poetry: "Was Troy lost for a kiss, / or a run of notes on a lyre?" (230). And then she asks:

> Was it Apollo's snare
> so that poets forever,
> should be caught in the maze of the Walls
>
> of a Troy that never fell? (232)

Helen suggests that her phantom status casts not just the motives for the war but the war itself in doubt. But she then reclaims ownership of the war's maze now that the (other) poets have failed:

> how could the lyre-string fail?
> I am called back to the Walls
> to find the answer,
>
> to wander as in a maze (232)

H.D.'s lyric is frequently cited as if it mobilized feminist resistance—as if a genre thwarted hegemonic narratives of identity and culture without reproducing its own problematics. It is the case that H.D.'s lyric does reinvent imagism; it does thwart epic; it does cross boundaries; it does undermine the Symbolic. These are all the sorts of claims that characterize much of the scholarship on H.D., on modern and contemporary women's poetry, and on lyric. But they also tend to privilege, and therefore abstract, something called lyric.[52] "Euripides is a white rose, lyric, feminine, a spirit," H.D. writes in 1919.[53] Euripides offered a rich vein of poetic expression which H.D. could mine to experiment with the self: her translations (or transliterations) of the choral lyric open deep possibility for reimagining the role of expression in modernist poetics, and for reimagining female and feminist subjectivity. But her lyric trade also activates an economy of lyric whiteness that brings into relief the pitfalls of genre for mythological and historical subjectivity.

3

"Movement, Rest, Repeat"

Cadential Lyric in "Paean to Place"

I have argued in the two previous chapters that long poems use lyric trade to reimagine the subject. For Gwendolyn Brooks, a lyric speaker negotiates the lineage of poetic form and the social and political demands of the contemporary moment; for H.D., feminist lyric installs an ideology of whiteness. Lyric trade articulates subjectivities that are by turns politically liberatory and limiting, that both align with and depart from received narratives of selfhood, or that make space for as well as foreclose certain identificatory modes. For Brooks, those identificatory modes include an explicitly antiracist Black feminist identity; for H.D., they include a feminist identity that relies on racial appropriation to forge its critique of Western female subjectivity. In this chapter I turn to a long poem by Lorine Niedecker, whose clipped ballads and torqued ambient cadences relay between human presence and nonhuman expression.

Niedecker's work often surfaces a number of connotations of the word "trade" in poems that deal directly with labor. In her three-stanza 1962 poem "Poet's work," for example, Niedecker links trade with the alienating effects of the labor market:

Grandfather
  advised me:
    Learn a trade[1]

The understated tercet undoes a number of narratives of aesthetic making: from its very title, it aligns art not with spontaneous or inspired creativity but with something called work. In the stanza's third line, the word "trade" swerves, signifying knowledge or skill. The remaining two stanzas enact the compressed materiality and looming precarity of the poet's trade:

> I learned
>   to sit at desk
>   and condense
>
> No layoff
>   from this
>   condensery

The poem condenses its own materials in real time, omitting the article "the" before "desk," jettisoning punctuation. It converts its compositional theory into a noun, "condensery," which could refer to poetic acts of revision and compression but which is also the word for a factory that processes milk products—condenseries were characteristic of Niedecker's home in the dairy-rich region of Jefferson County, Wisconsin. And if there is no "layoff" from such a practice of poetry, the artmaking that takes place here is inspired not by passion but by compulsion or obligation; poet's work is a laborer's dead end. Niedecker's verdict on poet's work may be more irony than indictment; she would not be the first poet figuratively to shrug at the obligatory qualities of artmaking. But her verdict could also be generative. It could be that the phrase "no layoff" keeps the pursuit of poetry safe from the vagaries of market forces that render certain kinds of labor precarious. Niedecker has complicated both the matter of labor and the matter of art by navigating a subject position for the poet that dwells ambivalently in multiple registers of making, precarity, and presence.

The posture of this particular poem toward artmaking and the subject may be an ambivalent one, but in its uses of words like "trade" and "layoff," and in its literal and figurative use of the condensery, Niedecker's poem aligns its linguistic materials with the lived realities of labor as well as the ideological imperatives of modernism. For Niedecker's modernist contemporary Pound, the slogan "Dichten = condensare" summarizes the notion of poetry as concentration (*Dichtung* in noun form; *Dichten* in verb form), a notion Pound attributes to Basil Bunting but which Pound also uses to elucidate the imagist principles of phanopoeia, melopoeia, and logopoeia as the three ways chiefly to "charge words with meaning."[2] For Niedecker's poem, on the other hand, the condensery allegorizes the precarity of the laboring subject at the same time that it suggests how artmaking might slip past that precarity. Niedecker's poem shuttles between labor and poetry's elusion by trading in condensation, expression, and presence: notions that attend a broad economy of supposedly lyric registers and forms.

Niedecker's intertwining of art and labor originates at least in part in her work as a research editor for the Federal Writers' Project, part of the Works Progress Administration, and her poetry during that time takes on what Niedecker called her "desire to get down direct speech":[3] a tendency to drop vernacular phrases, direct address, and proper names into the poem, imitating folk and ballad sound patterns that anticipate Niedecker's later remarks on the relationship between poetry and song. Elsewhere, Niedecker uses musical forms to reimagine the poetic beyond the laboring subject. In her long poem "Paean to Place," she uses the metaphor of a shorebird to interlock the work of writing with the act of flight:

> I was the solitary plover
> a pencil
>   for a wing-bone
> From the secret notes
> I must tilt[4]

The stanza confronts writing as a physical activity taken to the extreme: the substitution of "pencil" for "wing-bone" converts the bird into a machine made for writing. Writing is intimately, anatomically, equated with flight. The poem's speaker, planted in a broad canvas of lakes and marsh life, identifies more with bird kin than with human family. Whereas H.D. externalizes a swallow's wing in *Paint It Today* in order to cut through the "ether" of patriarchal forms, for Niedecker the plover wing does the writing of intimate expressive memory, the past of "I was" being followed closely by the present-future "I must." The expression of "Paean to Place" assumes the skeletal structure of the plover in order to articulate a poetics that is internal in the literal sense of the word. In substituting "pencil" for "wing-bone," Niedecker's lines sink the act of writing into the body's anatomy.

The plover, whose call is typically referred to in guidebooks as "plaintive," has become an emblem for Niedecker herself, something of a cliché, in fact, if the title of the Fort Atkinson, Wisconsin, newsletter published by the Friends of Lorine Niedecker is any indication (*The Solitary Plover*).

But this passage from "Paean to Place" also reveals the extent to which the embodied qualities of Niedecker's work are more conceptual than these descriptions of the plover's putatively expressive call. Niedecker's shorebird is an ornithological metaphor for writing, but also a musical one. In the last two lines of the stanza, the solitary plover tilts away from "the secret notes": "to tilt" can mean "to lean away from" but also "to run against." The line draws a picture of the plover issuing its song, its musical "notes," mid-flight. Those notes are contained and shaped within an interlocking five-line stanzaic structure that gives both rest and movement to the poem. Here are the five lines that follow:

> upon the pressure
> execute and adjust
>   In us sea-air rhythm
> "We live by the urgent wave
> of the verse"

These lines both conclude the first stanza—which ends with "From the secret notes / I must tilt"—and form a hinge between the first and second stanza—"I must tilt / upon the pressure." The enjambment of "upon the pressure" both exploits the tilting action of the bird (the line itself tilts down the page) and rests the speaker momentarily at the close of the syntactic unit before moving on to subsequent action. That speaker's single voice is decentered by a collective one, and further displaced by quotation marks.[5] In playing with rest, movement, and shifting speaking tones, Niedecker's stanzas enact what she describes in a 1965 letter to Cid Corman as a kind of musical cadence: "I'd say mostly, of course, cadence, measure make song."[6] Niedecker's cadence in "Paean to Place" aligns the rhythm of sea-air with the patterns of speech, a poetics that decenters human expression.

In this chapter I use the phrase "cadential lyric" to describe how Niedecker's long poem "Paean to Place" uses music to decenter the subject. The association of lyric with feminized birdsong is familiar, but I argue that Niedecker torques that link and invites a reconsideration of the relationship between music and modernism. Niedecker's interlocking five-line stanzas, which she provocatively describes as a "cremated" form, function as the crucible for a cadence in which multiple voices, human and nonhuman, sound. That polyphony shuttles between the presence of the human and the distance of nature, the poem's subjects dispersing into and emerging from a teeming landscape that mimics and inspires human forms, but which also materializes the nature of life spent in economically and ecologically precarious environments.

"An acre of music": Cadential lyric

Niedecker's cadential lyric begins with the dissociation of sound from subjective presence. In her 1928 poem "Mourning Dove," Niedecker cuts the notes of a songbird into discrete elements:

> The sound of a mourning dove
> slows the dawn
> there is a dee round silence
> in the sound.[7]

Niedecker begins by aligning the sound of the mourning dove with passing time: the dove's call "slows" the breaking of sun over the horizon. The following lines extricate birdsound as if it were a discrete object, breaking apart according to its orthography: "dee" recalls the whistling call of a killdeer, a bird native to the mourning dove's habitat, as well as the "d" in "dove," as if the dove were circling silence. Sound's proximity to nature reverses a Keatsian merging of self with nature—the colloquial, for the most part Romantic, association of "lyric" with the forlorn songbird is probably best summarized by Percy Bysshe Shelley in his 1821 "Defence of Poetry": "A Poet is a nightingale, who sits in darkness and sings to cheer its own solitude with sweet sounds."[8] Whereas Keats in "Ode to a Nightingale" looks to the bird as an exemplar of worldly transcendence before the bird's seeming immortality brings the speaker "back from thee to my sole self," Niedecker's speaker becomes nature, multiplying self. Niedecker continues:

> Or it may be I face the dull prospect
> of an imagist
> turned philosopher[9]

Niedecker apprehends sound of both bird and landscape, both figure and ground, before pivoting to a statement on her tenuous relationship to the modernist imagist movement, assuming the same kind of ambivalent posture toward labor and artmaking she takes in "Poet's work."

I am indexing Niedecker's uses of sound as well as her uses of terms like note, cadence, song, and measure—but there is an inevitable slippage between form and particularity when scholars use the terms of music to describe poetry. Often the language is simply figurative. The third of Pound's three principles of imagism reads "As regarding rhythm: to compose in sequence of the musical phrase, not in sequence of a metronome"[10]—the contrast he draws between something like the aesthetic qualities of the musical phrase and the rote machinery of the timekeeping metronome seems obvious.[11] Likewise, Adorno's lyric theory is accompanied by a theory of music that holds "Music is reducible neither to the mere being-in-itself of its sound, nor to its mere being for the subject."[12] Adorno uses music figuratively to make a point about the boundedness of poetic structure: discussing a poem by Stefan George, Adorno describes how "language escapes the subjective intention that occasioned the use of the word."[13] He uses a musical analogy: "Just as the greatest works of music may not be completely reduced to their structure but shoot out beyond it with a few superfluous notes or measures." The analogy contrasts subjective intention with superfluous materials—even if notes and measures are of course part of structure. Then there's Walter Pater's remark that "All art constantly aspires towards the condition of music," a position commonly taken to suggest music's special capacity among all the arts to obliterate the distinction between form and content.[14] Louis Zukofsky appears to echo this idea when he writes about Pound: "The order of the *Cantos* as the order of all poetry is to approach a state of music wherein the ideas present themselves sensuously and intelligently and are of no predatory intention."[15] And there is a way in which this is all a matter of genre: the differentiation of poetry from literature, as Rancière points out in his historicization of literary thinking about genre, often hinges on the differentiation of writing from music. What is often at stake is not the presence of musical techniques in literature, but the status of music as art.[16]

I call Niedecker's use of lyric cadential, but this is not quite the same thing as calling Niedecker's poems musical.[17] In a June 1957 letter to Zukofsky—with whom she was most creatively and socially embedded among the second wave of modernist poets, called the objectivists—Niedecker provides an example of the necessarily analogical function music assumes. She writes that the birthday gift of a music box "wasn't a *box*, just a tall, highly decorated pink and blue and yellow thing the top of which goes round as the music plays Brahms' Lullaby. Nice little pinkly tune."[18] Registering some disappointment, she continues, "My interest in music boxes is enormous but half the pleasure is the box, some highly polished beautiful little boxes I've seen." In the 1950 poem "Lugubre for a Child," a music box appears eerily as a martial object:

> Lugubre for a child
> but for you, little one,
> life pops
>   from a music box
> shaped like a gun.[19]

The poem likens itself to an unlikely piece of music. "Lugubre" is a term for a movement meant to be played slowly and mournfully, yet it has here been written "for a child" (Paul, Louis Zukofsky's son). A child's music box ought to play the sounds of liveness, but here is shaped like a weapon. This wartime image threads through the poem: flowers are likened to hammers of the construction and the piano kind; a hummingbird morphs from a bomber. The poem serves as a kind of lament for the "life" Paul has been born into, a life crosscut with atomic energies and anxieties of cold war containment.

Niedecker's stepped five-line stanzas function as forms—boxes— whose aesthetic work is inseparable from, if not more important than, the music the boxes play. When Niedecker writes in 1965 to Cid Corman that her views on poetic meaning have come to be informed by her thoughts on music, in particular cadence and measure, she performs a synaesthetic reading of a poem's effect on the senses. Her reading introduces the key terms of cadence: measure, song, and tone. She writes to Corman: "Yes, I see—'I picked a / leaf up'—I get for the first time that meaning has something to do with song—one hesitates a bit longer with some words in some lines for the thought or the vision—but I'd say mostly, of course, cadence, measure make song. And a kind of shine (or somber tone) that is of the same intensity throughout the poem. And the thing moves."[20] Niedecker's use of the word "measure" recalls a foundational definition of lyric: a spoken or sung genre. But Niedecker also anticipates a different sort of measure, one articulated in Charles Altieri's claim that objectivist poets such as Niedecker depart from the well-worn definition of self-staging lyric eloquence by conceiving of form as a flexible, porous "measure" rather than as a closed imposition of meaning. Altieri argues that objectivist sincerity resists ego-based lyric eloquence by "freeing imagist techniques into methods of thought based on notions of field, measure, and 'open form.'"[21] Niedecker anticipates Altieri's definition in the musical connotations of her remarks: while cadence can refer to the construction of any kind of rhythmical movement, whether speech, text, or some unit of sound, Niedecker uses cadence as a place where sound both rests and moves forward.

Some basic definitions of "cadence" from music theory illuminate its relationship to poetic measure. The cadence in one general definition refers to a moment in a musical composition that marks an end to a particular phrase, movement, or piece.[22] In music that is sung to a text, a cadence often coincides with a period; the original meaning of cadence pertains to the point at which a melody ends on the main note of the mode, or scale. A cadence has chiefly to do with a sense of rest and resolution, but a piece can contain many points at which a phrase comes to rest. The cadence itself can consist of any number of individual notes or chords; it can consist of a melodic or harmonic progression; and it can contain one or many voices. The cadence is chiefly a feature of tonal music, which is characterized by presence of a tonic, or a stable point of reference from which a piece's scales and chords derive. (For example, the tonic of a C major scale is the note C.) It is also characterized by the presence of a dominant, or the fifth note of a given scale. (For example, the dominant of a C major scale is the note G.) The most widely recognized sort of cadence in Western music, an authentic cadence, consists of a progression from the dominant, or the note that seeks the tonal center, to the tonic, the tonal center itself, which is the note upon which the scale is built. Atonal music, or music that does not seek a tonal center and that is driven instead by the principle of equivalence between the twelve tones of the chromatic scale, lacks a harmonic guide to distinguish a cadence from any other musical phrase. Yet atonal music—which has been a popular companion for many twentieth-century poets taken with its privileging of figures and motives over tonal hierarchies—might still allude to tonal cadences.[23] I offer this explication of tonality and atonality in order to clarify that cadence plays a role in both kinds of music, but also to note that the association of modernism with atonality is sometimes overstated—in the same way that, say, the characterization of a postlyric age can overstate a break from so-called lyric principles of an earlier century. In fact, what I call Niedecker's cadential lyric invites a reconsideration of the role of musical form in twentieth-century poetry and poetics.

Many of the earliest uses of "cadence," from the Italian musical term "cadenza," pertain to the measures of both speech and sung poetry, and the distinction between music and poetry that has characterized my discussion so far is a fairly recent one. The *clausula* of Greek and Latin rhetoric indicates, among other things, the terminal cadence to a sentence or clause, and structures the rhythm of prose, often quite strategically.[24] The colloquial expression "cadence of speech" transposes musical form to spoken form but actually draws on historical meanings of the word: a cadence of speech is not, strictly speaking, an analogy. A cadence primarily indicates a place to take a breath: particularly in vocal and wind music, the cadence follows patterns of inhalation and exhalation, and compositions frequently exploit this function in order to avert or contradict rhythmic patterns, varying phrasing and emphasis. The phrase "cadence of speech," then, indicates generally the rhythm of speech, the way its measures are ordered and phrased, the rise and fall of its sounds, or even more generally the measure of its rhythmical movement. And so, when F. S. Flint coins the term "unrhymed cadence" as a definition of imagist free verse, he figures received poetic forms as cadences—patterns—that find new and varied iterations in modernism's revolt. Flint also argues that free verse "has no measure, and it cannot, therefore, properly be called 'verse.' 'Cadence' would be a better word for it."[25] To say the least, the terms I am working with here, "cadence," "measure," and "verse," are mobile in their references throughout the twentieth century.[26]

Cadence in poetry often functions analogically not just as a description of breath and movement but also as an arbiter of aesthetic form itself for the modernist objectivist movement. Niedecker's relationship to music developed at least in part in response to the work of Louis Zukofsky. The "secret notes" of Niedecker's plover suggest birdsong but also the intense forty-year correspondence between the two poets, correspondence that includes descriptions of cadence as a formal feature that negotiates tensions between particularity and ideal poetic form. Both poets referred to performances and compositions they were hearing live in New York (Zukofsky) and on the radio in Wisconsin (Niedecker); both turned to the vocabulary of music to pursue a poetics steeped in associative sound and vernacular speech registers. The distinction between the two poets' approach to music can be characterized by their approaches to its metaphorical value.

Zukofsky conceptualized the elements of music as a formal boundary ringing the thematic and historical materials of the poem and in reciprocity with the demands of poetic form. He invites a metaphorical reading of music in poetry in his poem *"A"*-6, part of his long poem *"A"*: *"Can* / The design / Of the fugue / Be transferred / to poetry?"[27] Or in his more famous dictum, from *"A"*-12: "I'll tell you. / About my *poetics*— / music / speech / An integral / Lower limit speech / Upper limit music."[28] Or as Zukofsky remarks in 1930: "A poem: a context associated with 'musical' shape, musical with quotation marks since it is not of notes as music, but of words more variable than variables."[29] The fugal structure of Zukofsky's long poem *"A,"* as Mark Scroggins has insisted, refers to "the 'counterpointing' of linguistic, thematic, and conceptual units rather than a counterpointing of particular sounds or rhymes."[30] Zukofsky did not read music, and we know that Niedecker likely did, but not how extensively. *"A"* is not a score.[31] And yet cadence is a recurring metaphor of particularity and objectification for Zukofsky: in the "Objectivist" issue of *Poetry* magazine he edited in 1931, he claims poems of the new movement exhibit "objectivity of cadence" and defines objectification as "complete satisfaction derived from melody in a poem."[32] In *"A"*-6, Zukofsky writes: "The melody! The rest is accessory: / My one voice. My other: is / An objective—rays of the object brought to a focus, / An objective—nature as creator—desire / for what is objectively perfect / Inextricably the direction of historic and / contemporary particulars."[33] As Tim Woods has argued, Zukofsky cites melody and its contrasting particulars as a way to rid aesthetics of ego: the passage in *"A"*-6 performs an open-ended dialectic between the nonreferential voice of melody and the referential voice of historical and cultural particulars.[34] Zukofsky suggests that the cadence functions as a structure that allows the poem to move between the ideal and the particular, while behaving as an arbiter of objectification. The cadence structures particularity at the same time that it arbitrates it.[35]

Elsewhere, Zukofsky refers to "pure music": "Poetry has always been considered more literary than music, though so-called pure music may be literary in a communicative sense."[36] But given that Zukofsky describes the poem itself as a *particular* ("There are several kinds of poetic objects, i.e. poems; many particulars"),[37] I want to put pressure on "A"-6's contrast of "what is objectively perfect" with its "historic and contemporary particulars." In one of her few extant pieces of criticism, Niedecker shows how voice for Zukofsky persistently occupied a dual position for the ideal and the particular. Rather than invoking a binary made up of pure melody and a materialist poetics, Niedecker suggests, the dialectic for Zukofsky lies in the notion of voice itself. The "voice" that possesses "an impulse to master / music" is both "My one voice" and "My other."

"Everything sings (or becomes some art form) if you want to find the measure & the continuity?" Niedecker asks Zukofsky in a 1947 letter.[38] In her 1956 essay "The Poetry of Louis Zukofsky," Niedecker argues that the poetic voice takes form through musical genres. Writing about the way musical forms shape spoken tones in modernist poetry, Niedecker describes the "constant electronic interaction" within Zukofsky's uses of sung genres: " 'A' presents an order of succession but also of interweaving themes uniting with new and related matter, tightening often into such forms as canzones or ballades the tonality of our speech."[39] Niedecker juxtaposes lines from Zukofsky's "A"-8, a section whose design encompassing eight distinct voices Zukofsky borrows from "Bach's double chorus / Not paid a herring, eight themes spacing eight voices," with a passage from his "A"-6, in which Zukofsky contrasts melody with accessory. Niedecker suggests that there is something at the heart of both music and poetry—melody—apart from its particulars. Anticipating Williams's dictum that a poem is a machine built of words, Niedecker plays these two passages against each other as a demonstration of how poetic voice "moves to make the singing, living machine of our time."[40]

Niedecker's cadential poetics further departs from Zukofsky's music in a 1945 poem about labor that conceives of music as a historically bounded mode of cultural production. In that poem, Niedecker modifies Zukofsky's schema by zeroing in on a set of actors whose alienated labor correlates with their relationship to music. Zukofsky had sent Niedecker an early draft of his poem "Sequence 1944–6" and challenged her to write a poem in reply.[41] In the published version of that poem, Zukofsky writes:

We cross upon
One acre of music—
Asking
(So close who are cross)
Of acres and music:
Patience and time.[42]

Zukofsky provocatively spatializes music, first measuring it by acre and then placing "acre" and "music" in equivalent relation. Niedecker makes the acre of music into a scene of alienation. Titling her poem with Zukofsky's initials in parentheses—an intimate address literally set aside—she begins her poem with a modified version of Zukofsky's second line:

(L.Z.)

"An acre of music"
or a room closer to it
movement, rest, repeat,
for those making music
but not allowed to hear it
and those in peril
on the street[43]

Using both a line break and the conjunctive "or," Niedecker's poem splits the undifferentiated "acre of music" into acre and room. The poem's third line then uses formal terms to mark time—"movement, rest, repeat"—before swerving its gaze to "those in peril / on the street." Niedecker's poem bears traces of 1930s labor politics as well as 1940s warfare; it also functions as a subtle materialist analysis of the production of music, the peril outside a corollary for the disparity inside. The poem refuses to idealize musical form and instead zooms in on its practice, framing musicians as alienated workers, "making music / but not allowed to hear it."[44] Those who make music, after all, have historically occupied a different social and economic stratum than those who buy tickets.

"(L.Z.)" makes an argument about music and precarity in its content, but in its form it also anticipates the cadential poetics in "Paean to Place" that grapple with contested modes of expression and particularity. A few years after writing "(L.Z.)," Niedecker began refining a stepped, inter-locking five-line stanzaic structure in long sequences whose titles reflect her concerns with the history of place—*New Goose*, *My Life By Water*,

North Central, My Friend Tree. In 1956 Niedecker sent a manuscript of "For Paul and Other Poems" to Zukofsky and writes querulously about the shape the manuscript ought to take, wondering especially about what she called her "personal" ballads and the stepped stanza form that has often been read as a modification of haiku.[45] In brackets, Niedecker employs a provocative image for her new form:

> Question in my mind as to order—don't like the ballads mixed up with the serious—might make headings of groups e.g. Ballads—(whatever to call the more personal original ones)—(and the 5-liners with 2 words rhyming [did I create a new form or cremate?—influence of haiku I suppose] which form I'll be using often from now on if you like it)[46]

In suggesting that she might have "cremated" rather than "created" a new form, Niedecker, whose ear is frequently alert to puns, downplays her own innovation in favor of self-deprecation to a mentor ("which form I'll be using often from now on if you like it"). But Niedecker's remarks also belie a significant move toward seriality in the 1968 incarnation of the five-line stanza in "Paean to Place." Niedecker's choice of the word "cremate" suggests the way that new forms can both destroy and contain some element of the old, if not also the violent overthrow that can characterize modernist poetic innovation.[47] "Cremate" and "create" share no etymological bond, but here, paired as an off-rhyme, invoke how to render an object into different form.[48]

By 1968's "Paean to Place," Niedecker's characteristic stepped line structures had begun adapting into a distinctive interlinking serial style that combined modular cadences with extended form sequences: stanzas interlock and enjamb; syntactical units and phrases are made discrete with capitalization and indentation. Other poets of her moment, such as George Oppen, used seriality to explore nonteleological progression and the interplay of fragment and sequence. Niedecker's cadential seriality, on the other hand, confronts a central tension between expressive presence and ambient sound.[49]

"Not all that's heard is music":
Polyphonic cadence in "Paean to Place"

Niedecker's 1968 long poem "Paean to Place" uses forty-one serially interlinked five-line cadences to pin sound to the natural landscape.

The poem opens with an epigraph on the drifting nature of place and home:

> And the place
> was water[50]

"Paean to Place" progresses as family history, ecopoetic elegy, and poem of praise (paean) for Wisconsin lake country, as much as it elegizes the harsh material conditions of Niedecker's biography. Niedecker's approach to those material conditions attends to their settler colonial history: Niedecker spent most of her life near the small town of Fort Atkinson, where her mother's family owned a guesthouse and much of the other property on Black Hawk Island. Located in the Dells area of the western Great Lakes region, the island sits near the spot where the Wisconsin River empties into the Lake Koshkonong reservoir. Both Koshkonong and Black Hawk Island take their names from the Black Hawk War of 1832, in which the Sauk and Fox tribes, led by Black Hawk, fought European settlers in Illinois and Wisconsin to regain land taken by the US Army. In her early collection *New Goose*, Niedecker calls out the injustice of US land treaties: "Black Hawk held: / In reason / land cannot be sold, / only things to be carried away."[51] Those lines are echoed in other poems about the precarious nature of property: "Property is poverty— / I've foreclosed" she writes in 1962; "Do not save love / for things / Throw *things* / to the flood," she writes in "Paean to Place."[52]

The opening stanzas of "Paean to Place" use Niedecker's distinctive five-line cadences to dramatize the precarity of life in Wisconsin lake country. The poem's stanzas contain and measure at the same time that they serially enjamb and interlock. Niedecker's "cremated form" creates a space of cadential rest at the same time that it moves serially forward:

> Fish
>   fowl
>   flood
>   Water lily mud
> My life
>
> in the leaves and on water
> My mother and I
>   born

in swale and swamp and sworn
to water

My father
thru marsh fog
     sculled down
          from high ground
saw her face

at the organ
bore the weight of lake water
     and the cold—
he seined for carp to be sold
that their daughter

might go high
on land
     to learn
Saw his wife turn
deaf

and away
She
     who knew boats
          and ropes
no longer played[53]

Niedecker's poems insist on the mutually bound nature of art and labor; Niedecker's poetic subjects, as Elizabeth Willis has argued, "perform their identities, their ideological affinities, and their labors within a literary context that likewise considers itself as knowledge, as work, as relational system, as a product whose consumption demands even further labor."[54] In "Paean to Place," family relationships are thoroughly inflected by the harshness of fishing for sustenance, coping with regular flooding of the family home, hoping to enable the social mobility of a child (Lorine) who might go on "to learn," and the growing debility of a mother whose hearing loss would eventually keep Lorine on the island.

If Niedecker's cadential seriality uses music to decenter the subject, then "Paean to Place" also uses polyphony to invite and then complicate lyric associations of the voice. Polyphony relays between human presence and nonhuman expression, materializing economic and environmental precarity as a dilemma of subjectivity. Niedecker's polyphonic cadence is both form and analogy, and it draws attention to the way music functions in late modernist poetics, which entails a reconsideration of the role of music in reading practices. A number of scholars have taken music to be not simply linked metaphorically to questions within literary modernism but to be an integral part of basic questions of form and representation in the twentieth century.[55]

That discourse of music, form, and representation intersects meaningfully with discourses that consider what Min Hyoung Song describes as "climate lyricism," in which a poem torques "anthropocentric habits of expression" so that "the distinction between human and nonhuman becomes fuzzy and challenges the usual hierarchy of value that always privileges the well-being of the human over the nonhuman and that over-represents some humans at the expense of others."[56]

Lynn Keller likewise describes the "grammars of animacy" in contemporary ecopoetic work that writes self-consciously about and from the Anthropocene's current "crises and stalemates."[57] And Margaret Ronda has intricately traced how Niedecker's poetry in particular considers "the residual, attentive in both form and theme to what is left behind and what lasts," how it traces "a natural history of anthropogenic forces imprinted in various forms of matter."[58] Niedecker's ecopoetic polyphonic cadence reaches beyond the critical commonplace that the presence of multiple voices in a poem undermines the presumption of a single lyric speaker.[59]

In enlarging its soundscape beyond human speech, "Paean to Place" locates what Song calls the "moments of recognition" unique to climate lyricism's decentering of the human. Song shows how the notion of the human in twentieth-century poetry has become "increasingly turbulent with dispute" and how poetry that appears to decenter the human actually reconfigures human perception in a form of animism.[60] "Paean to Place" uses the central image of the mouth to reimagine the human:

> On this stream
> my moonnight memory
>   washed of hardships

       maneuvers barges
thru the mouth

of the river
They fished in beauty
   It was not always so
     In Fishes
red Mars (269)

The "mouth" acts as the conduit for "barges" that carry weight down or across a body of memory—across bodies of water both natural and manmade. Niedecker pulls back from the double meaning of mouth:

rising
rides the sloughs and sluices
   of my mind
     with the persons
on the edge

While it is to the mind and not to the body that the poem has returned, the mouth hovers in the final stanza of the poem. As with the pencil-wing of the plover, the poem moves the process of writing from the relative abstraction of a chronological act to the still-amorphous but embodied situation of the poem's speaker. The poem suggests that it is upon "the sloughs and sluices / of my mind" that the stream of memory continues to ride. But sloughs and sluices are not just objects that shape movement. They can both act as barriers to water's passage. The stream of memory that appears in the first stanza has by the third become the river of the mind; meanwhile, the mouth of body and river pivots between them, and the mind itself is likened to a series of boundaries that interfere with movement. What remains at the end of the poem is that "edge" that has been associated with watery memory and the source of speech: the mouth.

Niedecker's cadential poetics negotiates the fine distinctions between human presence and ambient sound, trading in supposed links between melodic centers and perspectival singularity using polyphony. Polyphony in Niedecker's poetry has typically been read in one of two ways: as a populist principle or as a form of musicality. Niedecker's uses of folk vernaculars, modified ballad stanzas, and Mother Goose nursery rhymes have been categorized according to modernist affinities for juxtaposition, mixture, and interruption—techniques that undermine principles of unity and representation. Scholars of modernist studies typically characterize polyphony as a technique that undermines the notion of a single, unified speaker; polyphony and polyvocality tend to be used interchangeably in literary studies, particularly when describing, for example, the plurality of different voices in canonical twentieth-century poetry such as *The Waste Land* and *The Cantos*.

Like cadence, polyphony is frequently defined in terms of its relationship to melody: in its most general sense, polyphony denotes the texture of a piece of music that sounds more than one melodic line. In his book on the Renaissance composer William Byrd, musicologist John Harley defines polyphonic cadence as a musical structure in which multiple voices act collectively to form a single unit while retaining their own sense of musical direction. Individual cadences of each voice may coincide or remain independent of one another within the larger structure: "Each voice is influenced by what is happening in other voices, but it has its own melodic cadences."[61] A plurality of voices in poetry, however, is difficult not to read as sequential, or "horizontal." Voices necessarily occupy stages or steps in a text according to the practices of reading and cannot be sounded at the same time. They do not appear simultaneously in the sense that musical polyphony makes it possible for more than one voice to occupy the same measure "vertically." Mark Scroggins goes so far as to insist that "in a musical fugue more than one voice can sound simultaneously, while in a poem only one voice can be heard at once."[62] Bob Perelman offers this example from the end of Zukofsky's *"A"*:

> *"A"*-24 ends with two voices speaking over a cadence in C minor. The Drama voice says, "Darling meet my mother. New gloves, mother?" as the Poem voice, concluding an apostrophe to ivy, says, "I wonder what makes thee so loved," with the typography showing that "gloves" and "loved" are to be spoken together. A misleading analogy could be made to two contrapuntal instrumental voices meeting on a C. But the verbal lines do not meet.[63]

Perelman's assessment that the rhyme of "gloves" and "loved" actually causes the words to interfere with each other when spoken together, rather than forming a "chord," illustrates the limits of using musical polyphony to read polyphonic poetry.

By tracking the nonhuman elements of land, water, organisms, and nonorganic matter, Niedecker's cadential poetics approximates horizontal polyphony. Niedecker's site-specific vocality can be understood as a variation on what Jonathan Skinner has described as ambient poetics. Drawing on principles of ambient musical composition, such as minimalism, the reversal of figure and ground, and saturation of the acoustic environment, Skinner identifies what he calls Larry Eigner's "soundscapes" in poems that function as stenographic landscapes of sonic texture and reference. As Skinner notes, the term "soundscape" was coined by the Canadian composer R. Murray Schafer, who defines it as any sonic field or environment to which a listener relates simultaneously as audience, performer, and composer. Against this concept Skinner contrasts Jean-François Lyotard's insistence that estrangement, or the effect of "losing oneself" in the indeterminate, absorptive qualities of landscape, is one of the key effects of this environment: Lyotard suggests in particular that in sound-based landscapes harmony and melody recede, and that timbre, or the sound quality distinct from pitch or rhythm, absorbs the listener's consciousness. Skinner argues that Eigner adapts the notion of "soundscape" to produce "listening maps": poems that invoke the spatial representation of sound, rendering aural facts by way of visual signs.[64] While the landscape so often appears precarious in Niedecker's work, at least during the flood—"River rising—flood / Now melt and leave home"—the first speaker of "Paean to Place" also inhabits that flooded plain, fully at home in it: "My mother and I / born / in swale and swamp and sworn / to water"; she "Grew riding the river"; "I was the solitary plover"; "You with sea water running / in your veins sit down in water."[65] If the "solitary plover" embodies the act of writing in its birdlike anatomy, Niedecker's site-specific vocality resonates with the features of an Eignerian soundscape in the bodies and flooded places of "Paean to Place."

Niedecker's work invests in the ambient textures of the soundscape, but her uses of aural collage, vernacular citation, and folk reportage also objectify sound as something material: the consequences for what lyric means in this work include what Lisa Robertson has called "acoustic subjectivity." Niedecker's diminishing eyesight in the late 1940s and early 1950s must have made her more sensitive to her aural surroundings, so that sound, for Niedecker, became not just perceptual but epistemic, a way to perceive, identify, and know her surroundings.[66] These two features of sound—sound as epistemic, and sound as object—can be understood as what Robertson calls a "dispersal" of the speaking I. Using the material history of sound reproduction technology to reconceptualize the act of listening as the act of composing (this emphasis on composition recalling Schafer's definition of soundscape as the field in which we listen as well as perform and compose), Robertson describes Niedecker's listening as a practice of reception and composition.[67] The acoustic subject, Robertson writes, "does not project identity, but loosely gathers identity's strands from all over the sonorous landscape"; the "I" furthermore "disperses across place to be washed in."[68]

Robertson's description of Niedecker's dispersed "I" accounts for important and striking reconsiderations of sound, perception, and subjectivity—and circles back to a number of lyric presumptions I have sought to unsettle throughout *Lyric Trade*. Niedecker's poem posits sound as object and sound as episteme, and it is because it does this through cadential and polyphonic structures—the musical terms revealing what the poetic forms are doing here—that it offers an intricate critique of subjective expression. In Niedecker's ambient soundscapes, disparate figures are consistently anchored in the voices of birds. Tracking the labor shared by the speaker's mother and father—"She helped him string out nets"; "He brought in a sack / of dandelion greens" (262)—Niedecker figures the precarity of lake country life in birdsound:

He kept us afloat

I mourn her not hearing canvasbacks
their blast-off rise
    from the water
        Not hearing sora
rail's sweet

spoon-tapped waterglass-
descending scale-
    tear-drop-tittle
        Did she giggle
as a girl? (262–63)

In the sora's "descending scale" the speaker both mourns her mother's loss of hearing and likens her mother's childhood giggle to the sora's call, the memory juxtaposing sound, body, and writing. While Niedecker may have meant "tittle" either to refer to the low voice of the sora or onomatopoeically to mimic the bird's distinctive staccato descending call, another meaning of "tittle" is a small diacritical or accent mark. In using "tittle," Niedecker returns the sound of the bird to the texture of the printed word, suggesting that the voice in the poem is written as well as heard. As an obscure form of contraction, a tittle also once functioned as a textual end or conclusion, not unlike a cadence. Bird and human merge again when the speaker describes:

> I grew in green
> slide and slant
>   of shore and shade
>   Child-time—wade
> thru weeds
>
> Maples to swing from
> Pewee-glissando
>   sublime
>   slime-
> song
>
> Grew riding the river
> Books
>   at home-pier
>   Shelley could steer
> as he read (264–65)[69]

The bird's call structures the lines that follow: "sublime" slides, glissando-like, into "slime- / song"; the alliteration predominates. Figures are remembered through song: the sora's descending scale, the peewee's glissando, the solitary plover's piping cry. The figures fold into the landscape and then resurface in textures of sound.

This chapter has traced a number of musical connotations—cadence, polyphony, and ambience—to show how Niedecker's lyric trade shuttles between the presence of the human and the expression of the nonhuman, materializing economic and environmental precarity as a dilemma of subjectivity. In a frequently quoted letter, Niedecker writes, "The Brontës had their moors, I have my marshes!":[70] Niedecker's ambient, place-based poetics can be understood as a form of regionalism that integrates metropole and province. "I grew in green / slide and slant / of shore and shade" (264): sonically mimicking the slide of stepped lines, "sl" and "sh" sounds shape an originary scene of lake-bound memory that allows Niedecker a few lines down to compare herself to her literary forebears. She "Grew riding the river," her "Books" stored "at home-pier," as Percy Bysshe "Shelley could steer / as he read" (265). But she also paints herself as a figure who seemingly came out of the marshes; Niedecker uses this method to sink memory into place as early as 1944's *New Goose*, in which a "long-billed pipe / on his red-brown vest" frames her grandfather as a marsh bird (92) and in which "Heirs rush in" to claim her father's property but resemble less people and more the "Ash woods, willow, close to shore" that "overflow each spring," the "woods" described in terms of "every board"—the wood of housing structures indistinguishable from standing trees (93).[71]

Under these harsh material conditions, Niedecker's poetics embeds the act of writing in the bodies and flooded places of Black Hawk Island as well as other, often more vast, landscapes nearby. As she pursued long serial poems that enlarged her close, focused attention on the object, Niedecker was reading extensively in natural history. Another long poem from around the same period assumes little separation between the human and the natural: 1968's "Lake Superior" forges a notion of world time based on geological imagery. After a road trip to the region, Niedecker wrote to Cid Corman that she felt herself taking a geologic retreat from circulation: "I need time, like an eon of limestone or gneiss, time like I used to have, with no *thought* of publishing."[72] Based on nearly three hundred pages of notes Niedecker took on the history and geology of the region, "Lake Superior" begins by linking the particulars of the local landscape with a generalized condition of being alive: "In every part of every living thing / is stuff that once was rock" (232). The poem associates the region's major geologic features with organic structures of being; rocks, minerals, and semiprecious stones are meticulously located within the physical structures of living things: "mash the cobalt / and carnelian / of that bird" (235). Niedecker's cadential poetics refuse to construct nature normatively. In 1950, Niedecker wrote: "Not all that's heard is music. We leave / an air that for awhile was good" (143). Niedecker's lyric cadences pursue a nonteleological epistemic approach to nature beyond the presumed subjective expression that otherwise might take hold there.

4

"I Looked Plural"

Lyric Others in *The Descent of Alette*

The previous chapter traces how a number of musical connotations—cadence, polyphony, and ambience—allow Niedecker's lyric trade to shuttle between the presence of the human and the expression of the nonhuman. While other poets use lyric trade to make space for as well as foreclose certain identificatory modes, Niedecker grounds her lyric trade in the conceptual spaces of expression and presence. For Niedecker and the other poets I have discussed so far, lyric trade is also a matter of negotiating literary inheritance: Brooks's uses of sonnets and ballads negotiate matters of audience; Niedecker's uses of music modify her relationship to objectivism; and H.D.'s lyric countermeasure spoke back to masculine epic.

This chapter picks up the thread of literary inheritance as a matter of racial othering. In chapter 2, I read the opening scene of H.D.'s 1955 poem *Helen in Egypt* in which a presumably white female speaker purports to blacken her face to thwart patriarchal narratives of female error. I read this scene through the colonial project of Egyptology, which detached Egypt from Africa and associated it instead with the Ancient Near East, in turn orienting the United States as the cultural inheritor of a sentimentalized, occupied Egypt. I then argued that *Helen in Egypt* activates an economy of lyric whiteness. Alice Notley's 1992 long poem *The Descent of Alette* also speaks back to a patriarchal version of modernism using an appropriation of Blackness. As in *Helen in Egypt*, lyric trade in *Alette* installs ideologies of the racial subject in place of the gender problematics it confronts.

In Notley's long poem *The Descent of Alette*, the poem's eponymous speaker awakens in a grassy meadow and encounters a decapitated woman sitting on a log. The woman's headless body features a "gruesome," "black well" of a neck, from which emit the "high & low tones" of her voice.[1] Alette realizes that the woman speaking in high and low tones is the archetypal "first mother." The first mother tells Alette a story about her speech:

> "She pointed suddenly" "A head sat" "several feet from us" "with open
>   eyes,"
> "frozen eyes," "& fixed" "frozen smile" "Brown skin lifeless," "dark
> hair wind-blown" "'I learned to speak from" "my throat," "from
>   darkness,"
> "not from behind the eyes" (91)[2]

The first mother tells Alette that having long ago walked into "darkness below the earth," carrying her own head, she came to be forgotten by those who remained above ground. Alette—whose own skin tone goes unmarked—spends much of the poem searching for the first mother. The first mother's brown skin could be attributed to the fact that Notley has said she modeled *The Descent of Alette* in part upon the Sumerian epic *The Descent of Inanna*; Notley's feminist retelling revises Inanna's journey underground in a number of ways, one of the most significant departures being to stage Alette's battle with her tormentor.[3] The eponymous hero of *Alette* draws agency from the brown first mother, scenes of whom structure a story about female voice: its primal loss and recovery; its binary genital inevitability; its power to undo tyranny; and its dissent from the high modernist epics that haunt *Alette*'s prehistory.

Alette's inclusion of the brown first mother emerges also from the high modernist epics to which *Alette* is indebted and from which *Alette* dissents. Specifically, modernism's formal claims necessitate the presence of racial others to reinforce the putative neutrality of its unmarkedly white subjects—such as the eponymous speaker, Alette. The poem initially encounters the first mother in a meadow, but Alette arrives in the midst of a long journey deep into the stations and tunnels of a subway, which serves as an elaborate trope for the poem's ideological intervention into the modernist long poem. Modernism's claims to new, revolutionary, or otherwise historically urgent poetic form were likewise often built in the subway, and modernism's formal interventions depended on the presence of othered subjects, a dependable presence woven into the lyric argument of *Alette*. Speech throughout *Alette* is segmented and enclosed in quotation marks, as if it were overheard, and the subway is segmented, too, by an underground system of passageways, temporary holds, and built and natural structures that all together are revealed to make up the mostly organic body of a nameless, patriarchal, all-seeing, and all-containing tyrant, structural patriarchy made flesh. Notley writes out of the legacy of modernist poetic encounters in and with the subway that treat it as a site of contrasts: between nature and technology; between the fragmentation of community and the cohesion of systems; between the intimacy of shared public space and the anonymity of urban masses; and between present-day modernity and the haunting effects of the past.

Modernist poems of underground transit figure the body as the object of exchange between past and present, an exchange that determines which bodies manifest and which are occluded. *The Descent of Alette* appropriates the modernist underground as a "space of dissent" from totalizing patriarchal form. Modernists used the subway as thematic ground for formal innovations in seriality, fragmented lyric, or the doctrine of the image—but their formal arguments, embedded in the material situation of underground transit, depend on the presence of racialized others. When Notley's poem culminates in the appearance of the lost first mother, her headless body and dark skin contrast with the unraced, presumably white, status of the poem's speaker. It becomes apparent how the thoroughly modern object of the subway must be populated by raced and classed others. The poem's turn to the racial other, or what Anne Anlin Cheng calls "the unassimilable racial other" who sustains an ideal of whiteness,[4] illuminates the imbrication of race with the history of US poetic innovation.

In this chapter I argue that *The Descent of Alette* reproduces the othering of racial identificatory modes by reading *Alette* against an earlier work by Notley that grapples with gendered literary inheritance. I first discuss a lecture Notley gave in 1980, titled "Doctor Williams' Heiresses," in which Notley cites feminist ambivalence toward the tangled genealogy of modernist predecessors. I show how the ambivalence at the heart of Notley's lecture is a matter of voice that anticipates the similarly genealogical ambivalence of *Alette*'s feminist lyric. I then turn to the 1992 long poem *The Descent of Alette*, which inherits from modernism the determining trope of the subway as the space of new form and adopts a feminist lyric that unfolds in the epiphanic textures of a highly citational practice of quotation. Through a reading of both texts against subway modernism, I argue lyric trade functions first to problematize and then to reproduce a central contradiction of modern and contemporary poetry: the way in which the avant-garde rejection of so-called lyric expression reinscribes ideologies of the subject. Modernism's subways figure as the architecture for *Alette*'s lyric ambivalence.

"As a poet I study my physiology": Descent in "Doctor Williams' Heiresses"

Like other poets I discuss in this book, Alice Notley's work manifests a certain dilemma of influence, one she refers to as "male forms." While Notley is associated with the second wave of New York School poets living in New York's Lower East Side in the 1960s and 1970s, she has expressed great skepticism toward being linked with that movement—she has said that she has "never quite identified with" the term "New York School."[5] She can at least be understood as one of the New York–based poets to emerge in the period that followed the publication of Donald Allen's *New American Poetry* anthology, published in 1960. After publishing a number of works in the 1970s, Notley left New York in February 1980 to spend three days in residency at the San Francisco artist space known as 80 Langton Street (later Langton Arts). In a report on Notley's visit to San Francisco, Kathleen Fraser writes that the New York scene in which Notley was embedded at the time was characterized by a distinctly masculine pattern of inheritance, one that Fraser calls a "fraternal laying-on-of-hands, from one generation to the next."[6] Notley herself characterizes this pattern of inheritance as a distinctly formal one: in a 1997 interview with Judith Goldman, she remarks that "It's also a fact that the ways in which poetry gets published . . . not to mention the whole idea of a literary movement, the academy, the avant-garde, are all male forms."[7]

Notley's posture toward the "male forms" of poetry institutions runs throughout a lecture on modernist inheritance she gave during her residency at Langton Street; the lecture was published later by Lyn Hejinian's Tuumba Press. As a meditation on literary history, "Doctor Williams' Heiresses" documents the rise in prominence of American women's poetry, a historical moment that happens to coincide with Williams's own late entry into the modernist canon.[8] As a piece of experimental historiography, the lecture ironizes the written record in order to confront the mixed position in which women poets find themselves writing after modernism. The lecture's uses of boundary-crossing libidinousness suggest a poetics of modernist affinity that refuses a polemical stance on the way formal inheritance enacts gendered marginalization—and possibly even eschews feminism. Instead, Notley's lecture assumes a posture of ambivalence.[9] This ambivalence anticipates the acute relationship between modernist inheritance and feminist critique in *The Descent of Alette*.

"Doctor Williams' Heiresses" opens by positing a basically conventional history of twentieth-century American poetry that is soon rendered strange and mythological by the presence of both divine intervention and male gestation. Notley writes:

> Poe was the first one, he mated with a goddess. His children were Emily Dickinson & Walt Whitman—out of wedlock with a goddess. Then Dickinson & Whitman mated—since they were half divine they could do anything they wanted to—& they had 2 sons, William Carlos Williams & Ezra Pound, & a third son T. S. Eliot who went to a faraway country & never came back. From out of the West came Gertrude Stein, the daughter of the guy who wrote the 800-page novel & the girl who thought maybe rightly that she was Shakespeare. Gertrude Stein & William Carlos Williams got married: their 2 legitimate children, Frank O'Hara & Philip Whalen, often dressed & acted like their uncle Ezra Pound.[10]

The passage begins as a perfectly conventional and quite linear narrative of American poetic lineage, featuring all the usual proper heirs: Poe begat Dickinson and Whitman, who begat Pound and Williams and, as an afterthought, Eliot, who went to a faraway country. (Notley does not mention that Pound also left America for the continent but did not, like Eliot, turn to New Criticism, formal conservatism, and the Anglican church, three moves that alienated Eliot from Poundian modernism.) Gertrude Stein seems to appear spontaneously, or to have descended from a different branch (that of Proust? Joyce? Woolf? herself?), only to marry Williams and give birth to O'Hara and Whalen. Notley suggests O'Hara's and Whalen's respective participation in the New York School and San Francisco Renaissance bears some similarity to Pound's self-fashioning as the harbinger of the new American poetry by imagining they dressed like Pound (Williams's brother). Stein's lesbianism has for the moment been elided; in fact, her so-called "marriage" to Williams converts the spuriousness of earlier poetic liaisons into heteronormative legitimacy: in the beginning of the passage, there is a lot of "mating" but no "marrying." The passage does not suggest seriously that Stein's William Jamesian commitment to textual surface and cognitive experiment shares a bond with Williams's relatively reckless Dadaist and impulsive vernacular. Rather, their union is simply one of many that Notley assigns to Williams, who is quickly taking shape as a kind of super-father to the poets of Notley's generation, and Notley's historiographic text becomes a kind of counterfactual claim against Williams's poetics of the destructive new.[11]

The lecture continues with Williams-as-Zeus spawning the larger-than-life Charles Olson. Notley writes:

> However, earlier, before his marriage to Gertrude Stein, Williams had a child by the goddess Brooding. His affair with Brooding was long & passionate, & his child by her was oversized, Charles Olson. Before Charles Olson's birth the goddess had also been having an affair with Williams' brother Ezra Pound. No one was ever absolutely sure who the father of Olson was. Now O'Hara & Whalen were males that were male-female, as were many of the children of Williams by various goddesses & of Gertrude Stein & some gods. Olson was too big to be as male-female as he would have liked; his female was always curling up inside his shoulder or wrist to take a nice dark nap. Anyway it was striking how there were no females in this generation; & the first children of the male-females & of Olson & their other brothers were all males, and there were very many of them because of their fathers' incredible promiscuity.

So far, most people who have given birth in Notley's text are men, although in the case of Whitman and Dickinson, the birth parent is not specified, and in the case of Olson, Williams's paternity (also cast as a sort of maternity) is later in doubt. Olson seems to have swallowed the "female" part of his "male-female" self: she naps contentedly in his shoulder. Whereas second-wave feminists such as Adrienne Rich posited matriarchal revisioning for literary inheritance, Notley adopts the attitude that all modernist progenitors are male who create other poets in their own image—and then ironizes that convention by suggesting they give birth vaginally rather than springing their descendants mythologically, fully formed from a forehead or thigh. Notley has in a sense feminized the male modernist body, a body whose offspring are sired by female goddesses. At the same time, Notley's historiography remains resolutely heterosexual. The roles have been switched, but there has been no queering of the tocogony. Stein has a child by male "gods," a story that muddles or erases her otherwise well-established modernist masculinism, to say nothing of her lesbianism, unless the lecture imagines a homosocial liaison for Stein imagined as a "male-female" like the gay poets Frank O'Hara and Philip Whalen.[12] Stein doesn't get to have a baby with a goddess, or to have a homoreproductive relationship with a god; she is basically lumped in with the femme goddesses. It is also striking who is missing from this narrative. There is no Marianne Moore, no H.D., no Mina Loy, no Virginia Woolf, no Djuna Barnes. There is Poe's unnamed goddess, and one goddess called "Brooding," but no other instance of allegorical personification. When Notley writes that "it was striking how there were no females in this generation," she wryly understates how she has reproduced the densely masculine story of modernist lineage, replete with fully fleshed out male personages; nameless, invisible female ones; and the indeterminacy of Stein. It would seem that the "male forms" of literary inheritance impart a typically masculine—and white—narrative.

When Notley's generation of women poets shows up, they cannot recognize themselves in the faces of their eccentric human fathers, and they find their goddess mothers remote and unavailable. So the women poets invent their own lines of kinship. As Notley writes,

> These females could not understand how they came to be born—they saw no one among their parents & brothers who resembled them physically, for the goddesses their fathers mated with were evaporative nonparental types. As a matter of fact these females couldn't even believe that their fathers *were* their fathers. They came to indulge in a kind of ancestor worship—that is they each fell in love with a not too distant ancestor. One of them, Bernadette Mayer, fell in love with Gertrude Stein. And the one named Alice Notley fell in love with her grandfather, William Carlos Williams.

Rather than looking to the immediately preceding generation of their fathers, the women poets reach further: to their grandparents, Stein and Williams. Their attachments enact taboo—queer, incestuous—liaisons and clichés of (grand)father-worship. Notley's and Mayer's attachments to Williams and Stein at once satisfy and vex the conventional narratives of modernist influence. This sense of vexed, libidinal poetic attachment establishes the lecture as a historiographic intervention into the written record of modernist influence, even as the gender binary survives largely intact, and even as a number of female figures—goddesses—manifest as "evaporative non-parental types." Are the goddesses simply unnamed and functionally interchangeable and ephemeral, or are they, having sired the poets, inscrutable? Are they as inscrutable as the absent women of Notley's generation who do not appear in the lecture (there is no Anne Waldman, no Barbara Guest, no Maureen Owen, no Ann Lauterbach, no Hannah Weiner, etc.)? Do they represent an antireproductive turn—the infertile or nonreproductive female? If heteronormativity and the gender binary limit by turns the feminist imagination of Notley's modernist inheritance, it is difficult to say whether that limit is discursively unavoidable.

The lecture hews to patrilineal and heteronormative rules of genealogy, yet there is one way in which the genealogy expands historical critique, and that is in its use of parody. "Doctor Williams' Heiresses" offers a speculatively literal genealogy; it is a work of poetics about literary history. But it can also be understood to undertake the kind of genealogical critique of history Michel Foucault describes as a "history of the body." Notley's approach toward parody in particular helps makes sense of the ambivalence at the heart of her text by illuminating its political entailments. Notley's lecture keeps the generations of poetic inheritance intact but crosses their temporal and desirous boundaries, leaves questions of influence unanswered, and parodies authority in the fashion of Foucault's genealogical method. Foucault describes how genealogy, or what he calls the "gray, meticulous, and patiently documentary" method of history, rejects linear development and transcendent origins. Genealogy has little interest in the "monotonous finality" of imagined or projected origins; it looks instead to the "entangled and confused parchments" of the past.[13] Key to genealogy's approach to history, for Foucault, is its use of parody. Genealogy "teaches how to laugh at the solemnities of the origin": it reminds us that historical beginnings are not "modest or discreet" but "derisive and ironic, capable of undoing every infatuation."[14] The parodic modality of history, which Foucault traces back to Plato, is imaginatively, parodically "directed against reality."[15] The status of monuments as transcendental origins is revealed to be a fiction, as is the practice of looking at them from a position of unwavering faith.

Notley's historiography ironizes and undoes its infatuation with modernist mastery, using parody as critique. When the text turns its attention to the female body, both metaphor and material, it suggests a very mixed feeling about being desired by a forebear:

> And you like my poetry for my body, & I admire it in the mirror to write my poetry, though it is aging, though it is aging & that is admirable. As a poet I study my physiology, I don't discourse on the evils of alcohol & drugs. I would give you in my poetry all the delight that my body might give your eyes & hands or that any lively body might there are so many — as a poet I study my physiology.

The scene of the female poet admiring her aging body in a mirror wittily alludes to Williams's poem "Danse Russe," in which the poet as "happy genius" dances naked in his north room "grotesquely" before a mirror, gazing on his own arms, face, shoulders, flanks, and buttocks "against the yellow drawn shades," self-parodying his aging creative body as his family sleeps.[16] Notley's use of the word "physiology" also alludes to the doctrine of physical science that grounds Foucault's genealogical critique. Foucault writes that descent is not a form of "acquisition" but an "assemblage of faults, fissures, and heterogeneous layers" paralleled by the fragilities of the body: descent "attaches itself to the body. It inscribes itself in the nervous system, in temperament, in the digestive apparatus; it appears in the faulty respiration, in improper diets, in the debilitated and prostrate body of those whose ancestors committed errors."[17] Notley's mirroring of physiological decline with literary descent will become much less parodic in her later poem *The Descent of Alette*, which depicts the structures of male poetic lineage as macabre, fleshy forms that pose mortal threats to women. But for now, Notley catalogs how drying skin and mucus membranes, graying hair, thinning pubes might deflate Williams's desire: "My blood & my breathing, my vision, my walk, the chapping of my lips, the greying of my hair, my flowers becoming less sticky more silky, the birds in my nests, etc." In tracking her own body's decline, Notley's speaker curries her forebear's approval and braces him for its decline.

When Notley's lecture turns to the matter of tone, her text becomes even more vexed under the sign of gender and subjectivity. Notley writes first that Williams's conception of the "variable foot" inflects her own speech-based poetics: "We still haven't caught up with what Williams meant by the variable foot, which has to do with scoring for tone of voice." In the variable foot, Williams insists, traditional forms of "fixed" poetic rhythm instead vary "with the demands of the language," particularly everyday speech.[18] Notley uses Williams's formulation first to differentiate her speech from classical, Romantic, or twentieth-century models of poetics and then to concretize her speech as something physical, before, finally, she confirms it as something gendered. And this binding of tone, physiology, and gender torques the approach "Doctor Williams' Heiresses" takes toward poetic subjectivity. Notley writes:

> I'm not an oracle or a musical instrument or a tradition or a stethoscope or a bellows or even a typewriter: I am a tone of voice, warming, shifting, pausing, changing, including, asserting, exulting, including, including, turning & including.

Within and against a catalog of precursors—as Perelman notes, Notley catalogs Homer's oracle, Shelley's and Coleridge's aeolian harp, Eliot's tradition, Olson's projective bellows, and a typewriter that "possibly" signals the materialist poetics of Language writing[19]—Notley positions first-person tone: "I am a tone of voice." A few pages later, she invites and then disavows the link between tone and gender:

> Being a woman the poet? Well it's a tone of voice that people aren't used to. You have to hit these tones of voice that people are going to say are this or that, strident or shrill . . . [. . .] I'm not all that interested in being a woman, it's just a practical problem that you deal with when you write poems.

Notley's terse linking of tone with misogyny—shrugging that a woman poet's "tone" will inevitably be judged "shrill"—flips to outright refusal ("I'm not interested") of the aesthetics of tone. That disavowal might actually align with Williams's own poetics, or at least the version of Williams cited by Adorno in his elaboration of poetry that polemically argues against conventional notions of poetic tone. In a discussion of tone, lyric, and subjectivity in *Aesthetic Theory*, Adorno writes that Williams "sabotages the poetic and approximates an empirical report": Adorno takes Williams's poetry to be a corrective to what Adorno later calls "the semblance of the self-evidence of poetic subjectivity."[20] It indeed might be useful to read a poetic work like "Doctor Williams' Heiresses" as a sequence of empirical sentences written as a "polemical rejection of the exalted lyrical tone"[21]—that is, Notley's empirical sentences in the style of Williams. And Notley's dismissal of a female subject position could easily be read as a dismissal of the kind of identity-based literary analysis I have been tilting toward here in even considering the extent to which the text is "interested in femaleness"—or implying that a text should be interested in femaleness. By "tone" Notley ostensibly refers to the sound of poetic speech; Notley's text could be read as a flippant swerve away from representative identity politics, "I'm not interested in being a woman" akin to "I'm not interested in being read as a woman poet." And yet in so dramatically rejecting "being a woman," Notley's lecture both reinscribes and studiously avoids anything like an "exalted lyric tone"—both because the rejection implies something will take the place of the tone projected upon the woman poet, and because, read another way, the rejection insists upon its own tone not as subjective but as critically discursive.

By "critically discursive" I mean Adorno's characterization of tone as it entails aesthetic judgment in poetic speech, but I also have in mind Sianne Ngai's critique of Adorno's own ambivalence toward the term. Ngai posits that literary tone be understood as a relational feeling: tone encompasses the attitude a literary text holds toward the social. Affective tone ought to be understood as a way to "generalize, totalize, and abstract the 'world' of the literary object, in a way that seems particularly conducive to the analysis of ideology."[22] And she skewers Adorno's own posture toward feeling as a reminder that "tone's generality and abstractness should not distract us from the fact that it is always 'about' something."[23] While Notley might seem to embrace, and then abstract and reject, tone in "Doctor Williams' Heiresses," the lecture roots its abstraction in the affective and ambivalent contours of the relations of poetic inheritance.

"It is a curious odor, / a moral odor," Williams writes in "Asphodel, That Greeny Flower" of bringing flowers to his wife.[24] He writes elsewhere: "The beauty of girls seemed the same to me as the beauty of a poem."[25] Notley invites these sorts of moments when she describes the experience of reading "Asphodel" while pregnant and depressed in an epistolary passage addressed to Williams:

> I'm looking for a passage from "Asphodel" about a "field of women like flowers & what should you do but love them?" Everything that's catching my eye though, in this poem, is something that's beautiful & makes me cry. But to a pregnant woman, I repeat, your reasoning was useless & enraging. We poets take all words personally. But I wrote my poem & I used for its form your *Paterson* & an O'Hara ode & those Cantos . . . & it is held together by flowers, as "Asphodel" is—we had a bewilderingly luxuriant garden there—& by the presence of the opposite sex "you" & by the will to write poetry.

Here the lecture turns most explicitly emotional in its critique of Williams's failures. Shuttling between anger and affection, Notley concretizes the problem of poetic inheritance as the thing that binds not only her own poetry but her very ability to write it. The etymological roots of the word pregnant refer to the state of being imaginative, compelling, inventive, cogent, or even variant. Notley's pregnancy at the end of "Doctor Williams' Heiresses" recontextualizes the text's earlier posture toward reproduction as it literalizes the normative female body and the feeling registers pregnancy produces. Whereas birth in the lineage section of "Heiresses" produces more and more poets, here pregnancy entails immobility. In a poem of the same period, 1979's *Songs for the Unborn Second Baby*, Notley writes, "I feel pretty androgynous / on paper [. . .] otherwise it's just still me here [. . .] Pregnancy most literal or flat state."[26] Notley distinguishes between the "androgyny" of paper and the "literal state" of pregnancy, describing androgyny as a kind of nonliteral textual state, if not a fiction—whereas pregnancy is literal (and, presumably, female).

Naming androgyny a *feeling* in this epistolary address to Williams (signed "Yours, Alice") situates Notley's work within a larger discourse about affective ties to gendered modernism, imitating Williams's own appropriative strategy in *Paterson* to include, uncited, letters from the then-obscure poet Marcia Nardi. Williams's use of the Nardi letters in *Paterson* is frequently described as a usurpation of female writing. Notley's strategy does not necessarily reverse this tactic; this tactic may not even be a sufficient way to describe the letters in *Paterson*. But Foucault's invocation of the nervous system in his description of genealogy also chimes with Nardi's 1942 letter to Williams in which she describes "my having been born with a sick nervous system."[27] As Nardi wrote in 1950 about modernism as a gendered mind/body problem: "I feel dumb— inarticulate, and like those in your *Paterson* who do not know the language and who die incommunicado. Perhaps I am all body."[28] (Another letter Nardi sent in 1943 associates the underground with gender and class privilege, calling to mind the subway in Notley's *The Descent of Alette*: "You've never *had* to live, Dr. P.—not in any of the by-ways and dark underground passages where life so often has to be tested. The very circumstances of your birth and social background provided you with an escape.")[29]

Notley identifies herself and Mayer less as the grandchildren of Stein and Williams and more as their "heirs." But to be a female heir, too, carries its own gendered histories: Notley chooses the feminized word "heiress" rather than the masculine or neutral "heir," suggesting a parodic redeployment of the nineteenth-century sentimental term "poetess." The difference between descent and inheritance, or between genealogy and inheritance, is also the difference between the past and the future. Genealogy, as Foucault writes, endlessly adjusts to accommodate new details and connected branches of origin. Inheritance on the other hand has to do with the transfer of property, title, or office; it tracks some source of power that usually remains intact in the transfer, and its inheritors are only a chosen few—which may explain why so many women are missing from this version of the Williams legacy, and why "Doctor Williams' Heiresses" does not obviously articulate either an assimilative or a radically divergent poetics for the woman poet. My invocation of Foucauldian genealogy recalls Wendy Brown's reminder that method does not necessarily engender politics. Genealogy affords discursive space for thought, judgment, and intervention, but that space "is precisely a space free of the notion of necessary entailments."[30] The entailments are yet to come. If Notley's genealogy in "Doctor Williams' Heiresses" serves primarily to "map the discourses,"[31] as Brown might put it, rather than entailing an intervention—such as what I have been calling feminist critique—the genealogical method may be the best way to theorize the lecture's abiding ambivalence toward modernist inheritance, and its investments in the ideologies of the subject that manifest in Notley's later long poem *The Descent of Alette*.

"The world is" "his": Form and racial othering in *The Descent of Alette*

The parodic ambivalence that characterizes poetic attachment to the past in 1980's "Doctor Williams' Heiresses" contrasts with the affectively pessimistic contours that shape Notley's 1992 long poem *The Descent of Alette*, whose central figure embarks on a Dantean journey set in an underground subway. Whereas "Doctor Williams' Heiresses" articulates Notley's poetic family tree as a space of intellectual and emotional play, *Alette* posits modernist lineage as a horrific prison lit with fantastical visages and ruled by a murderous tyrant. And whereas "Heiresses" declines either to indict "exalted lyrical tone" or to embrace a female identificatory subject position, *Alette* uses lyric for critical ends while reproducing the subjective othering of the modernism it interrogates. In its vision of underground poetry as emerging from literary history, Notley's text invokes Pound's attempts to "detach Dantescan light"[32] from modern poetry and make his *Cantos* into a wholly contemporary new epic. In its attitude toward received forms of knowledge as spaces of bodily and psychic harm and its insistence on the escape from hell as the path to new forms of being, Notley's *Descent* also invokes Williams's *Kora in Hell* and *Spring and All* as journeys to hell that culminate in necessarily destructive creation of truly new literature.[33] In her climactic final confrontation with male poetic authority, the poem's central speaker undergoes a traumatic catharsis in which she articulates her name and her private memory of grief, trading lyric epiphany for an exit from patriarchal form. But the poem also trades modernism's racial othering for an exit into new form.

I read *Alette* against the specific modernist lineage of poems that draw on the determining trope of the subway to stage their formal argument, but apart from its being set in the subway, the most explicit formal argument *Alette* makes is its use of quotation marks. Quotation marks surround phrases and lines, guiding the poem's structure and establishing its mode as oral but also deeply citational; they also cite and trouble literary inheritance. Notley's quotation marks gesture again and again toward a "way out" of literary inheritance in their dual approach to citationality: as marks that "sound" as well as "cite" what they enclose, the quotation marks enact what Derrida calls the "duplicity" of the sign, identifying voice as appropriated even as it signals supposedly lyric individualism. However, this initially capacious, reiterative approach to voice capitulates under the racial othering of subway modernism.

The book's opening introduces immediately its distinctive formal intervention:

> "One day, I awoke" "& found myself on" "a subway, endlessly"
> "I didn't know" "how I'd arrived there or" "who I was" "exactly"
> "But I knew the train" "knew riding it" "knew the look of"
> "those about me" (3)

The opening establishes Alette's descent as otherworldly and alienating, yet also recognizable: within the world of the poem, she remembers only (for now) that she awoke one day on a subway whose space and inhabitants feel familiar, even if how she came to be riding there remains a mystery. What is also familiar is that the subway is ruled by a "tyrant" whose price for leaving the subway is so high no one would ever ask to pay it, for it is "all of you, & more" (3). The collective "we" of the poem is, Alette says, trapped in an endless cycle of "ongoingness" as they move from station to station, traveling in a variety of fantastical subway cars: a car full of suited men with animal heads; a car whose inhabitants are on fire; a car filled with doubled bodies; a car of garbage; a car of invisible voices; a car of blood. The stations, too, hold their own mysteries: at one subway stop, a giant snake guards the exit; at another, Alette looks into a black mirror on the platform to see her own face covered by a plain wooden mask. As the poem progresses, Alette encounters supernatural beings, trials and riddles, and demands for self-sacrifice. She moves from the subway through other kinds of caves and cavelike spaces before her journey ends, but her quest culminates in a collective exit from the underground transit system into an ancient yet unmade world, toward the possibility of "something new now" (148). The quotation marks signal the speech-based text of Notley's poem as much as they ironize it. The marks suggest that the poem is a form of citation: to cite is also to draw on something as an authority or as a discursive history, and Notley's marks create an authorial and authoritative distance between speaker and reader.

The quotation marks' reiterability—their frequency, their unrelenting texture throughout this book—are of a piece with the architectural trope of the poem's setting, a trope that also happens to materialize literary inheritance: the subway. The quotation marks link the poem with the orality of epic, the musicality of lyric, and the textuality of historiography as they segment the supposedly individual voice of the poem.

But the quotation marks do not behave as expected. They do not segment speech conventionally; they do not distinguish between speakers; they do not enclose normative grammatical units of speech. They contain phrases, embed different voices, and enact parataxis at the same time that they interrupt lines and syntactical units. Sometimes the quotation marks take the place of other punctuation or a coordinating conjunction, such as the comma or the word "and" that might otherwise appear between the phrases: "But I knew the train" "knew riding it." In other places, the quotation marks disrupt syntax and separate referents from one another, as where in the quotation "those about me" is pulled away from "of." The quotation marks interrupt normative structures of grammar and syntax.

The interruptive function of Notley's quotation marks likewise aligns with a recurring theme in which subjectivity alternately coheres and fragments. In the second section of the poem, the bodies of Alette's companions suddenly become part of her own:

> "I saw that" "my hands' outlines" "were several" "& seemed blurred"
> "Likewise" "my arms & legs—" "I looked plural" (47)

The transformation of the single speaker into a "plural" one—and back again—is consistently described in *The Descent of Alette* as delineation: specifically, delineation of the body. Here, the outlines of Alette's own body appear "several" and "blurred," as if many bodies were overlapping at once in companionship or usurpation. Later, the reconstitution of the plural body back into a single one is again articulated in terms of delineation, when Alette looks down and sees that her arms and hands are no longer "plural":

> [. . .] "Instead," "a clear single edge" "delineated them" "I
> became sad" "sadder . . ." "Until" "I fell asleep:" "& dreamed of
>   falling" (61)

The resolution of Alette's body back into the singular via a "single edge," a single line, leads to misery; over the course of the book, the resolution into a single body advances and then is undone, over and over, as if one of the features of Alette's quest were to negotiate repeated, failed individuation. That negotiation would also seem to contradict what I describe as the status of Alette as a communal, rather than individual, speaker.

The overlay of delineation, desubjectification, and torment is dramatized in a scene in which Alette and a male companion detach their genitals and affix them to the fleshy walls of a cave in order to find out what it is like not "to have a sex" (57). The reconstitution of their selves punctuates the scene's genital inevitability.

> [. . .] "We disattached them then—"
> "my vagina," "his penis" "Pulled them out of" "our bodies" "like
> rocks stuck into clay—" "& inserted them" "shallowly" "in the
>
> cave walls," "where they stayed fast" "And then all at once" "I
> couldn't see," "see anything" "except vaguely" "a brown-pink flesh tint"
> "I seemed to swim in it," "ride waves of it" "uncontrollably"
> "I couldn't think" "at all" "Was formless," "was in chaos" (57)

Even with the suggestion of orgasm (the detaching of genitals enabling a kind of ambient pleasure), Alette's response indicates the terror of losing form: she has "become lost" and "unfocused"; all is "in chaos." Alette becomes disconcerted without her genitals, without her "form," shrieking that she wants "my sex back" and that they must "replace" their sex between their legs, at which point identity is restored. Lineation, reconstitution, and genital coherence are restored:

> [. . .] "My sex" "was then replaced" "between my
> legs," "instantly back" "The man's" "was too;" "& we were then
> delineated," "formed," "ourselves again" (57)

The scene reinforces the idea that subjects are delineated in poetic form: subjects in *Alette* become "ourselves again" once they are "formed"— sexed male or female. The quotation marks intensify the line's segmentation: the quotation marks break up the line into smaller units, as if the selves were being fragmented at the same time that they regained their integrity. The quotation marks further link poetic form to corporeal form as explicitly sexed. Notley's poem becomes a highly gendered version of what Lacan describes as the subject's fear of fragmentation and its flight toward unity. Describing the outrageous figures in Hieronymus Bosch's paintings, Lacan writes that the fragmented body "manifests itself in dreams when the movement of the analysis encounters a certain level of aggressive disintegration" before it "appears in the form of disjointed limbs, or of those organs represented in exoscopy, growing wings and taking up arms for intestinal persecutions."[34]

Quotation marks in *The Descent of Alette* serve at least three major functions: first, they formally enact epic quest by emphasizing orality, even as they bristle beneath the rules of typography. Second, they establish the poem as a form of historiographic citation. Third, they visually structure, segment, and re-form the poem's alienated and fractured subjects. It is this third function to which my reading is attuned. Quotation marks link poetic and corporeal form to binary gender. The discursive history of quotation marks informs this link: as scholars such as Margreta de Grazia and Marjorie Garber have written, the citational function of the quotation mark has always been unstable. Early printed quotation marks, or "inverted commas," as they came to be called in the seventeenth century, were originally used to indicate emphasis; they were not associated with quotations until the eighteenth century.[35] Yet, as Garber argues, even before the eighteenth century, they raised the question of the relationship between punctuation and speech. In the early modern period, Puttenham's *English Poesie* describes the comma as a pause given to every word, whereas Ben Johnson's *English Grammar* describes the comma as an aid to the breath. The difference between these two Renaissance views, Garber writes, hinges on whether the quotation mark is chiefly aural or written, elocutionary or syntactical, an indication to the reader or a guide to grammatical construction.[36]

Notley's own remarks on the quotation mark resonate with both Puttenham and Johnson, as she puts it in an author's note in *The Descent of Alette*:

> [T]hey're there, mostly, to measure the poem. The phrases they enclose are poetic feet. If I had simply left white spaces between the phrases, the phrases would be rushed by the reader—read too fast for my musical intention. The quotation marks make the reader slow down and silently articulate— not slur over mentally—the phrases at the pace, and with the stresses, I intend. (v)

But, Notley suggests, the marks also establish narrative legitimacy: "They also distance the narrative from myself, the author: I am not Alette. Finally they may remind the reader that each phrase is a thing said by a voice: this is not a thought, or a record of thought-process, this is a story, told." The question of who speaks in *Alette* derives from the question of how the quotation mark confers discursive authority. In the late eighteenth century, Garber writes, the use of the inverted comma came to be accompanied by a certain amount of anxiety around the authenticity of "extracts" or quotations in learned texts; even in contemporary writing, she suggests, "In some ways quotation is a kind of cultural ventriloquism, a throwing of the voice that is also an appropriation of authority."[37]

The extent to which quotation marks appropriate authority in *Alette* depends on how they leverage the elaborate trope of the subway as a sign of literary inheritance. The quotation marks serve as visual cues; they mimic both the tracks and the segmentation of underground transit; they suggest the halting, fragmentary conversation underground. The marks graphically mimic the subway as a metaphor of both containment and momentum: quotation marks enclose, but they also traverse the page. Likewise, they contain—they cite, and sound—Alette as well as the various "shades" in her landscape: "My name is" "Alette." The subway's segmented, serial architecture echoes in the poem's formal textures—its stanzaic patterns, its phrases surrounded by quotation marks, its fragmented and recohering subjects—and serves as a gridlike, clacking backdrop to the poem's trajectory. Notley's figures take, change, and lose shape: the figures take their material and poetic lines from the tracks and segmented cars of the subway system.

Waiting on a platform, Alette encounters a begging woman whose body has begun to manifest signs of the subway's dual function as linguistic and physical form:

> [. . .] "She wore a ragged blouse" "that was map," "that was
> printed as" "a red-lined map" "'What map is" "on your blouse?' I asked"
> "'Map of" "Map of" "Map of the subway,' she said" "'But it looks,' I
>   said,"
> "'so arterial—" "the lines so red & thick'" "They seemed to thicken"
>   (132)

The woman tells Alette that what she sees is a subway map that, thickening upon her chest, is also the veins, the "lifeblood," of the tyrant's body. A transit map not just imprinted upon but sunk beneath and pulsing through the flesh of a begging woman is an abject image of mortal decay, and Notley's use of the word arterial suggests the literal flow of organic material just as the quotation marks in this passage suggest the halting, fragmentary speech within the subway machine. In its corporeal unity, Notley's subway tracks at least two different histories of public transit. A 1941 Encyclopaedia Britannica film called *Arteries of New York City* announces that the major cities of the United States rely on "arteries [that will] carry men and goods in a steady flow of commerce."[38] To illustrate the anatomical networks of New York's transit system of trains, buses, and subways, the film depicts a graphic of Manhattan as a "heart" that draws workers through its valves and out again, with the subway as its main artery. More recent visualizations of the subway capitalize on rhizomatic growth, lost tunnels, routes that dead-end in forgotten spaces. Notley's poem returns to a moment when circulatory language expressed the efficient and triumphant consolidation of multiple transit systems into one body: in *Alette*, a body that serves as the governing image of epic descent, gender, and modernity.

The way Notley's figures fragment and cohere also recalls a specific history of subway modernism as a space in which, as Michael Warner might say, we recognize strangers "as transient participants" whom we address in "impersonal forms."[39] The subway can be considered a specific ongoing public in its own right, one to which poets have turned as a site for working out experiments in impersonal poetic form. The subway's history is characterized by the ubiquitous integration of art and everyday life, that integration illuminating the aesthetic ideals of interwar modernism, as Michael Saler has argued. The 1928 reopening of the London Underground signaled the subway's affinity with the idea of a mythopoetic construction of a distant community—not so unlike the Egypto-modernism I discuss in chapter 2 of this book. Subway architect Charles Holden directed that sculptors carve designs directly onto the London subway walls, "rather than use plaster casts, as direct carvings had been the practice in the Middle Ages."[40] At the same time, chief executive Frank Pick drew on the social and aesthetic ideals of nineteenth-century figures like John Ruskin and William Morris in constructing the Underground as a work of public art, one stocked with museum exhibits and cultural propaganda that "should be considered as the culminating project of the nineteenth-century English arts and crafts movement, a union of the arts designed for the pleasure and the use of the common individual," as Saler describes.[41] Saler traces how the Underground helped define a specifically English avant-garde that, like the modernism of Pound and Benjamin, "sought to reinvigorate earlier traditions as a way to negotiate the present."[42] The subway remained indebted to nineteenth-century efforts to restore the city to a state of social and spiritual integration, an integration mapped back onto nineteenth-century interpretations of the Middle Ages. That anachronistic approach to history signaled the subway's affinity with what Peter Bürger identifies as a specifically avant-garde attack on the status art had come to occupy in bourgeois society: literally, in this case, the act of bringing art from the museum to the underground in exhibitions and promotional materials. As Saler points out, art was housed in the new modernist London Underground in a design that "would herald 'modern London'" at the same time that it harkened back to an earlier historical era in its integration of art and architecture.[43]

Underground transit in Paris and New York, the primary sites of Anglo American modernism, includes several examples of poets who experienced the subway as a socially charged public space that hosted new kinds of expression and a different relationship to the past. This does not mean that modernists necessarily celebrated the subway in the ways London designers did; rather, the subway offered a social situation to be problematized. The subway has stood as a site of cultural production at several moments in modernist poetry: as a charged transnational space for Pound's Paris Metro haiku, as a locus of class discourse for Zukofsky's MTA sestina, as a scene of literary haunting for Crane's descent under the Brooklyn Bridge, and as a theatre of American decline for Williams. In each case, poetic innovation hinges on the need to leave certain subjects underground: the othering of certain subjects underground enables poems to stage their arguments for poetic newness, poetic innovation, or exit from the poetic past. *The Descent of Alette* inherits modernism's othering of racial and classed identificatory modes to stage its exit from patriarchy made flesh.

One prominent icon of subway modernism is Pound's "In a Station of the Metro," in which Pound uses the underground to argue for an antilyric imagism that draws on orientalist accounts of the ideograph. First published in 1913 in *Poetry* magazine, the poem consists of two lines:

> The apparition   of these faces   in the crowd   :
> Petals   on a wet, black   bough   .[44]

In *Gaudier-Brzeska*, his 1916 memoir of the French Vorticist sculptor, Pound describes his Metro poem as responding to the "sudden emotion" he felt upon sighting the crowd: "Three years ago in Paris I got out of a 'metro' train at La Concorde, and saw suddenly a beautiful face, and then another and another, and then a beautiful child's face, and then another beautiful woman."[45] Pound then "made the following *hokku*-like sentence" that he published as "In a Station."[46] Pound had been seeking a form in which readers construe relationships between disparate parts, what he calls a "form of super-position, that is to say [. . .] one idea set on top of another. [. . .] In a poem of this sort one is trying to record the precise instant when a thing outward and objective transforms itself, or darts into a thing inward and subjective."[47] While critics such as Hugh Kenner have suggested that Pound depicts a banal technological present against which the poet contrasts the fecund, feminized face-petals, Marianne DeKoven argues the female face-petals in Pound's poem are actually "a product or appropriate denizen of the metro, an eruption into displaced representation of the fecundity of that maternal cave. They are *of* the underground cave just as much as they are its antithesis."[48] If Pound sought to record the transformation of the objective into the subjective, then, that transformation doubly objectifies the female face as it figures the metro as both technological new and primitive past.

Pound's underground objectifies the figure of the female, but it also depends upon a racialized other in order to achieve super-position. Pound's notion of a "mythic past" for imagism allies modernism's visual ambitions with his "speculative ethnography of East Asia," in Christopher Bush's phrase, as well as with his poetics' simultaneous "orientalist transparency and penetration," as Jahan Ramazani puts it.[49] Pound locates the foundations of imagism in ancient Greece and China while revising a classic catalog of poetic genres: Pound writes that "There is a sort of poetry where music, sheer melody, seems as if it were just bursting into speech," and that "There is another sort of poetry where painting or sculpture seems as if it were 'just coming over into speech.'" The first sort of poetry, he writes, "has long been called 'lyric.'" The other "is as old as the lyric and as honourable, but, until recently, no one had named it. Ibycus and Liu Ch'e presented the 'Image.'"[50] Pound's "In a Station of the Metro" claims for modernism a poetry that would return to an "honorable" historical chapter, just as it insists on the resolutely new structures of the present. And while Pound rejected techniques of excess in a Victorian lyric past that he took to obfuscate rather than center the image, he draws on an imagined Eastern past in order to argue for the imagism he invents in the modern Paris subway, a poetic form rooted in what David Leiwei Li calls "compensation" for the West's own desires.[51] Pound's image in "In a Station of the Metro" in particular enacts what DeKoven identifies as a form of *sous-rature*, the mechanistic subway emotion simultaneously locating itself in and erasing the face of the other. In DeKoven's words, female and racial otherness coincide in the image of the bough as Pound's poem trades in the lyric emblem of feminine death: "The wetness and the blackness of female, racial otherness are reassigned to the bough, a figure of rugged masculine potency, over which the light-colored, feminine petals now presumably droop."[52]

Louis Zukofsky's 1934 poem "Mantis" likewise occasions a subway scene to advance an argument about poetry's sufficiency or insufficiency to reckon with the present. For Zukofsky, it is the repeated phrase "the poor" that connotes the subway's othered subjects. Spotting a praying mantis among the stone banks of the subway, Zukofsky's speaker renovates an Old World—medieval, in fact—form, the sestina, to read the mantis as emblem of poverty:

> Mantis! praying mantis! since your wings' leaves
> And your terrified eyes, pins, bright, black and poor
> Beg—"Look, take it up" (thoughts' torsion)! "save it!"
> I who can't bear to look, cannot touch,—You—
> You can—but no one sees you steadying lost
> In the cars' drafts on the lit subway stone.[53]

In "Sincerity and Objectification," a de facto objectivism manifesto, Zukofsky writes that poetry ought to focus not on the subjectivity of the poet but on the objectivity of the poetic work.[54] While Pound's orientalizing imagism objectifies the world outside in the space of the poem, Zukofsky's objectivism stresses the poem itself as object. It also, like *The Descent of Alette*, stresses poetic lineage: both "Mantis" and the seven-page free-verse critical commentary Zukofsky appends to his poem respond to

Pound's own 1909 "Sestina: Altaforte," written only a few years before Pound and Richard Aldington laid out the principles of imagism and in which Pound pays homage to his own putative forebears, Dante and Petrarch. Unlike the symbolism that burdens Pound's sestina, Zukofsky insists that his mantis is not symbol but occasion: "The mantis itself only an incident, *compelling any writing*."[55] Incidental or not, the mantis is exhorted in the poem's concluding lines to build a future otherwise apart from "the poor":

> Fly mantis, on the poor, arise like leaves
> The armies of the poor, strength: stone on stone
> And build the new world in your eyes, Save it![56]

To fly "on" the poor and then "arise": Zukofsky's incidental emblem articulates a social poetics underground. While not overtly racial, as are Pound's orientalized face-petals, Zukofsky's dialogue between formalism and critique is likewise curiously populated by others in an underground setting described most frequently—because it is one of the end-words that must recur according to the laws of the sestina—as "stone." The mantis sits on "stone banks"; the subway is lined with "stone seats"; the mantis will "Graze like machined wheels, green, from off this stone": it is almost as if the modern subway were becoming ancient, and the trope of the mantis more mechanized: Zukofsky describes the mantis at one point as an "android."[57] As a deliberately open-ended treatment of class division, "Mantis" and its commentary necessitates the subway as a space of othered subjects delineated by antique form.

Like Zukofsky, Hart Crane turns to the subway to express anxieties about the American condition; the poem also alludes to a lynching, in the most burdened reference to violent othering for the modernist subways discussed here. In the "Tunnel" section of *The Bridge*, which he began writing in 1926, Crane characterizes the underground motion of the subway by contrasting the "overtone" of the individual car with the "monotone" of faces, the din of chatter presumably overtaking the melody of the individual. Whereas Pound's face-petals recede underneath the weight of remembered images, and Zukofsky's begging poor appear as the reflective surface of an "invoked collective,"[58] the others in Crane's subway behave more allegorically within the poem's argument for part and whole. "The Tunnel" links literary forebears with innovation: Walt Whitman and the airplane, Herman Melville and the sailor, and Edgar

Allan Poe and the advertising age. Poe's ghostly visage looms as Crane's poem turns to the circulatory language of public transit:

> Whose head is swinging from the swollen strap?
> Whose body smokes along the bitten rails,
> Bursts from a smoldering bundle far behind
> In back forks of the chasms of the brain,—
> Puffs from a riven stump far out behind
> In interborough fissures of the mind . . . ?[59]

Crane invokes both the physiological subway and eschatological epic. The language is circulatory in its referentiality, but also in its form, which seeks coherence for its fragments, or what Crane himself describes in a letter to Waldo Frank as the "notes and stitches" from his own nights as a straphanger.[60] The Poe lynching may be ambiguously racialized, but elsewhere in *The Bridge*, Crane's poem refers to "A homeless squaw— // Perhaps a halfbreed" with "eyes, strange for an Indian's," which are "not black / But sharp with pain // And like twin stars," as one among a catalogue of the poem's outsiders.[61] The squaw figure appears in the "Indiana" section of *The Bridge*, whose settler-colonial ("pioneer") narrator invokes a mythic Indigenous past in uneasy tension with the straphanger's urban present. Several lines later, the speaker in "Indiana" seems to have been converted in old age back to natural form, as in Zukofsky's underground: "I'm standing still, I'm old, I'm half of stone!"[62]

Williams's argument for the poetic fragment characterizes an overtly racialized modernist focus on Blackness on public transit. In 1955's "Asphodel, That Greeny Flower," Williams's speaker sees an African American man on the subway who comes to stand in for the speaker's father, for the speaker's own face, and finally for a universal subject:

> And so, by chance,
>   how should it be otherwise?
>   from what came to me
>   in a subway train
>   I build a picture
>   of all men.[63]

Williams turns, as many Anglo modernists did, to Blackness to construct a number of different fantasies in the subway: one of the past, one of the confining present, and one of the possible human future.[64] In a section from his 1962 series *Pictures from Brueghel*, Williams instrumentalizes the figure of a Black man to ask how to "escape" a suffocating modernity:

> returning home
> late at night
> I saw
>
> a huge Negro
> a dirty collar
> about his
>
> enormous neck
> appeared to be
> choking
>
> him
> I did not know
> whether or not
>
> he saw me though
> he was sitting
> directly
>
> before me how
> shall we
> escape this modern
>
> age
> and learn
> to breathe again[65]

Here the modernist poetic subject experiences rapid transit's technological new as ominously contradictory. The "Negro" whom Williams's speaker sees appears like Poe on the strap in Crane's *The Bridge*, the choking of his collar also reminiscent of a lynching. In his use of the pronoun "we" Williams could seem to try, at least, to turn away from the facile stereotype of the "Negro"—and instead toward the recognition of the subway as a social space in which the experience of modernity's rejection of America's past failures is a shared one. Yet the encounter with the Black man is one-sided: "I did not know / whether or not // he saw me." The scene triggers lament for the stifling effects of the modern airless age. That lament, coupled with the blurring of singular and plural "I" and "we" in Williams's terse lines, resembles what Cheng describes as the naturalization of the affliction of racialization. Williams's unmarked speaker struggles to forge a new relationship to the past that overlaps with a "diligent system of melancholic retention" of liberal white identity.[66] While the melancholy of race can be understood, Cheng shows, as the structural formation of racial identification for minoritized subjects, melancholy can also be attributed to white US subjects.[67] While Williams's subway poem volleys for an empathetic version of poetry for "all men," that volley depends on the presence of a racialized other.

US modernist poets depended on the presence of othered, impersonal subjects to host innovation in the subway underground. They used the subway as object, as site, and as formal enactment of an inability to leave the past completely. Which is why a 1992 long poem using the subway to dramatize the feminist quest of writing out of modernist form is so illuminating—and ambivalent in its politics. When Alette looks into the "shadowed" face of the tyrant, he tells Alette:

> [. . .]"The darkness—" "this darkness—" "scares me,"
> "always scares me" (132)

The tyrant recalls the darkness in the figure of the lost so-called "first mother," whose dark skin and brutalized, headless body figure a complicated past for Alette, whose race goes unmarked. Earlier in the book, the first mother has told Alette an origin story: humans once existed in an undifferentiated whole of flesh, but they then divided into two sexes, male and female, the "edges" of their "forms" sharpening and differentiating in primal, orgasmic sensation. The existence of these two sexes then led inevitably to their estrangement: the male became a "thinker" and a "war-maker," and he fetishized and degraded the female, who was made to "dance naked alone" as a decorative reminder of human creation. Over time, the female's head became detached from her body, which continued to perform before the men as an object of display and subservience (91). In the midst of telling Alette this story, the decapitated woman points to her own head, which is lying several feet away:

[. . .] "A head sat" "several feet from us" "with open eyes,"
"frozen eyes," "& fixed" "frozen smile" "Brown skin lifeless," "dark
hair wind-blown" "'I learned to speak from" "my throat," "from
    darkness,"
"not from behind the eyes"

Read in light of the modernist legacy *Alette* is built to resist, the passage reveals how the supposedly thoroughly modern object of the subway—which structures these poems thematically and formally—actually turns on the trope of a "brown" other, illuminating the imbrication of race with the history of US poetic innovation.

Like some of the modernist predecessors, Notley's epic speaker originates underground. She wakes and descends further into the subway, whose veins and arteries belong to the body of the tyrant who is both of the subway and the creator of everything within its passages and chambers, including both artistic and human forms. Creative activity inside the subway is from the outset tightly conscripted by the tyrant's ownership of creative output. Early in the poem, Alette encounters a woman artist struggling with this dilemma of making, not so unlike H.D.'s treatment of statuary in "Pygmalion" and "Helen":

"I asked her who she was" "& why" "she was crying" "She
said: 'I" "am a painter" "I have been trying" "to find"

"a form the tyrant" "doesn't own—" "something" "he doesn't
know about" "hasn't invented, hasn't" "mastered" "hasn't
made his own" "in his mind" "Not rectangular," "not a
sculpture" "Not a thing at all—" "he owns all things,"

"doesn't he?" "He's invented" "all the shapes" "I'm afraid he's"
"invented mine," "my very own" "body'" (25)

It is not only artistic form the tyrant has mastered, the woman tells Alette; her own body is also inscribed and determined within his subway. The space of the subway dramatizes the link between corporeal and poetic form, a link that, as Susan McCabe points out, can be traced back to Plato's *Timaeus*, in which the feminine is posited as matter while women are refused the possibility of possessing form. Judith Butler takes up this link in *Bodies That Matter*, arguing that "to invoke matter is to invoke a sedimented history of sexual hierarchy and sexual erasures"—the feminine being actually "a nonthematizable materiality" beyond both form and matter.[68] Notley's subway likewise makes female matter a kind of impossible thing: however, the subway is also the passageway to a new democratic formal space. Like the subways of modernism, Notley's subway forges paths to forms that are old or forgotten, but her poem refuses a verdict on the feminist efficacy of form or formlessness, instead offering an ambivalent exit from its quest.

The ambivalent end of *Alette* is anticipated by a scene in which Alette hears a woman describe having once found a temporary exit from the subway. Opening the door, the woman tells Alette, she found a scene shot through with blackness: figures dressed in black against the snow, with "guarded, / dark eyes." The woman then says she remembered entering a library also shot through with decaying black matter, even in the midst of a blooming spring:

> [. . .] "The books were decayed matter," "black & moldy" "Came apart"
> "in my hands" "All the books were" "black rot" "Were like mummies"
>
> "More body of" "the tyrant" "It is all his body" "The world is" "his
> mummy" "Up there, up there" "Down here it is" "a more desperate"
> "decay," "as if" "rich emotion," "pain," "could still transform us"
> "despite him" "despite his power, &" "tyrannical" ". . . ignorance,"
>
> "passing as" "knowledge—" "And so of course I" "re-entered" "re-
> entered" "the subway—" "I can't leave it" "ever" "unless"
> "we all leave—'" (21)

The woman in this passage describes a false escape from epic: when, through temporary error, she was able to ascend from the tunnels, she found not some ideal place lit by freedom but a wrongly seasoned cityscape, snowy and blooming at the same time, populated by mourners. She realizes the whole world is a "mummy," a prefiguring trauma in the midst of which she left the university for the subway, or the Enlightenment for Hell. Both the books and the subjects remain "frozen" in memory. As Williams shows in the second book of *Paterson*, the library is decaying before our very eyes; only a "new line" will halt its cycle.[69] In Notley's poem, the rotting library makes up another part of the hellish subway, a form of false knowledge we must inhabit; only "rich emotion" will "transform us." The woman says she can't leave the subway unless "we all leave": only a collective exit can obviate the power of the underground.

Public transit in *The Descent of Alette* has the curious effect of invoking the historically situated modernist public at the same time that it aspires to a mythopoetic imaginary. If, as Adorno claims, all epic poetry is anachronistic, out of harmony with the present moment, Notley's subway likewise cites a curious anachronism.[70] Alette searches for the first mother through a series of caves underneath the subway tunnels, caves made of stone described as the "middle psyche": recall the lapidary surfaces of "Mantis," Brooks's "rapture in stone," or Niedecker's "living rock." When she meets her again in book 3, she helps the first mother repair her severed head and regain the power of her voice:

> [. . .] "her face" "began to change"
> "Color" "poured into it:" "her skin was golden brown" "her eyes
> deep-set & brown," "tender" "beneath fierce eyebrows" "She was
>   young"
> "Younger than I" "& yet she was, I felt," "truly" "our mother . . ."
>
> "Wide nostrils, wide lips . . ." "She smiled at me" "warmly" "'I'm not
> afraid" "anymore,' she said" "'My voice has not lost" "its power'" (98)

Like the antilyric modernism it interrogates, *The Descent of Alette* has drawn on the figuring of a racial other in order to drive its formalist quest underground.

Touching on at least three iterations of dead matter—the bloodied remains of the first mother, the zombielike passageways of the tyrant's subway, and the rotting library—the book's teleological focus on escape draws on a putative lyricism to engender new life, new growth, beyond male form. In its invocation of the modernist subway, the modernist long poem, and the long history of male form, *The Descent of Alette* takes on the avant-garde rejection of so-called lyric expression and converts it into a kind of extreme: the near-totalizing structure of the poem's quotation marks foregrounds exquisitely cathartic expression in the hero's final confrontation. The end of Notley's poem coalesces putatively lyric elements in a scene in which the retrieval of private memory is the act that ultimately shatters male form. Alette and the tyrant stand by a river that resembles Lethe, the river in Hades from which the shades of the dead drink in order to forget. The tyrant confirms to Alette that the red waters of this river are his blood; on the waters' surface, Alette spies a "black tatter" of fabric (135). Alette plucks the fabric out of the river, swallows it, and realizes it is a scrap of her own memory. Once she consumes the scrap, Alette gives an outpouring of speech spliced by quotation marks in which intimate grief unfolds from the grim finality of warfare:

> [. . .] "My name is" "Alette"
> "My brother" "died in battle'" "I sank" "to the ground &" "sat,"
> "sat & thought of him—" "his pure profile," "his head's shape" (136)

The tyrant, "deeply moved" by Alette's memory, assumes a "military" demeanor. The exchange between them constellates the same kind of ambivalence around male form and female creativity Notley explores parodically in "Doctor Williams' Heiresses," but here with an urgent, even mortal, weight. Both the tyrant and Alette remark on how the "intensity" of masculine battle sources the imagination and the aesthetic. Their exchange turns argumentative over the nature of beautiful speech. "Men fight," the tyrant tells Alette;

> [. . .] "'Men fight" "Don't you
> think they must sometimes?" "And there's a shape to—" "an intensity"
>
> "to battle—" "to war—" "a proximity to life & death—" "that
>   captures
> many men's" "imaginations . . .'" "'That's exactly what women" "are
>   enslaved to,'
> I said dully" "'But this is all a cliché" "All a cliché, anyway"
> "I don't" "want to live" "in a cliché,' I said" "'Your" "house of insults"
>
> "of science," "of art," "your trivial politics," "your inspiration"
> "drawn from the hardships" "of others . . ." "my grief for" "my
>   brother"
> "so moving" "to you . . ." "I must" "have been searching" "for him"
> "as well" "Or I was searching" "for her voice—" "the headless"
>
> "woman's voice—" "so that I could" "speak to you'" "'Beautiful,'"
> "he murmured" "'It is not *beautiful*" "It is what was!'" "I was nearly"
> "screaming now" (136, italics in the original)

Handily reducing the male forms of imagination, science, art, politics to "cliché," Alette asserts the ontological and historical fact of her speech-memory, recovered from the first mother: it is not beautiful, she tells the tyrant; it is not moving; it is what was.

Alette turns catharsis into a public weapon, retrieving emotion from the repository of male form in order to restore her community above ground, to a space where new embodied forms can emerge from the corpse of epic. The first mother, presumably, has been left behind, her voice reincorporated by Alette. The quotation marks take a dual approach to citationality: as marks that "sound" as well as "cite" what they enclose, they suggest the "duplicity" of the appropriated sign, displacing what we might otherwise read as an appeal to authenticity.[71] As Garber notes, in order to be recognized *as* signs, linguistic and nonlinguistic signs "have to be able to be repeated—to be iterable and citational. (In French the word *citation* means 'quotation.') And since every repetition is a repetition with a difference, duplication becomes 'duplicity.'"[72] "I am a tone of voice [. . .] including, including, turning & including," Notley writes in "Doctor Williams' Heiresses." This reincorporation of voice depends on the racial othering inscribed throughout modernist inheritance and then reiterated in the passages and chambers of *Alette*'s own subway, even in a final scene that punctures the cliché of male forms. *Alette*'s open forms dwell in intensely ambivalent relation to the antilyric history it exits; their own relationship to lyric likewise remains ambivalent even up to the moment at which an unnamed voice in the crowd asks, on the last page of this book, "'"But can't we make" / "something new now . . .'"" (148). The wavering affections of Notley's "Heiress" anticipate the way *Alette*'s affective registers—the rage, disgust, embarrassment, and, again, ambivalent affection—culminate in a cathartic release of new form, followed by abiding faith in which voices can sound above ground.

5

"A Mutual Duration"

Civil Lyric in *Civil Bound*

As I have shown in the previous chapters, a number of modern and contemporary poets experiment with what happens when a long poem draws on apparently lyric forms, such as the melodic, the personal, the interior, the private, or the otherwise apparently ahistorical. What I have called lyric trade negotiates competing narratives of experimentalism, politics, and the subject; or it activates an economy of whiteness; or it dissociates sound from subjective presence; or it reproduces modernist ideologies of racial others even as it imagines liberatory spaces for the subject beyond the circulatory structures of patriarchy. The lyric trade I discuss in my last chapter, on Myung Mi Kim, is doing something different. Kim's works frequently draw on terms that have surfaced in my previous chapters—including subjectivity, speech, body, and form—in poetry that assumes a critical posture toward language's translative and identarian functions and that invokes and unsettles discourses of the civil subject.

A number of passages in Kim's 1988 book *Dura* use the language of the proposition. Framing its page with a pair of colons that suggest calculation, ratio, or analogy, *Dura* brings together a number of political concepts in uneasy relation:

:　:

Propose: constant translation. Propose: the
application of the compass to navigation. Propose: from
a settlement, a capital grows. Propose: foray, expansion.
Propose: as relates to an America. Propose: as relates
to immigrant. Propose: knowledge becomes the parlance
of the state. Propose: sound combinations. Propose:
nameless days.[1]

Two pages later, Kim includes the lines:

33.0   The subject is a proposition
34.6   Impulse of vocal air[2]

When Kim writes both "Propose: constant translation" and "The subject is a proposition" as numbered axioms, she leverages the rhetorical-mathematical figure of the proposition to suggest the moveability of identity.[3] *Dura* invokes an array of political terms—including settlement, capital, expansion, America, immigrant, and the state—before collating axiomatic declarations about the translative nature of language with the notion that language might be atomized to central elements of impulse and air. *Dura* then turns to a sequence of mathematical and geometrical forms, which Stephen Hong Sohn describes as unmasking "the way race and racial difference are structured onto economically exploitative gradients."[4] The word proposition carries with it a number of etymological associations with problem, riddle, or parable; a statement of logical truth or fallacy. In one of the last pages of *Dura*, Kim writes: "*State* is, for instance, *having armor on, having shoes on.*"[5] Kim encircles the notion of identity with the rhetoric of both the state of being and the nation-state.

In this chapter, I use the phrase "civil lyric" to describe how Kim's work uses lyric to engage with the subject and the state. In her 2002 book *Commons*, Kim describes lyric this way: "The lyric undertakes the task of deciphering and embodying a 'particularizable' prosody of one's living."[6] On its face, Kim's line rehearses a commonplace of lyric: that it is a form that enables the expression of discretely individual life, distinct from the social or political. Yet by characterizing living as an instance of prosody, Kim instead frames lyric as the exquisite expression of both personal and social form, one whose expressive particularizability is in fact both established and destabilized by a pair of quotation marks around the word "particularizable." The form of lyric becomes a social condition, itself, that does the work of subjectivity. Seventeen years after the publication of *Commons*, Kim's long poem *Civil Bound* takes up the question of "the prosody of one's living" in a long poem that enacts the formal gestures of fragmentation, translation, and documental appropriation. The book's opening page uses imagistic lines in a spare, connotative invocation of migration:

the oceans held up a snarling dog

eardrum bramble

salty necks, heaven hung

an according bargain

short luck's business

limbs or lives   horns together

savagery's judge[7]

These aphoristic lines, with their surprising yet logical pairings—a dog at sea, an ear clogged with debris, a neck brined with sea water, luck run short with consequence for life and limb—combine the dryness of catalog with the halting and haunting effects of a fragmented poetics in a kind of—to borrow a phrase Kim uses elsewhere in *Civil Bound*—"debris architecture."[8] In Kim's work, the interrelated operations of fragmentation and documental appropriation invite a critique of the supposedly lyric "particularizability" of the subject.

In *Commons* Myung Mi Kim describes lyric as the particularizable prosody of the subject, but in that same book she also offers what Michael Leong calls a theory of the long poem: "Desire for the encyclopedic // Interrogation of archive."[9] Across a number of long poem works, Kim has bent the supposedly lyric concerns of the speaking voice against the encyclopedic, the archival, the historical, the durational, and the broadly sociopolitical, often staging this concert of concerns through the combination of English and Hangul. Shot through the work are translingual poetic enactments of the ongoing traumas of immigration, assimilation, globalization, and xenophobia. I take the phrase "translingual poetics" from Sarah Dowling, who uses this phrase to describe what happens when poetry stages "confrontations" between different languages.[10] Terms such as "bilingual" and "multilingual" tend to reproduce the logics of neoliberalism, which cast certain languages as dominant and others as alien. The word "translingual" instead captures the ways in which languages interact and influence each other, and the ways in which poetry in particular can attend to processes of domination and refusal.[11]

Where Kim's poetry tends toward the spare, fragmented line, it also creates vast spaces on the page for accounts of flight and rest, of migration and stillness, of stalled and halted transnational journeys of the subject. Snatches of speech coexist alongside documental catalogs of objects, governmental records of expansion, microaggressions, and experiments with text alignment and punctuation that demarcate the field of the page. This contrast of the spare line and the vast field often surfaces a putative contrast of lyric expressivity and the long poem's tendency toward historiography. In this chapter I argue that in the 2019 long poem *Civil Bound*, Kim's lyric trade operates within and across spatial and conceptual fields to apprehend the civil subject and its absence as a social form. First I place Kim's lyric critique of the civil subject in the context of discourses that theorize form and the social. I then trace how Kim's civil lyric unfolds across documental and fragmented forms.

"What sound do we make":
The forms of social conditions

A line from Kim's 2009 book *Penury* invokes the catastrophic effects of militarization on the speaking I:

> : the place I'm from is no longer on any map[12]

By introducing the line with a colon, Kim suggests both an axiomatic function of the poetic line and the halting effects of fragment: the colon is preceded by a long gap on the page, as if that gap mapped the missing origin. Kim's work is frequently read as doing something different with first-person speech: Sohn describes Kim's poetics as a sort of "historicist lyric imaginary" that braids together the details of historical crisis—such as the historical dearth explored in *Penury*—with a "lyrical meditation on subjugation, colonization, and violence."[13] To move laterally from an adjectival "lyrical meditation" to the analytical phrase "lyric trade" attends to how Kim's work deals with the subjugative economies of colonialism: something called lyric is not simply mobilized, but circulates. To describe the way lyric circulates attends to the politics of work like Kim's—which stages a critique of global trades and trafficking—as well as to the difficult and differential relations that shift into gear when a long poem adopts multiple formal registers. To take this example from *Penury*, then: thinking about the appearance of the I as an instance not just of lyric but of lyric trade suggests how Kim's work activates an economy of genre in order to posit the subject as a social form.

Reading lyric trade in Myung Mi Kim's work as a matter of subjectivity invokes two discourses that link lyric with the civil subject: one, the discourse of lyric theory, and the other the discourse of aesthetic inquiry that has frequently characterized the field of Asian American studies. Jacques Rancière, in considering the first discourse, lyric theory, asks in *The Flesh of Words* what "necessity" might link "the modern stance of poetic utterance with that of political subjectivity."[14] The answer lies at least in part in how the term lyric circulates: for Rancière, the modern lyric is "a new political experience of the physical world, or a physical experience of politics."[15] For Rancière, lyric subjectivity is accompanied by a "horizon of community," the distinction between the two being made possible only by a "critical effort that separates the 'wandering' of the poetic 'I' from the poetic utopia of politics."[16] Rancière reads "the new liberty" of Wordsworth's *The Prelude*—that classic instance of supposedly lyric wandering inside a long poem—as an example of modern lyric's unique posture toward both subjectification and figuration.[17] Rancière draws on Kantian formalism to make this theoretical and literary-historical argument: "It is the modern aesthetic revolution on which Kant focuses at the time: the dismissal of the *mimesis* and the abolition of the distance between the *eidos* of the beautiful and the spectacle of the perceptible; the ability of the beautiful to make itself be appreciated without concept; the free play of the faculties that proves, even if it neither can nor must determine any concept, a power of reconciliation between nature and liberty."[18] Rancière is Kantian in his belief in a priori forms, even as his approach to genre and subjectivity is acutely historical—and as Kandice Chuh shows, Rancière's formalism is ultimately political both in its conditioning and in its a priori structures. As Chuh writes in *The Difference Aesthetics Makes*, Rancière's aesthetics, as Kant's, is both political and conceptual. Just as for Kant, "a priori concepts translate experience into understanding," for Rancière, aesthetics "are structures that proffer and frame what can be heard and seen." Aesthetics are themselves political, but also are "the grounds upon which the political is constituted and perceived": this is why aesthetic inquiry is such a powerful tool to confront power and authority.[19]

Chuh's description of the aesthetic and the political in Rancière's thinking illuminates not only what I have been describing as the forms of social conditions but also the exemplarity of the lyric. I have questioned the assumption of that exemplarity, and I have asked whether reproducing the notion of lyric's exemplarity simply reproduces the ideology of an ahistorical, transcendent subjectivity that theories of lyric putatively undo. Linking poetic utterance with political subjectivity in the way Rancière does, and attending to Chuh's characterization of the politics of aesthetics as both grounds for the political and the political itself, offers a way to trouble lyric's supposed exemplarity—and offers a different way to think about the lyric subject.

The second discourse that links lyric with the civil emerges from the field that Chuh also describes: the discourse of inquiry that has frequently characterized the field of Asian American literary studies. To take one key example: Chuh's book *Imagine Otherwise: On Asian Americanist Critique* unpacks the way grounding assumptions of Asian American studies, such as the homogenization of peoples and their histories, "have faced repeated interrogation"; Chuh points out that the discourses of transnationalism and postcolonialism make explicit the implicit principles of nation-based fields like Asian American studies.[20] Chuh's approach is instead to foreground contingency and irresolution, to emphasize difference itself as "anterior to and irresolvable in identity."[21] Chuh conceives of the field of Asian American studies as an anti-essentialist "subjectless discourse," one able to "create the conceptual space to prioritize difference by foregrounding the discursive constructedness of subjectivity."[22] Asian American literary studies, in particular, for Chuh, can trace the "internal work (the deconstruction) of individual disciplines necessary for Asian American studies to work interdisciplinarily in more than name alone."[23]

The discourse of the subject and aesthetic inquiry intersects with the way poetry and poetics was dealing with voice and expressivity around the time Kim began publishing work. Kim's literary oeuvre has long been aligned with two significant moments that emerged in 1970s and 1980s US poetic practice: Language writing's conceptual-material openness as a redress for the fixation on personal, expressive lyric, and a number of new anthologies of Asian American writing that, as Timothy Yu puts it, "exposed the mainstream voice as a white voice."[24] Yu has delved into the ways in which these two moments in US literary practice—Language writing and the rise of Asian American literary publishing—inform and challenge each other, in particular how certain Language poets frequently could not sustain the tensions between radical form and interpretation that revealed a bias toward white identarian individual speech, while the rise of Asian American writing presented certain pitfalls of narrative voice for poets whose personal ruminations risked being absorbed and commodified as ethnic markers by mainstream American culture.[25] Yu cites the work of Chinese American poet John Yau as an example of poetry that stages "a playful emptying out" of the signifiers of ethnicity as well as looking toward work by other Asian American poets—including Theresa Hak Kyung Cha, Mei-mei Berssenbrugge, and Tan Lin—in which "the impulses of experimental and Asian American writing meet in mutually critical fashion" and stage questions of identity and poetic form.[26] Yu's work on the variegated relationships between Language writing and Asian American poetry takes as its central stakes the status of literary value.[27] Although different in its theoretical inflections, Yu's framing of Language writing and Asian American poetry does, like Chuh's, posit aesthetic inquiry as a necessary pathway into central questions of form and subjectivity. Park has also written about how instances of field formation for Asian American studies have confronted the "tendentious and tenuous nature of the category 'Asian America'" and have inspired scholars "to revel in the critical possibilities afforded by this very instability."[28]

Chuh's critique of citizenship provides a useful set of terms for lyric studies. "At the same time, and despite how enormously enabling citizenship continues to be in the garnering of access to certain material resources, subjectivity itself, alone, cannot remedy injustice," Chuh writes; "Subjectlessness, as a conceptual tool, points to the need to manufacture 'Asian American' situationally. It serves as the ethical grounds for the political practice of what I would describe as a strategic *anti*-essentialism—as, in other words, the common ethos underwriting the coherency of the field."[29] While Chuh's aesthetic inquiry focuses on narrative literary forms, especially those of the novel, her characterization of a subjectless field of Asian American studies shows how a reading of social forms must take into account the constructedness of the subject and the pitfalls for a version of literary studies that seeks simply a different kind of subjectivity, thereby reproducing essentialist or liberal notions of the subject. Very often Kim's work is read as a kind of autobiography of Asian American or Korean American subjecthood, but these readings can limit analysis of what else forms like lyric are doing to pose productive questions about the histories of citizenship.

Kim's modernist-inflected long poem practice, as well as her approach to the text-oriented practice of materialist poetics, frequently invokes the subject and its absence. Kim's first book, *Under Flag*, published in 1991, offers a dense and fractured series of poems about Korean immigration to the United States that spotlight the role of monolingualism in constructing citizenship. Drawing on a tradition of twentieth-century Anglophone long poems that bear a heightened relationship to citizenship—as Adalaide Morris writes, "the epic solicits the ear of the public"—Kim's earliest work takes on both the bardic hailing of a rapt audience and the cultural ambitions of a poetic voice speaking for that audience, especially in times of crisis.[30] Morris describes the statist contours of that poetics: "Epic composers speak as citizens to other citizens, engaging a tribe, community, nation, or alliance." Kim opens *Under Flag* by setting the distance between voice and subject against the distance between two continents, fracturing the citizen-to-citizen exchange Morris proposes. Kim's poem "And Sing We" shores up the way language enacts relations of power:

> Must it ring so true
> So we must sing it
>
> To span even yawning distance
> And would we be near then
>
> What would the sea be, if we were near it
>
> > Voice
>
> It catches its underside and drags it back
>
> What sound do we make, "n", "h", "g"
>
> Speak and it is sound in time[31]

The lines conflate geography with anatomy: the "yawning distance" of land and sea doubles as the wide opening of a mouth mid-breath or -cry; the one-word line "Voice" behaves as an object as well as a command, linking the indeterminacy of "our" nearness to the sea ("if we were near it") with an invitation to speak or narrate that subjunctive proximity. Kim writes, "It catches its underside and drags it back": the voice catches without leaving the mouth, producing instead more silence—and distance. The poem dissociates sound from voice with disaggregated letters "n," "h," and "g" that fall short of semantic meaning. If Lorine Niedecker's poetry features discrete bits of sound that take on nonhuman subjective meaning, Kim's marks out the gaps and silences that mark civil subjectivity. Kim's poetry maps the linguistic trauma of migration, interrogates language as a tool of assimilation, and cites the frustrated work of language to cite both state and subject.

Several passages in *Under Flag* tie language acquisition to the assimilating operations of history, trading in the gestures of expression and musicality. In "Food, Shelter, Clothing," a section of *Under Flag* whose title recalls Thoreau's suggestion in *Walden* that the necessities for man may "be distributed under the several heads of Food, Shelter, Clothing, and Fuel,"[32] Kim writes:

> She could not talk without first looking at others' mouths (which
> language?)
> (pushed into) crevice a bluegill might lodge in[33]

In lines that mimic the operations of language acquisition—watching another person's face speak in order to learn—Kim suggests how a language can fit uncomfortably inside a mouth, like a fish stilled in a crevice. Near the end of the poem, after intervening passages that depict scenes of war and arrival, Kim writes:

> Stricken buoys
> Span no tongue and mouth
> Scripting, hand flat against the mouth[34]

Quieted by the "scripting" hand, the poem's voice goes adrift, and the poem conflates silence with geographical distance:

> Up against bounty and figured human
>   allaying surge
>
>   neighboring

Geographical trodden shelter
Locate deciphering

> by force

As contour
Hurls

> ga ga ga ga[35]

The dissociated sound—ga ga ga ga—could be an epithet hurled at a newcomer whose language sounds illegible; it could signal the slow acquisition of a new language; it could be a placeholder for meaning for a mouth disoriented and estranged; or it could be a gesture toward the romanization of written Hangul or spoken Korean.[36] The poem that follows, "Into Such Assembly," distorts official rhetoric designed to assess one's linguistic suitability for US citizenship:

Can you read and write English? Yes ____. No ____.
Write down the following sentences in English as I dictate them.
> There is a dog in the road.
> It is raining.
Do you renounce allegiance to any other country but this?
Now tell me, who is the president of the United States?
You will all stand now. Raise your right hands.[37]

The mashing up of texts (a questionnaire, but also a series of spoken commands) distorts the rhetoric's juridical power. As Dowling has argued, "Into Such Assembly" not only torques but "corrupts" multiple kinds of found texts—one from English language instruction and the other from a US naturalization ceremony—such that "citizenship and linguistic facility almost appear coterminous."[38] The found texts also, Dowling argues, interpellate the "you" of the poem, a speaker "we are invited to assume is the poet, as a would-be American, an immigrant desirous of citizenship." Later in *Under Flag*, Kim will write: "This is the body and we live it. Large as I. Large as."[39] In a kind of reverse Whitmanianism, Kim suggests a body large and multiple enough to contain a globally diasporic we, rather than an I large enough to contain American multitudes. Kim's formulation reveals the state in fracture.

Kim's critique of citizenship interrogates the linguistic forms of state violence—and the biopolitical aspects of her critique invite alliance with scholarship from postcolonial and ethnic studies theorists who have complicated Foucault's original thinking about biopolitics, drawing out racial, colonial, and gender-based facets of the state's effects upon the body.[40] Kim's work also makes a specific argument about empire. In a December 1997 interview called "Generosity as Method," Kim argues for a poetics that refuses to follow the narrative logic of opposition. One of the challenges with opposition as a politics, she tells Yedda Morrison, is that opposition is so often linked to narratives of empire. Kim describes a poetics that instead provides multiple points of entry for radicalization: "if we could simply acknowledge that any move towards radicalization doesn't always look like just one thing, that then we can begin to talk to each other," she tells Morrison. Yet when opposition invokes the machinery of empire, it compromises its radical capacities by reproducing empire's epistemologies:

> To thematize opposition for me is a direct replication of the whole machinery of the narrative of empire making, the narrative of sense making, the narrative of power-making. I think of the last decade [i.e., the 1990s] as a time of trying to develop some way of acknowledging that there's an arc along which people are at different points of understanding their own meaning of opposition. If we can respect this in each other, especially around issues of ethnicity and those things which are more thematically recognizable, they don't simply become part of a whole language of opposition.[41]

When Kim emphasizes ethnicity as "thematically recognizable" in modern and contemporary poetry, she gestures toward how the literary text might be capable of unsettling the identificatory structures of race and gender without reinscribing those structures of otherness in poetic form.

Kim's description of ethnicity as "thematically recognizable" anticipates the methodological critique made by Dorothy Wang in her book *Thinking Its Presence: Form, Race, and Subjectivity in Contemporary Asian American Poetry*. Wang's critique seeks a way beyond disciplinary oppositions—including lyric/avant-garde or historicist/formalist—as well as ideological ones—politics/testimony; historical/personal. Her critique leverages intricate close readings of poetic form in a range of work by Asian American poets for what that form reveals about the social world. In what she calls a "praxis-based methodology of theorizing,"[42]

Wang uncovers the interlinking of race, ethnicity, and poetic form in work by a number of poets not often grouped together in literary studies, poets who come from a number of different aesthetic lineages and affiliations: Li-Young Lee, Marilyn Chin, John Yau, Mei-mei Berssenbrugge, and Pamela Lu. Wang instead reads poets with diverging relationships to avant-garde poetry and canonical literary institutions—for example: Lee, canonized in the mainstream Norton anthology, and Lu, published by Language writer Lyn Hejinian's small Atelos Press. In doing so Wang engages one of the questions Kim asks in the 1997 interview: "How can we keep making wider the terms by which we politicize or radicalize?" Attending to the incremental formal work of poetry allows Wang to consider as fundamental a poetic category as metaphor alongside the highly specific, even idiosyncratic, category of the subjunctive mood. But Wang's book also challenges the longstanding critical tendency to treat race and ethnicity as a matter of theme, rather than of form. Wang points out in detail in her introduction that scholars of avant-garde poetry frequently locate structures of class or gender difference in the structures of form, but that "race alone seems unspeakable."[43] Wang's book disrupts the notion that there is something called "form" and something called "the social world" and that the scholar's task is to discover the intersections between them.[44] In her call to regard ethnicity as something other than simply "thematically recognizable," Kim's argument about opposition makes a claim for subjectivity that resonates particularly with Wang's formal critique. Form "isomorphically captures the structural logic governing social and psychic processes," as Wang puts it in the chapter on metaphor in Lee's work, or "mirrors the structure[s]" of "subjectification," as Wang puts it in the chapter on the subjunctive mood in Lu's work.[45] By emphasizing structure in each case, Wang's work sails beyond a genre of criticism that Divya Victor, interviewing Kim, has described as one in which "formal strategies are analogies for life experience."[46] In that same interview, Kim responds to the critical tendency to trace formal decisions back to "the person" by asking how critics might "leave room for what is *not* equivalent, *not* correspondent between those two terms" of form and experience.

Wang's formalism, read against Kim's lyric critiques of monolingual citizenship and political opposition, offers a critical framework for how Kim has described the notion of divestment. Kim posits divestment as a formal alternative to the narrative logic of opposition: "I think there is always some kind of invisible, constant, millisecond-by-millisecond negotiation between the form and its divestment, between the poem and the world, that you're engaging every time you decide to write anything."[47] Literary scholarship often positions the poem as the form and the world as something else: this is the essence of the supposed relay between form and content, or form and the social, or the poem and the experience. But Kim's work lays bare the ways in which forms themselves enact, probe, and lay bare their social conditions—and the ways in which social conditions inscribe the subject. If that "divestment" lies beyond the form, poetry has the capacity to negotiate the spaces around and between.

"abjure mouths":
Lyric divestment in *Civil Bound*

If, for Kim, the poem is an incremental and precise negotiation between form and divestment, her 2019 book *Civil Bound* more explicitly turns to the notion of the civil self as an unstable figure. The title of the book does not use the word "citizen" or "citizenship": it slides, instead, to the related but distinct concept of the civil. Citizen is civil's etymon; the words share the connotations of belonging, rights and privileges, legal status—and recognition by the city or state. But as Claudia Rankine shows so thoroughly in *Citizen: An American Lyric*, the pernicious effects of American empire are felt at multiple points across the spectrum of citizenship, citizenship's denial, and the way civility—the order of, or behavior between, citizens—is shaped by what Rankine elsewhere calls a "racial imaginary," or the broad spectrum of effects of the construction of race. By choosing to center "lyric" in *Citizen: An American Lyric* (as well as in her earlier work *Don't Let Me Be Lonely: An American Lyric*), Rankine, like many of the other poets I discuss in this book, uses the long poem to invite and then torque any number of associations with that word within the particular nexus of political exclusion that accompanies "citizen."[48] When Kim chooses the word "civil" for the title of *Civil Bound*, she locates her book within this same nexus but exploits the term "civil" for its ability to reach for a number of additional meanings related to civil behavior, social order, and collective identities.

As in many of Kim's other works, *Civil Bound* uses fragmentation and documental appropriation to materialize the effects of language on political and social identity. In *Civil Bound*, poetry becomes what Kim calls a "pronunciation key for suffering"[49] as well as a staging ground for the complicated and painful notion of what it means for a self to be bound: to nation, to empire, to the collective, to rule. Kim's 2009 book *Penury* ends on a couplet that suggests the precarious and intimate nature of this subjectivity, and that anticipates the title of her 2019 book:

Nestled close
Civil bound[50]

These lines from *Penury* unsettlingly swing between the comforts of community and the ominous bonds of civil subjectivity. Ten years later, *Civil Bound* uses the truncated line in an aphoristic gesture toward conditional statements about language:

sounds produced by using air from the lungs

if the air is pushed out

if the air is sucked in[51]

The "sounds" here suggest speech, song, or an inarticulate cry, and the two conditional "if" lines that follow clarify—sound is produced if air is pushed out or if it is sucked in—but also further complicate—the definition is shot through with precarity; it's unclear whether a sound is actually being described or omitted. These lines could serve as a universal definition of language; they could indicate the estrangement of a voice whose sounds are not legible as communicative language. Later on, another clipped line invests the voice with the ability to repudiate the interpellative functions of the state:

abjure mouths | | (55)

To abjure is to repudiate a right or a privilege, often one associated with citizenship. By placing the word "abjure" in unsettling syntactical relationship to "mouth," Kim makes it into a modifier as well as an active verb, as if the sense of the line were as gnarled and difficult as what it connotes.

These descriptions of Kim's form are all ways to understand how a truncated line connotes meaning beyond its denotative sense: often a fragment means something because of what hovers, occluded or omitted, beyond it. But these lines also follow the book's exegesis of what Kim calls the "hemispheric lust" of colonial expansion. That exegesis consists of a poetic catalog of the traces left by that expansion upon landscapes and bodies:

platform of moveable objects

for live spectacle

arch of armaments and charts

stronghold | prowess

a link of people sorted—size, strength, age

bellflower broth, liver broth

hemispheric lust (13)

The pages that follow catalog the architecture of colonialism's genocide: "thrown down the wells / scoured off the foundation"; "taught to make coffins for each other" (15, 17). "Hemispheric lust" resolves inevitably in a quote from an 1872 document concerning the isthmus of Tehuantepec, a major above-ground transport route for global mail and goods: "It is conceded that an interoceanic canal through any of the isthmus passes of the western hemisphere is a necessity for the present and prospective commerce of the world."[52] The quotation summarizes what Kim has just written about globalism's appetite for hemispheric consumption, literalizing the poem's metaphorical language around passage, transport, channel, and the spaces between bodies and land.

As an intertext, the 1872 quote performs the multiple historical functions of citation, summary, and enactment. A few pages later, Kim appropriates a US government document commonly cited as a key archive in the history of forced English monolingualism as a tool of assimilation and white supremacy. In 1886 Commissioner of Indian Affairs E. A. Hayt wrote in the annual report for the Office of Indian Affairs:

In the extract from my first report, already quoted, I expressed very decidedly the idea that Indians should be taught the English language only.

From that position I believe, so far as I am advised, there is no dissent either among the law-makers or the executive agents who are selected under the law to do the work. There is not an Indian pupil whose tuition and maintenance is paid for by the United States Government who is permitted to study any other language than our own vernacular—the language of the greatest, most powerful, and enterprising nationalities beneath the sun. The English language as taught in America is good enough for all her people of all races.[53]

The commissioner goes on to write that day schools present the biggest challenge to enforcing English language instruction in the United States, as children return to their "oftentimes savage parents" and "relapse more or less into their former moral and mental stupor."[54] Characterizations such as these were used to bolster the United States' increased emphasis on the boarding school model as the best way to isolate Indigenous children from their communities—including their linguistic culture—in favor of assimilation to US English.

In *Civil Bound*, Kim truncates and renders this 1886 governmental document vertically so that the text reads not from right to left but from top to bottom—which is one way to write Hangul. The document's letters appear in lower case and are shot through with extra gaps and spaces; all punctuation and case changes have been stripped out. Truncated, stripped down, and rotated on its original English axis, the document becomes a kind of grid poem that refuses the communicative function of its initial word, "expressed." Rather than denoting utterance, declaration, or representation, expression here instead connotes the ways in which the state alters habits of the eye and ear and mouth, as the presumably Anglophone reader's eye must pivot and adjust to read down the page. The state's expression halts legibility and communicative possibility.

To render the 1886 document in this way is to make a statement about the document's historical significance: it could be said that Kim aestheticizes the document, furnishing it into a visual object, with the understanding that "to aestheticize" can mean not to remove an object from its social and historical fetters but instead to heighten their effects. By truncating the 1886 quote so that it begins with the word "expressed," rotating it on its axis and converting reading into a scene of difficulty and illegibility, Kim's poem recapitulates the definitional and precarious work

```
e t   n w e t h g d   a   a
x h   l h d t a e   r u a
p a   y o   e n   e   g l h
r t     s s d   o n t h l a
e   i t e t   o f t h t   y
s t n h   a t u   e e   h t
s h   e t t o r t r   i e
e e t r u e     h p s n r
d   h e i s s o e r u
  i e   t   t w   i n a p
v n   i i g u n g s   m e
e d e s o o d   r i t e o
r i n   n v y v e n h r p
y a g n   e   e a g e i l
  n l o i r a r t     c e
d s i t s n n n e n e a
e   s     m y a s a n   o
c s h a p e   c t t g i f
i h   n a n o u   i l s
d o l   i t t l m o i   a
e u a i d   h a o n s g l
d l n n   w e r s a h o l
l d g d b h r   t l   o
y   u i y o   t   i l d r
  b a a     l h p t a   a
t e g n t i a e o i n e c
h   e   h s n   w e g n e
e t   p e   g l e s u o s
  a o u   p u a r   a u
i u   p u e a n f u g g 1
d g   i n r g g u n e h 8
e h   l i m e u l d     8
a t     t i   a   e a f 6
            t   a   s o
                n     r e
                    t
```

FIGURE 1. Excerpt from *Civil Bound* by Myung Mi Kim (Omnidawn, 2019). Courtesy of Omnidawn Publishing.

done by the lines "sounds produced by using air from the lungs // if the air is pushed out // if the air is sucked in" (23). Kim cites the history of Indigenous language suppression in US settler colonialism by appropriating and rematerializing its archive.

Kim's work on sound, voice, and breath braids together spoken and expressive modes with documentary ones—but it is not just the combination of these modes that constitutes its civil lyric. Rather, it is precisely because her poetry trades in supposedly lyric expression—ironized in documentary appropriation—that the poetry makes a larger argument about linguistic trauma. Kim's engagement with the 1886 document appears among other documents in *Civil Bound*, including a 1919 letter from Theodore Roosevelt to the president of the American Defense Society in which he declares that there is "room for but one language," and photographs and other documents from the Carlisle Indian School in Pennsylvania (37, 65–66). On another page, Kim appropriates the text of a 1913 *Popular Science* article on the construction of the Panama Canal. The original passage notes that the construction of the canal "is the greatest assault ever made upon nature; but the white man, brushing aside all obstacles and scorning danger, will soon have finished this greatest of all monuments of marching civilization."[55] The passage Kim lifts from begins this way:

> It is an inspiring sight to witness this unseemly, death-ridden tropical country, changed into a place of beauty and a veritable health resort, right in the midst of disease and death. The Panama Canal is a wonderful feat of engineering, and we can easily imagine civil engineers attempting in the near future to conserve and utilize the motor power of the ocean waves and the trade winds.

Like the 1886 document, here the celebration of the Panama Canal as a feat of white (US imperial) engineering is turned on its head.

These two engagements with documents in *Civil Bound* can be understood as a specifically contemporary North American poetic practice that Leong calls the "documental turn," a turn he traces to the emergence of two key texts: Charles Reznikoff's *Testimony* and Theresa Hak Kyung Cha's *Dictée*. Leong points out how the transformation of material documentation is typically read in literary criticism as a series of "antagonisms to originality, self-expression, and creativity"; however, he argues, certain

w   a r d t a g a g t s ma w n
i i   c   n e s h   i s i h e o n i k
n t d o a d s t   w n i n e r t   n f
s n e u   o   t o e l e   v o w d o
p e a n p a r o h n e y e n e r a s r
i s t t l   t f e d r   r e   v   d
r s h r a v   e i i s a a p e d
i   r y c e r d p r n m   r n o s r
n t i   e r i i a f g a a   d w
g h d c   i g s n u   g t f   e a 1
  i d h o t h e a l a i t u u r n 9
s s e a f a t a m   n n e t t   d 1
i   n n   b   s a f d e mu i o   3
g u   g b l i e   e   p r l f t
h n t e e e n   c a w c t e i   h j
t s r d a   a a t e i i   z t e o
  e o   u h t n n   v n t e h   h
t e p i t e h d a o c i g o   e t n
o mi n y a e   l f a l   t   r
  l c t   l   d   n   i c h o a l
  y a o   t me i e   e n o e c d a
    l   h i a s n e n   n   e e

FIGURE 2. Excerpt from *Civil Bound* by Myung Mi Kim (Omnidawn, 2019). Courtesy of Omnidawn Publishing.

documental poets actually return their texts to the public sphere.[56] In attending to the inherent sociality of the document and of the documental poetic practice, Leong's study crucially goes beyond the way uses of the document have often been theorized in terms of "the phenomenalization of voice."[57] A critical focus on the voice—what is amplified, what is displaced, what is emptied out—also reinscribes a notion of lyric as the central term for this kind of poetics, even as that focus purports to probe what is antilyric or postlyric about it.[58] Instead, the transformation of documents can be understood as what Kim describes as the "negotiation between the form and its divestment": rather than resolving a document as a phenomenon of voice, poems like Kim's keep open their circulation in implicit and explicit critique.[59]

Poets often use erasure to transform material documentation; for Kim, erasure is a formal and thematic turn, as she puts it in this line in *Civil Bound*:

> effacement of oh father, mother, the, we (28)

This line puts two crucial pieces of texts in relation with *Civil Bound*: "Who is mother tongue, who is father country?" Kim asks in *Under Flag* (29). Likewise, "And Sing We" is the title of the first section of *Under Flag*, "And Sing We" invoking the epic-odic contours of poetic address in both its subject pronoun and its verb. *Civil Bound* suggests the effacement of that cluster of meanings around speech, the state, and the "we" of shared experience, that effacement leaving fragments in its wake. For modernists like Eliot and Pound, the fragment aspired toward both the representation of a disoriented, fractured world and the practice of stripping away patterns of meaning that imposed a fictional coherence. For poets like Niedecker, the fragment features in serial form that relays between its fracture and sequence as well as the decentering of human speech.[60] For Kim, the twin operations of effacement and translation that produce a fragment—including fragments of documentary sources as well as of translations—are part of a larger thesis about form's social conditions.

Kim articulates very clearly a thesis of the lyric fragment in an exegesis that appears at the end of *Commons*. Kim ends the book with a section called "Pollen Fossil Record," which takes its title from the term for how the remains of an organism are preserved in sediment (form as sedimented content, again). Kim's record functions as a set of scholarly notes to the book that range from the straightforwardly citational to the allusive. Kim in this section writes about form and identity in lines that formally behave all at once as aphorisms, propositions, and annotations to the book that precedes them. Kim attends especially to the role of the fragment and cites Adorno, for whom fragmentation is linked to displacement of the lyric subject. Kim writes:

> Because isolations occur
> Uncover the ear
> To give form to what is remote, castigated
> The necessity of carving out [intuiting/enacting] one's own treatment
>   of a particular arena of language
> Social and psychic identifications that disrupt and (re)envision, to throw
>   into question conventions of codifying
> Form as interplay of mobile elements, actuated by the ensemble of
>   movements developed within it
> The comportment is one of experiment
> The poem infiltrates, filters, avulses   :   nuance and gradation
> "The fragment is that part of the totality of the work that opposes
>   totality." *Aesthetic Theory*, Adorno
> The contrapuntal, the interruptive, the speculative[61]

Beginning provocatively with a command to "uncover the ear" in order to "give form" to what happens under isolation, disruption, or castigation—as if the act of listening gave shape to what is cast out, and as if what is cast out were first formless—Kim's passage goes on to argue for the necessity of carving out, intuiting, and enacting "a particular arena of language" that questions norms of social and psychic order. Kim describes form as the "interplay" of elements and the poem itself as something that "avulses"—tears away—and then juxtaposes that claim with Adorno's thesis that the fragment opposes the totality to which it belongs. The "arena of language" cited here anticipates a line *Civil Bound* takes from a newspaper article about the extinguishing of nonhuman sound due to habitat loss and human encroachment. In *Civil Bound*, Kim quotes this line from the article: "if a species cannot find a sonic niche of its own, it will not survive."[62] The line invokes the phenomenon of vanishing biodiversity as an analogy for language suppression and loss—suggesting how civil language suppression literally threatens human survival.

Kim's engagement with Adorno is as revealing for its appropriation of his words as a poetic fragment as it is for its argument: an argument about the fragment, about language, about art. In the opening pages to *Aesthetic Theory*, Adorno writes: "Artworks detach themselves from the empirical world and bring forth another world, one opposed to the empirical world as if this other world too were an autonomous entity."[63] And yet, he also writes both that "The concept of art is located in a historically changing constellation of elements; it refuses definition" and that "Art acquires its specificity by separating itself from what it developed out of; its law of movement is its law of form."[64] Artworks in Adorno's view are both historically bound and uniquely forged to teach something about form: artworks are "afterimages" of the empirical but also "alive"; they are "products of social labor" but they also—in fact, because of this—"communicate with the empirical experience that they reject and from which they draw their content."[65] Art communicates in this way—Adorno says "opposes"—through its form: if above he writes that art's law of movement is the law of its form, these are the same opening pages to *Aesthetic Theory* in which he also famously (and imagistically) writes of "form as sedimented content."[66] Adorno's intervention is to argue that art is as historical as any other productive labor even as it retains a certain kind of autonomy in its relationship to empirical reality.

When Adorno writes later, then, about the ways in which an artwork refuses coherence, he does so with careful attention to how something like the fragment sediments content. In the section from which Kim selects Adorno's claim regarding the fragment, Adorno alludes to Prospero's famous line in *The Tempest*—"I'll drown my book"—commonly cited as an allusion to Shakespeare's own departure from artmaking.[67] "Artists discover the compulsion toward disintegration in their own works," Adorno writes, "in the surplus of organization and regimen; it moves them to set aside the magic wand as does Shakespeare's Prospero, who is the poet's own voice."[68] For Adorno, art is "simply identical with form," as he writes later.[69] And yet, as Gerald L. Bruns points out, Adorno was "a dialectical rather than an analytical thinker; that is, his practice was not to clarify concepts but to put them into play." For Adorno, "form is never a concept that stands on its own; it is always mediated."[70] Form itself inheres in the relay of the artwork, much like the appearance of "Pollen Fossil Record," Kim's index of annotations, citations, and notes to the long poem *Commons*. Or, like the operation of the fragment in Kim's description of translation in "Pollen Fossil Record":

The ideas of translation, translatability, transliteration, transcription:

> Bit, part, scattered phoneme, suggestion of sounds, a glitch of ear
> and tongue occurring in unrecognizable patterns: for a long time
> I dismissed (or couldn't fold in or hold) these random, skittish
> stutterings. However, once perceived as (made audible and tactile as)
> potential sounds in Korean or, for that matter, any number of languages
> (Middle English, Latin, French) that constitute "English," these
> roaming fragments fall into the writing.[71]

The fragment, as intertext, snippet of speech, truncated line, or indeed trans-lingual enactment of the "glitches" that Kim posits as "potential sounds," stages an argument about linguistic authority. As Warren Liu notes, Kim's focus is not on the literary but on the enunciative: "For Kim, the power resides not in the settled, received text, but in that which in fact cannot be read, that which remains 'illegible.'"[72] As Kim continues in *Commons*:

> It is not the actual translation or even the state of translatability between
> the two texts that is intriguing but the possibilities for transcribing what
> occurs in the transversal between the two languages (and, by extension,
> between the two "nations," their mutually implicated histories of colo-
> nization, political conflicts, and so on). What is the recombinant energy
> created between languages (geopolitical economies, cultural representa-
> tions, concepts of community)?[73]

Kim's Adornian opposition creates a poetics of the transversal between languages.

Kim writes in *Commons*: "What *is* English now, in the face of mass global migrations, ecological degradations, shifts and upheavals in iden-tifications of gender and labor? [. . .] What are the implications of writing at this moment, in precisely this 'America'?"[74] In these lines from *Civil Bound*, civil bodies whose languages split, sever, and join each other jostle alongside fragments:

silt   slit   syllabaries

ob   /a   s/r

traduction

fin and aspen grove

persons to appear
persons who made

debris architecture (29–30)

The sounded syllabaries of these lines seemingly burst from a deposit of clay—silt is typically deposited by moving waters, as in those that divide continents—as well as from an incision—*slit*, a wordplay on *silt* whose second and third letters are simply transposed but also a narrow aperture or cut—as in Korea's 38th parallel. The word "traduction" (also: translation) alludes to the conveying of persons and things from one fractured land/language to another, an aspen grove appearing nestled not beside fir trees but beside the word *fin*, an allusion to the watery body left behind as well as to the French word for *end*. And in the last three lines quoted here, which conclude the book's second major section, Kim offers a catalog of persons both potential and past followed by the image of discarded debris made into architecture of the built environment. Those persons, poised to voice the "state of translatability" inherent in the fragments "*ob /a   s/r*," are "propositions," as Kim puts it in *Dura*, articulated by a form that keeps the terms of its coherence open and imagines minute negotiations between literary form and the world that might form that world differently.

If debris—scattered, remnant—can function as architecture, then Kim's fragments make an argument about how language can both fall apart, or fall short, and still make up a built environment. *Civil Bound* contemplates the possibility of binding one person with another in civil formation, asking:

what is   a mutual duration (79)

With the word "duration" Kim invokes her 1998 book *Dura* as well as a key line from Cha's 1982 book *Dictée*: "She makes complete her duration."[75] In Kim's line, the caesura enacting a proposition's wait, civil lyric negotiates the spaces between forms of mutuality and their divestment, between the self and its mutually constituted others, between form and a world shaped by fractured syllabaries.

CODA

Sometimes the word "lyric" seems to appear everywhere: in part because it is often used interchangeably with the word "poetry," and in part because, as I have endeavored to show, its errors—its taxonomical slipperiness, its ideological baggage, its historical misconstruals and debates whether it ought to be considered a genre, a mode, a style, a structure of address, a remnant of classicism or Romanticism or modernism or something else—mobilize its specialness, its exemplarity, its distinct power, and its frequent circulation in poetry and poetics. The longstanding difficulty of fixing a definition of lyric is an error written into its role as structural marker of the speaking subject. Poems that engage lyric can both reproduce that error and convert it into new possibilities for imagining the subject. They can also dissolve the notion that the error somehow matters, except for what it reveals about the uses of taxonomy to sort texts and sort selves—and they can think far beyond received notions of how experience is organized and made legible.

This book has included in each chapter a discussion of how a particular poet engages with literary inheritance and has pointed out that the notion of a postlyric or postgenre work actually ends up reproducing narratives of a white Western literary tradition. Sometimes that tradition is coded as "the literary" or "the poetic." In this brief coda, I want to ask whether an alternative lyric genealogy might be useful. What if we used a different term? What if we read the self in a different way? What if we expected something different from the speaking subject in a poem?

All the poems I have discussed in this book have argued the need for a different kind of language adequate to the self, to history, and to the conditions of living; I have looked to those poems to do the theorizing work of lyric, and so the poem I turn to in this coda is no different. In the prefatory note to their 2021 book *Maroon Choreography*, fahima ife writes that their book is "preoccupied with anachoreography," a term they describe this way:

Anachoreography is a recursive practice of refusal. I refuse the choreo-
graphed apparatuses of coloniality, its methodologies, its origin stories,
its naming rituals, and its movements. To move elsewhere and practice
otherwise, I retrace my breath, loop back, and move with the opaque air.
In the unseen, unknown expanse of blackness, I move inside the palimpsest of what exists prior, or beside us.[1]

With the formal terms of recursivity, refusal, and palimpsest, ife gestures toward the way in which *Maroon Choreography* is a deeply citational
work—shot through with quotation, homage, and riffings on a catalog
of different poets and theorists in Black studies, affect studies, dance,
poetry and poetics, and elsewhere—as well as a graphically daring one—
the poems range from lineated tercets and couplets to durational para-
graphs to a coda that functions as a visual bibliography, its authors and
book titles arranged and rearranged in horizontal, vertical, and angled
lines in what ife elsewhere calls the practice of "(queer)black radical traditions of breaking form and from, of making new forms derived from
those prior fugitive movements undocumented as the wind."[2] The title
Maroon Choreography invokes the metaphor of maroonage to refer to
the fugitive or emancipated figure on whom many thinkers have drawn
to refuse the abstractions of the transcendental subject—as Fred Moten
and Stefano Harney write in *The Undercommons*, "The maroons know
something about possibility. They are the condition of possibility of the
production of knowledge in the university—the singularities against the
writers of singularity, the writers who write, publish, travel, and speak."[3]
    When ife invokes the lyric in *Maroon Choreography*, it is against this
backdrop of refusal, palimpsest, and poetry as the production of knowledge. In a poem called "of being nameless,"[4] ife uses curly brackets to
segment and pause:

{ we drag our bones } {in the long lineage of spite }
        { the rage inside the specter} { liquid heat }
            { you cannot see us as i am }

                    { the lyric has gone black } (77)

When ife writes a line about lyric that follows a "long lineage of spite,"
after lamenting that "you cannot see us as i am," that line collapses the
politics of (individual subjective) recognition into the difficult task of

recognizing a collective subject by switching personal pronouns mid-sentence. They suggest the ways in which the lyric *descends* from a long history of subjectification. The lyric in ife's line also *dissents* from that long history: it has "gone black" as in a film picture fading to a black screen, or as in the I speaking out of the "unseen, unknown expanse of blackness" of ife's prefatory note. The line "the lyric has gone black" refracts its own visuality, historicity, and formal postures (as if the cinematic screen of lyric had gone dark), suggesting both the appropriation and the refusal of a term, lyric, that has tended to sediment the content of white Western subjectivity.

When a poem both refuses and enacts the formal entailments of something called lyric, that exchange between refusal and enaction can be understood as a kind of trade; to read ife's poem in this way is to cite the context of the afterlives of the transatlantic slave trade in relation to the way the term trade functions to shape and foreclose subjects. The lines of this poem bring into stark relief the links between lyric form and histories of race, gender, nation, and empire—in their invocation of the refusals and dissents that make a different kind of lyric, and subject, possible.

In a way, my reading of this poem undercuts many of the logics of the book I have just written—including the modernist archive to which each chapter has turned; including the archive of women poets I have discussed, a female and feminist archive I have declined to rationalize; including the insistence on categorical genre as both an arbitrary and a meaningful area of study, an insistence I have tried to provoke into a diagnostic method. In part this has been a book about literary inheritance, although it is not a book about coteries; it has been a book about genre, although it is not a book that offers a new definition of lyric genre; it has been a book about form, although it insists on collapsing distinctions between form and the world that have reproduced ideologies of the subject that run contrary to the imaginative and political work poems can otherwise do. To make that work possible is both to multiply its archives and to allow them to think between and beyond each other, to enlarge the field of genres and subjectivities, and to "move elsewhere and practice otherwise" (ix), as ife writes—in writing the poem, and in enlarging our readings of it.

NOTES

Introduction

1. Shockley, *Semiautomatic*, 43.
2. Rich, *The School Among the Ruins*, 97.
3. Hughes, *Selected Poems*, 127.
4. Wellek, "Genre Theory, the Lyric, and *Erlebnis*," 51.
5. Riley, *The Words of Selves*, 18.
6. Mackey goes on to say this meaning of lyric has always been with us, its musical "strings attached," and describes the long poem as an "extended lyric" (*Blue Fasa*, xii, italics in the original).
7. Bernstein, *Recalculating*, 123–24 (capitals in the original).
8. While "a-lyrical ballad" and "Wait" are not themselves long poems, the distinction between long poems and short poems is perhaps becoming less relevant. At "Boundary Conditions of the Long Poem," a 2017 MLA roundtable, Shockley suggested that a "long-poem logic" informs the way we now read and write political and historical contexts into "lyric" poems in the twenty-first century. Shockley's comment suggests a complement to the claim in lyric theory that "lyric reading" reads all poems as lyric.
9. Myriad sources offer an overview of the modern and contemporary long poem as a distinct form with a distinct relationship to narrative, seriality, collage, and hybrid genres—all crossed with a fundamental antilyricism or alyricism. For a discussion of the submerging of narrative within the modernist long poem, see McHale, "Telling Stories Again"; for a discussion of the "world-creating" visionary qualities of modern epic, see Conte, *Unending Design*; and for a discussion of the modernist long poem as a post-Romantic genre, see Gibson, *Epic Reinvented*. Lynn Keller's *Forms of Expansion* argues that the collage long poem is the major genre of twentieth-century poetry and that contemporary women poets use it to write out of and against the modernist tradition. Other key full-length studies of the long poem include McHale's *The Obligation Toward the Difficult Whole*; Jim Keller's *Writing Plural Worlds in Contemporary US Poetry*; and Carbery's *Phenomenology and the Late Twentieth-Century American Long Poem*. Jaussen offers a rich survey of criticism on "the history of the long poem's formal deviance"—where "deviance" often means either the inclusion or the rejection of lyric—in his introduction

to *Writing in Real Time* (10). Many of the fullest articulations of the long poem's antilyricism are made by Rachel Blau DuPlessis, whose own long poem *Drafts* draws both on the "hardness" of modernism and on the "ethicality" of second-wave feminism. DuPlessis describes the process of coming to the long form in resistance: "But whatever did I mean by the lyric? [. . .] Was it a glyph for resistance to shortness, closure, beauty, and a female place inside it, and not to 'it' itself? Did I resist the unitary tone, the coherent speaking subjectivity, the sense of elegant closure [. . .]?" (*Blue Studios*, 221–22).

10. Niedecker, "The Poetry of Louis Zukofsky"; Williams, "A New Line Is a New Measure," in *Something to Say*, 161. Williams writes that Zukofsky's *Anew* radically revises lyric as well as the relations between music and poetry: "It is invention of a kind that music cannot and need not copy. But like music it is capable of being adult—to the day of its creation. It is capable of going *with* invention in music which almost all modern verse is definitely NOT capable of doing. Almost all modern verse is metrically sterile" (italics in the original).

11. Park, *Apparitions of Asia*, 23.

12. For an overview of the new formalist studies and modernist studies, see the introduction to Lewis's *Dynamic Form*. See also Ellen Rooney on the essential question of critique and form: "I begin with the proposition that the possibility of rethinking critique entangles us with the question of reading. And once we turn to the question of reading, we confront the question of form" ("Symptomatic Reading Is a Problem of Form," 129).

13. de Gennaro, *Modernism after Postcolonialism*, 13. See also Sonya Posmentier, who in *Cultivation and Catastrophe* sets out to use the term lyric to describe "near-sonnets by Claude McKay and Gwendolyn Brooks, documentary poems by Sterling Brown, musical lyrics by Bessie Smith and Lloyd Lovindeer, long poems by Brooks and Derek Walcott, and fragmentary book-length poems by Brathwaite and M. NourbeSe Philip" in order to invoke "a different history of the lyric generated on the margins of American and European modernity" (4). And see also Cameron Awkward-Rich's reading in *The Terrible We* of trans writers' uses of "the capacity of lyric speech to sustain temporal and categorical paradox" (137).

14. Shockley, "Notes," in *Semiautomatic*, 104.

15. Rankine, *Citizen*, 134–35. The first printing of *Citizen* included just four names—Jordan Russell Davis, Eric Garner, John Crawford, and Michael Brown—while subsequent printings of Rankine's book have seen that list grow. The suggestion is that the list will grow perpetually, always to be followed by Rankine's lines "because white men can't / police their imagination / black men are dying" (135).

16. Rich, "Five O'Clock, January 2003," in *School Among the Ruins*, 95.

17. See, for example, Frow's description of genre's "broad economy" in *Genre*, 143.

18. McCaffery, *North of Intention*, 201.

19. Derrida, "The Law of Genre," in *Acts of Literature*, 230.

20. The phrase "lyric trade" also gestures toward the discourse of economic theory in poetry. That discourse is taken up more extensively in works like Rebecca Colesworthy's *Returning the Gift*, which reads the literary gift as a form of market currency, and Paul Jaussen's *Writing in Real Time*, which uses systems theory and economics to read the long poem from Walt Whitman to Nathaniel Mackey.

21. DuPlessis: "We could say that a lyric poem haunts the long poem even as the long poem surrounds it, trumps it, smashes it, and envelops it (these moves are different of course). Even when it is made to disappear, or to become untenable, the ghost of lyric may haunt the long poem" ("Lyric and Experimental Long Poems," 42).

22. Ferreira da Silva and Desideri, "A Conversation between Valentina Desideri and Denise Ferreira da Silva," 7. Adorno, *Aesthetic Theory*, 5. Creeley, quoted in and popularized by Olson, "Projective Verse"; Creeley clarifies in a 2003 interview that "Well, content is never more than an extension of form and form is never more than an extension of content" ("Robert Creeley in Conversation with Leonard Schwartz"). Willis, "Work This Thing." Moten, *The Feel Trio*, 4.

23. Just a few works that take the argument against dehistoricized formalism as axiomatic include Jeon's *Racial Things, Racial Forms*, Shockley's *Renegade Poetics*, Ponce de León's *Another Aesthetics Is Possible*, and Keller's *Writing Plural Worlds in Contemporary US Poetry*. Exceptions to this sort of scholarship include Levine's *Forms*, which rehearses a claim that "forms are not outgrowths of social conditions; they do not belong to certain times and places" (12). Levine does differentiate between "form" and "genre" and suggests that genre is the act of classifying texts in a historically specific way in the service of interpretation, whereas form is both interpretive and an abstracted principle of organization (13). Yet the claim that forms "migrate across contexts in a way that genre cannot" (13) renders this distinction a fallacy, to say nothing of the unacknowledged allusions of a word like "migrate" and its invocation of, for example, poetic genre's relationship to borders.

24. Rancière, *The Flesh of Words*, 9.

25. Rancière, 14.

26. Genette, *The Architext*, 59, 5.

27. Genette, 7.

28. Foucault, "What Is an Author?," in *Language, Counter-Memory, Practice*, 113–38.

29. Friedlander, *Simulcast*, 280; Riley, *The Words of Selves*, 2.

30. Seth Perlow refers to lyric's "exemption" in the way it is valued in opposition to the notions of information or knowledge in his book *The Poem Electric*, which offers a generative study of the "technologies" of lyric.

31. Jackson, *Dickinson's Misery*, 10 and 11.

32. Jackson, 100.

33. One of the most frequently cited texts for the new lyric studies is a special section in the January 2008 issue of the *PMLA* in which a number of literary scholars respond to Marjorie Perloff's address as outgoing president of the MLA. In that address, Perloff charges that growing interest in interdisciplinarity marginalizes the literary, and that in hiring and recruitment practices "there is one discipline that is conspicuously absent, and that discipline is what the Greeks called *poetike*, the discipline of poetics" (Perloff, "Presidential Address 2006," 655). For Perloff, "poetics" has to do with something she calls "the specifically literary," as when she surveys an array of dissertation titles and concludes that "only a handful have any specifically literary component" and that most use the literary as "means to an end—they are windows through which we see the world beyond the text, symptoms of cultural desires, drives, anxieties, or prejudices" (654). Perloff suggests that "the classical and medieval rhetorical triad—*docere, delectare, movere* ('to teach, to delight, to move')—has been reduced to a single one: the teaching function" (654). Perloff's remarks set off a series of responses from scholars working in cultural studies, transnational modernism, critical race studies, and feminism, with defenses and critiques of lyric ranging across subdisciplines within literary studies. But these responses were collected not under the heading "The New Literary Studies" or "The New Poetics" but "The New Lyric Studies."

34. Jackson, *Dickinson's Misery*, 128.

35. Jackson, 129.

36. Jackson, "The Cadence of Consent," in Glaser and Culler, *Critical Rhythm*, 99.

37. Jackson, *Dickinson's Misery*, 143.

38. Dickinson, "706: I cannot live with You—," in *The Poems of Emily Dickinson*, 316.

39. Jackson, 155–57.

40. Jackson, 158. Jackson does cite Diana Fuss's reading of the poem's address as an instance of "ontological suspension" that Dickinson produced from the interiors of her family's Amherst, Massachusetts, homestead, a dwelling shot through with white wallpaper, white marble, white linens—

Fuss, citing Thomas Foster, remarks that Dickinson's relationship to the home "clears a space for poetic production by redefining, from the inside, a white middle-class woman's relation to domesticity and the private sphere," the whiteness of the page colluding with the signs of white femininity. See Fuss, "Interior Chambers: The Emily Dickinson Homestead," 42n19.

41. Jackson, *Dickinson's Misery*, 137.

42. Jackson, 158. I have inserted, within brackets, the open quotation mark before "White" that is missing in the 2005 printing of *Dickinson's Misery*, as if the text unwittingly built an ambiguous relationship of the phrase "White Sustenance" to Jackson's own words, enacting what Derrida calls the "duplicity" of the sign, as I discuss in my reading of quotation marks in this book's chapter on Alice Notley's *The Descent of Alette*: quotation marks identify a voice as appropriated, even as they also signal atomized individualism or presence.

43. Jackson, *Dickinson's Misery*, 159, 171.

44. Other works in lyric studies seem to naturalize whiteness. Jonathan Culler devotes the final chapter of his book *Theory of the Lyric* (which includes an extended critique of Jackson) to "Lyric and Society," shifting from an effort to provide a transhistorical theory of lyric genre to an examination of lyric as a "device" for exploring "social issues." As is often the case, the word "society" seems to stand in for nonwhite otherness, while the prevailing universalized identificatory modes of lyric, including its whiteness, go unmarked. Gillian White, whose book *Lyric Shame* uses the notion of shame to tease apart strands of antilyricism in modern and contemporary poetics, acknowledges the problem only briefly when she writes at the very end of her book that "the legibility of nonwhite 'lyric' subjects would add significant dimension to my account of lyric shame" and that "the perhaps overwhelming nondiversity of the lyric shame articulators I've engaged here is not quite an accident, as the beginnings of the lyric shame situation I seek to historicize are in fact located in forms of entitlement bound up with histories of minority oppression and white privilege" (268). How might a theory of lyric shame account fully for such "nondiversity" as a part of lyric's naturalization of whiteness? Kamran Javadizadeh points out how a critique of lyric might align with a critique of whiteness when he writes that "Jackson's account of the historical consolidation of a normative lyric as 'temporally self-present or unmediated' resonates with whiteness's implicit claims to universality and unmediated identity, whereby to be white in the United States is to be, apparently, without race and without a role in the erasure of whiteness's racialized others" ("The Atlantic Ocean Breaking on Our Heads," 476).

45. Keene, "White Silences." In a review of Jackson and Prins's anthology, Lytle Shaw notes that the logic of *The Lyric Theory Reader* suggests that "critical race theory seems to play no role in modern poetics" ("Framing the Lyric," 405). More recent work recalibrates the field of lyric theory to account for those questions and issues: Jackson's book *Before Modernism: Inventing American Lyric*, for example, posits a history for American lyric grounded specifically in late eighteenth- and early nineteenth-century Black poetry and argues that the "lyric social imaginary" is "racialized to its core" (47).

46. Ashton, "Lyric, Gender, and Subjectivity in Modern and Contemporary Women's Poetry," 530.

47. Scappettone, "Bachelorettes, Even," 180–81. Scappettone's essay is a pointed response to Ashton's essay "Our Bodies, Our Poems," in which Ashton argues that "even though the recent commitment to women as formal innovators has been accompanied by a critique of essentialism and a celebration of the performative, the logical basis of its agenda is utterly and literally essentialist" (177).

48. Rankine, "On Lyric."

49. Rankine, *Citizen*, 90.

50. Rankine, 112.

51. Keegan Cook Finberg argues that "*Citizen* manipulates received structures of the lyric as both a racializing and a carceral apparatus" ("American Lyric, American Surveillance, and Claudia Rankine's *Citizen*," 2). Tracing the expressivity and temporality at the heart of lyric theory, Finberg demonstrates how Rankine's formal structures appear as forms of surveillance that shape and foreclose subjectivities—how lyric can be understood as "a method to understand the cell and the person in it" (10). Lyric and the cell are at the center of Andrea Brady's book *Poetry and Bondage*, which asks, "What would happen to our understanding of the history and practice of lyric if we confronted these claims about constraint with poetic witnesses to actual bondage? How does the poet's freedom and individuation look from the perspective of slavery or the prison?" (4).

52. *Lyric Trade* joins several pieces of scholarship in seeking a way beyond a seeming impasse between twentieth-century experimentalism and marginalized subjectivities, most often located in Ron Silliman's well-known remark from an 1988 essay in *Socialist Review* that "Progressive poets who identify as members of groups that have been the subject of history— many white male heterosexuals, for example—are apt to challenge all that is supposedly 'natural' about the formation of their own subjectivity" by calling into question the conventions of narrative, referentiality, and persona in their writing, whereas "poets who do *not* identify as members of groups that have been the subject of history, for they instead have

been its objects"—writers and readers who are "women, people of color, sexual minorities, the entire spectrum of the 'marginal'"—instead "have a manifest political need to *have their stories told*," producing the phenomenon "That their writing should often appear much more conventional" ("Poetry and the Politics of the Subject," 63, italics in the original). The relationship between this comment, Language writing, and marginalized writers—as well as the numerous poets and critics who challenged Silliman's formulation—is thoroughly unpacked by Timothy Yu in his essay "Form and Identity in Language Poetry and Asian American Poetry" as well as in the conclusion to his book *Race and the Avant-Garde*.

53. Derrida, "Before the Law," in *Acts of Literature*, 181, 185.

54. Derrida, "The Law of Genre," in *Acts of Literature*, 224 (italics in the original).

55. Derrida's emphasis on the law also grounds a historical approach to genre. Ralph Cohen, for example, responds to Derrida by arguing that genre always serves a historically bounded human need for institutionalized, discursive classification and interrelation: only in the nineteenth century did literary genre definitively take the place of "kind" or "species." Equating those terms erases the social history of generic classification itself, which involves what he calls a "process of sedimentation" as genres change and alter over time ("History and Genre," 217). Similarly, Dominick LaCapra has argued that classification is always ideological: "the defense or critique of generic definitions typically involves a defense or critique of discursive and social arrangements, since genres are in one way or another inserted into sociocultural and political practices" ("History and Genre: Comment," 221). A number of critics have debated what a historical poetics might actually look like for the study of the lyric, but lyric seems consistently to give rise to the debate in the first place; Simon Jarvis offers a clarifying overview in "What Is Historical Poetics?," noting that the "mediation" of lyric so problematized in lyric studies is also endemic to the act of criticism: "The relationship between thinking *about* verse and thinking *in* verse is not necessarily a cooperative one. It may instead be a powerfully antagonistic, repressive, or deceptive one" (115). Likewise, Kimberly Quiogue Andrews bracingly trains the lens on the discipline itself when she writes, "To critique a thing, from oneself to entire expressions of historiography, is to throw oneself upon the gears of language-as-usual. How many people would it take to get those gears to stop? What else, in that silence, might start to move, or to sing?" (*The Academic Avant-Garde*, 214).

56. Derrida, "The Law of Genre," 227.

57. While lyric is a frequent topic of feminist formulations of poetic subversion, the masculinism of materialist lyric theory is less discussed. An

exception is DuPlessis's reading of Adorno's essay on the lyric subject, which returns a theory of the avant-garde to a critique of gender. Adorno writes about lyric in order to defend materialist criticism against the charge of formalism, and his essay is widely cited in essays on experimental lyric. But, DuPlessis shows, his focus on the vague utopianism of poetry's otherness undermines his essay's own analytic propositions. See Adorno, "On Lyric Poetry and Society," in *Notes to Literature*, 1:37–54, and DuPlessis, *Genders, Races, and Religious Cultures*, 8–10.

58. Judith Butler's early articulation of gender performativity was also a critique of the model of subversion articulated by French feminism and psychoanalytic theory; her argument along these lines in *Gender Trouble* cites Derrida's work in "Before the Law." As Butler puts it in the preface to *Bodies That Matter*, "how might one formulate a project that preserves gender practices as sites of critical agency?" (x). How, indeed, does a project, such as a poem, approach genre as a site of critical agency? In *Gender Trouble*, Butler highlights the difficulty inherent in using the taxonomy of gender to do feminist work: "The problematic circularity of a feminist inquiry into gender is underscored by the presence of positions which, on the one hand, presume that gender is a secondary characteristic of persons and those which, on the other hand, argue that the very notion of the person, positioned within language as a 'subject,' is a masculinist construction and prerogative which effectively excludes the structural and semantic possibility of a female gender" (16). I argue that this double bind is shared by a poetics that struggles both to resist hegemonic genre and to offer an alternative language model, whether that alternative is conceived as avant-garde, postgenre, or resistant in some other way.

59. Butler, *Gender Trouble*, 187–89.

60. Wynter, "The Ceremony Found," 196n20 (italics in the original).

61. Wynter, 216 (italics in the original). With the phrase "Human Others" Wynter refers to Jacob Pandian's *Anthropology and the Western Tradition: Towards an Authentic Anthropology* (1985).

62. Wynter, "The Ceremony Found," 216. See also Wynter's writing on how the "epochal rupture" between "the new genre of the novel and the old genre of chivalric romance" enabled a new discourse of "secularizing variants / models of human being" ("On Disenchanting Discourse," 211).

63. Ferreira da Silva, "Hacking the Subject," 25.

64. Hejinian, *The Language of Inquiry*, 42, 43.

65. Hejinian, 41.

66. Hejinian, 43.

67. Michael Leong suggests that the charge of racism leveled at Conceptualism, particularly following Kenneth Goldsmith's notorious remixing of

Michael Brown's autopsy report at a 2015 performance, might be understood lyrically: "Perhaps Goldsmith's 'The Body of Michael Brown' was a performance aiming for consolation but without sorrow even if it does critique—at grievous cost—conventions of lyric expressivity" (*Contested Records*, 153).

68. Hejinian, *The Language of Inquiry*, 44.

69. Hejinian, 42. Hejinian writes that Carla Harryman's long poem *The Middle* offers a subject position that "is in the middle" of authority and invention, a subject that takes form as "an uncontainable presence making meaning" (40).

70. Perloff, "Language Poetry and the Lyric Subject."

71. Silliman et al., "Aesthetic Tendency and the Politics of Poetry," 262.

72. Silliman et al., 266 (italics in the original).

73. The essay makes frequent reference to ways in which visual art of the late twentieth century follows from the experimental advances of modernism, whereas poetry does not: "On analogy to the visual arts, where the 'avant-garde' is felt to be a virtual commonplace, the situation of poetry is as if the entire history of radical modernism—Joyce, Pound, and Williams notwithstanding—had been replaced by a league of suburban landscape painters" (262).

74. Silliman et al., 263, 266.

75. Silliman et al., 266.

76. H.D., *Helen in Egypt*, 227.

77. See, for example, T. S. Eliot's association of poetic feeling with the feminine: "The craving for the fantastic, for the strange, is legitimate and perpetual; everyone with a sense of beauty has it. The strongest, like Mr Joyce, make their feeling into an articulate external world; what might crudely be called a more feminine type, when it is also a very sophisticated type, makes its art by feeling and by contemplating the feeling, rather than the object which has excited it or the object into which the feeling might be made" ("London Letter," 216). This opposition of the object and motion appears also in Pound's sexualized and gendered terms "hard" and "soft" to argue against the emotion of French poetry: in rejecting what he calls descriptive "slush" and emotional "slither," Pound, as Jane Malcolm argues, uses these terms to "encode a universalizing literary masculinity grounded in the metaphors of hard and soft." See Pound, *The Literary Essays of Ezra Pound*, 285–89, and Malcolm, "Hard Women, Hard Modernism," 12.

78. Chuh, *The Difference Aesthetics Makes*, 6. The question of lyric as a matter of history is explored at length by Jerome J. McGann in *The Romantic Ideology*. Two distinct types of Romantic criticism have been confused,

McGann writes: "journalistic and polemical criticism whose focus is the present" (2), and "scholarly and historical criticism which operates in the present only by facing (and defining) the past" (2–3). This confusion, McGann argues, is particular to Romanticism, "whose ideology continues to be translated and promoted, and whose works continue to be taught and valued for that ideology" (3).

79. See, for example, Jackson, *Dickinson's Misery*; Culler, *Theory of the Lyric*; White, *Lyric Shame*; Levine, *Forms*; Kornbluh, *The Order of Forms*; Barletta, *Rhythm*; and Glaser, *Modernism's Metronome*. For two different sorts of examples, see Edward Allen's introduction to *Forms of Late Modernist Lyric*, in which he argues that the "pluralistic category" of lyric persists despite "the desire to conflate poetry's internal differences" and despite "the persistent impositions of narrative, the narrativising instinct, and questions of a narratological cast" (12), as well as Chris Scott's "Beyond Theory of the Lyric": "It is possible to write about lyric poetry while giving in neither to the relaxations of a totalising historicism nor of a totalising theory (but nonetheless preserving less totalising forms of both)" (94).

80. Kornbluh, *The Order of Forms*, 3.

81. Levine, *Forms*, 12.

82. Jackson appears to diagnose, if indirectly, the cultural studies–poetics debate as a symptom of lyric reading in her essay "Who Reads Poetry?" See also Jennifer Ponce de León's elegant explication of the relationship between aesthetic practices, social orders, and anticapitalist and anticolonial social transformation in Argentina, Mexico, and the United States: "Aesthetic practices aligned with movements can work to affirm and defend this other world by producing conditions that allow others to perceive it *as a real world*. This is, of course, precisely what hegemonic aesthetic practices do for dominant capitalist and colonial social orders: they make these seem natural, desirable, or, at least, like the only possible, or even imaginable, reality" (8 italics in the original).

83. Hunter, *Forms of a World*, 5. Hunter notes, drawing on Saidiya Hartman: "the very premise, the very idea, of a bourgeois lyric subject is made possible by the existence of a (lyric) object: the commodified human, the Atlantic slave trade, and the ongoing racialized violence necessary for the continuation of capitalism. This is one way in which the process of 'lyricization,' through which the lyric is made by our reading it as such, occurs in concert and in complicity with global capitalism" (11).

84. Wang, *Thinking Its Presence*, 19.

85. Kim, "Generosity as Method."

86. Mackey, "Breath and Precarity," 10.

87. Mackey, 13.

88. Mackey, *Blue Fasa*, xii.

89. Mackey, xii.

90. Jahan Ramazani writes about the need to think sharply about identitarianism in ways that do not reproduce the "too-sharp contrast between a poetics of identity and a non- or even anti-identitarian poetics" ("Poetry and Race," xi) and that bear in mind that "'Identity' isn't inherently progressive or conservative. Along with its potential for collective uplift from below, it has also been imposed or fomented from above by autocrats, dictators, and populists who oversimplify the past and homogenize nations" (xii). Ramazani's work, along with work by other critics such as Dorothy Wang, Evie Shockley, Urayoán Noel, and Anthony Reed, attends to the need for an expansive approach to identity and poetic form: "While poetry has been a space for imagining and building identity among dominant and oppressed peoples, its transnational and intercultural crosscurrents at the levels of form, language, and memory complicate one-sided identitarianism. Poetry's cross-cultural complexities require attention to identity's multidimensionality" (xiii).

91. Kim, *Commons*, 111.

Chapter 1

1. In 1955, fourteen-year-old Emmett Till was accused of flirting with a white woman cashier as he walked out of a local grocery store in Money, Mississippi, and was tortured and executed by two white men who left his body mutilated beyond recognition. His killers were acquitted.

2. Brooks, "A Bronzeville Mother Loiters in Mississippi. Meanwhile, a Mississippi Mother Burns Bacon," in *Blacks*, 333, and quoted in Shockley, *Semiautomatic*, 41.

3. Brooks, "The Last Quatrain of Emmett Till," in *Blacks*, 340. Unless otherwise noted, citations to *The Bean Eaters*, *Annie Allen*, and other collections by Brooks are to the editions printed in Brooks, *Blacks*.

4. In 2008, Carolyn Bryant told historian Timothy B. Tyson that her testimony against Till had been fabricated (*The Blood of Emmett Till*, 6). Bryant's remarks in Tyson's book were later contested, and the US Justice Department closed its inquiry into Till's murder in December 2021. In 2022, a grand jury declined to indict Bryant in any charges related to the case. She died in 2023.

5. Madhubuti, "Gwendolyn Brooks: Beyond the Wordmaker—The Making of an African Poet," in *On Gwendolyn Brooks*, ed. Wright (82). This essay first appeared as the preface to Brooks, *Report from Part One*. "Bronzeville" refers to the neighborhood of the same name on Chicago's South Side.

6. Brooks, "Marginalia," in *Report from Part One*, 183.

7. Baraka, "SOS," in *The LeRoi Jones/Amiri Baraka Reader*, 218.

8. Pound, *Cantos*, 538.

9. Culler, *Theory of the Lyric*, 245.

10. De Man continues: "Our claim to understand a lyric text coincides with the actualization of a speaking voice, be it (monologically) that of the poet or (dialogially) that of the exchange that takes place between author and reader in the process of comprehension." See de Man, "Lyrical Voice in Contemporary Theory: Riffaterre and Jauss," in Hošek and Parker, *Lyric Poetry*, 55.

11. Genette, *The Architext*, 58. After all this, Genette declares simply: "There are modes (for example, the narrative); there are genres (for example, the novel); the relationship between genres and modes is complex and doubtless not, as Aristotle suggests, one of simple inclusion. Genres can cut across modes (Oedipus recounted is still tragic), perhaps the way individual works cut across genres—perhaps differently; but we do know that a novel is not solely a narrative and, therefore, that it is not a species of narrative or even a kind of narrative" (71). The word "genre" does not appear in *Poetics* (72–73).

12. To cite just two discussions of African American lyric that index its multiple cultural forms: Ford writes about Brooks's ballads in "The Last Quatrain" and in "The Sonnets of Satin-Legs Brooks," and Müller offers a survey from the nineteenth century to the present in *The African American Sonnet*, noting especially Brooks's sonnet as "synthetic form" (86).

13. Jackson, "The Cadence of Consent," 99.

14. Brooks, "Summer, 1967," interview by Paul M. Angle, in *Report from Part One*, 139 (see also *Report from Part One*, 66–67, for a description of Stark's workshop). Yet Brooks also remarks in 1967 that "I thought that Ezra Pound was a master of English—that he knows what to do with words" and in 1969 that "I don't even admire Pound, but I do like, for instance, Eliot's 'Prufrock' and *The Waste Land*. [. . .] When I start writing a poem, I don't think about 'models' or about what anybody else in the world has done"; see Brooks, "Summer, 1967," 142; and Brooks, "March 28, 1969," interview by George Stavros, in *Report from Part One*, 156. (This text appears in *Report*'s table of contents as "March 29, 1969," but it is titled "March 28, 1969.")

15. It is a critical commonplace to set the elements of treatise, argument, or history against first-person "lyric"; Peter Baker, for example, writes that modernist long poems "deliberately turn the notion of the lyric speaker inside-out in order to establish a new kind of text production based on *exteriority*" (*Obdurate Brilliance*, 1, italics in the original). Baker takes

"interiority" to be an interpretive model derived from a theory of the Romantic and post-Romantic lyric speaker.

16. Brooks, *Report from Part One*, 56. See also Brooks, "Spring, 1971," interview by Ida Lewis, in *Report from Part One*, 169. In her essay on Dunbar's uses of georgic verse, which deals with rural and agricultural themes, Margaret Ronda argues that critical focus on Dunbar's orthography and rhythms as racial performance overshadows his georgics' treatment of "the material effects of the uneven modernization of racialized labor in the post-Reconstruction era" ("Work and Wait Unwearying," 864).

17. See discussions of Brooks's relationship to literacy in Fisher, "I Don't Want Us to Forget the Fire," and Flynn, "The Kindergarten of New Consciousness."

18. For George E. Kent, writing a preface to *Report from Part One* in 1972, Brooks's "black particularism" may have been assimilated to a white literary genealogy ("I've been reading those essays now appearing in the white 'learned journals,' which are picking up on black autobiography and, probably with good intentions, instantly relating it to Benjamin Franklin, the Great White Father of American autobiography; to European traditions of the spiritual biography; to the American materialistic success drive, to the role of symbolic blacks as exemplars—all that sort of thing"), but her success is above all proof of her "genuine universalism." Kent attributes Brooks's "balance" to a "lyrical strain" of the "private woman as an extension of her community." Kent, "Preface: Gwen's Way," in Brooks, *Report from Part One*, 33.

19. Madhubuti, "Gwendolyn Brooks: Beyond the Wordmaker," 84.

20. Shockley argues that *Annie Allen* alters epic in two ways: by foregrounding an unconventional epic subject, and by reworking the rhyme royal stanza form. These two formal interventions reconcile Brooks's "potentially competing interests in literary legitimacy and the honest treatment of black experiences in World War II–era Chicago" (*Renegade Poetics*, 28).

21. Schultz, *The Afro-Modernist Epic and Literary History*, xiii. In chapter 3 of that book, Schultz carefully lays out Tolson's uses of Black vernacular as the compositional structure of *Harlem Gallery*, particularly the dozens, which Tolson leverages in an interrogation of race. As Nielsen notes, "Those who would oppose Tolson's modernism to an oral, vernacular tradition, clearly favoring the latter, make at least two mistakes. First, they neglect to consider fully the implications of the fact that the oral tradition is represented by poets *in writing*. Second, they present a grossly reduced vernacular for our consideration. Tolson's turning to the heritage of African proverb and the traditions of pulpit performance is part of an aesthetic that celebrates and continues the richness of verbal signifying practice

among the people" ("Melvin B. Tolson and the Deterritorialization of Modernism," 247, italics in the original).

22. Tolson, *"Harlem Gallery" and Other Poems*, 309 (ellipses in the original). As Raymond Nelson writes in his notes to *Harlem Gallery*, the letter *q* is an anomaly in Anglo-Saxon (441n185).

23. In his use of the word "dilemma," Tolson refers to Gunnar Myrdal's landmark 1944 book *An American Dilemma*, which describes race relations in the United States as a "moral situation" (lxxx).

24. Generally recognized as a reference to Richard Wright's 1945 autobiography *Black Boy*, "Black Boy" was also how Tolson addressed his audience in the columns he wrote for the *Washington Tribune* from 1937 to 1944.

25. Althusser explains: "Assuming that the theoretical scene I have imagined takes place in the street, the hailed individual will turn round. By this mere one-hundred-and-eighty-degree physical conversion, he becomes a *subject*. Why? Because he has recognized that the hail was 'really' addressed to him, and that 'it was *really him* who was hailed' (and not someone else)" (174, italics in the original).

26. Fanon, *Black Skin, White Masks*, 109. Schultz argues that by creating the racially indeterminate "Afroirishjewish" Curator as his poem's central speaker, Tolson turns the "pressured place" of the African American dilemma into a space of creative possibility: "It is the Curator's very liminality between blackness and whiteness, and his ability to negotiate various cultural positions, that gives him the perspective and insight to evaluate art" (*Afro-Modernist Epic*, 70).

27. Fanon, *Black Skin, White Masks*, 138.

28. Shapiro, introduction to Tolson, *Harlem Gallery: Book One, The Curator*, 13.

29. Shapiro, 13.

30. Shapiro also suggests that Tolson was "outpounding Pound" in *Harlem Gallery*, a remark that would seem to celebrate Tolson's modernist mastery rather than celebrate his departure from it (12). As Nielsen notes, Tolson's own response to Shapiro's "outpounding" remark was, "Well, I did go to the Africans instead of the Chinese" (quoted in "Melvin B. Tolson and the Deterritorialization of Modernism," 249).

31. Brooks, "Summer, 1967," 136.

32. Early critical assessment of *Annie Allen*'s "abstraction" is summarized in Bolden, *Urban Rage in Bronzeville*, and collected in Wright, *On Gwendolyn Brooks*.

33. Redding, "Cellini-Like Lyrics," in Wright, *On Gwendolyn Brooks*, 6.

34. Redding, 7.

35. Brooks, *Report from Part One*, 84.

36. Brooks, "Marginalia," in *Report from Part One*, 183. For example, Brooks
    writes these ode-like lines in the title poem of her 1980 book *Primer for
    Blacks*:

    > Blackness
    > is a title,
    > is a preoccupation,
    > is a commitment Blacks
    > are to comprehend—
    > and in which you are
    > to perceive your Glory. (9)

37. As John Lowney points out, while "*In the Mecca* is usually identified as
    the book that enacts Brooks's literary 'conversion' to the Black Aesthetic
    in the late 1960s," its historical consciousness can be traced back to
    Depression-era African American cultural discourse: "As the Depression
    devastated African American urban communities, the utopian vision of
    the city as a promised land for migrants was displaced by a dystopian
    vision: impoverished, deteriorating black urban communities became
    increasingly identified with the [Hughesian] African American 'dream
    deferred'" (*History, Memory, and the Literary Left*, 130–31). As James
    Edward Smethurst argues in *The Black Arts Movement*, Brooks's 1967
    moment must also be understood within the context of a long history of
    radicalization, which included her involvement with the Communist Left
    of Chicago.
38. Baker, *The Journey Back*, 110.
39. Baker, 108.
40. The formal break in Brooks's work is mirrored in her publication history.
    She would publish eight volumes of poetry, including *Annie Allen* and
    The Bean Eaters, with the mainstream publisher Harper and Row before
    moving in the late 1960s to the African American-run Broadside Press
    in Detroit and Third World Press in Chicago (founded by Madhubuti).
    James D. Sullivan notes that for Brooks, "Sloughing off [. . .] great
    stretches of her mainstream-poetry-buying public was a profoundly anti-
    economic move," but the switch was also a political-aesthetic act: "The
    domination of the whole communicative process by African Americans
    greatly decreased the likelihood of anyone's reading the poem through a
    lens of universal white humanism" ("Killing John Cabot," 557, 558).
41. Madhubuti, "Gwendolyn Brooks: Beyond the Wordmaker," 82. Madhu-
    buti further describes Brooks's pre-1967 work as written for white readers:
    "*Annie Allen* (1949), important? Yes. Read by blacks? No" (84).
42. Madhubuti, 88.

43. Madhubuti, 85.

44. Madhubuti, 89.

45. Madhubuti, 92. Madhubuti's remarks from 1973 recall Langston Hughes's 1926 essay "The Negro Artist and the Racial Mountain," in which Hughes writes: "I am ashamed for the black poet who says, 'I want to be a poet, not a Negro poet,' as though his own racial world were not as interesting as any other world. I am ashamed, too, for the colored artist who runs from the painting of Negro faces to the painting of sunsets after the manner of the academicians because he fears the strange un-whiteness of his own features" (*Collected Works*, 35).

46. Du Bois, *The Souls of Black Folk*, 38. Descriptions of double consciousness in Brooks's work include a 1945 review by Paul Engle that praises Brooks as "the first Negro poet to write wholly out of a deep and imaginative talent, without relying on the fact of color to draw sympathy and inter-est" and a 1972 account by Houston Baker that repeats Du Bois's phrase when he describes Brooks's work as "comprised of 'white' style and 'black' content—two warring ideals in one dark body"; both are quoted in Gery, "Subversive Parody in the Early Poems of Gwendolyn Brooks," 45. Unlike some critics, for whom Brooks's double consciousness consists of Euro-pean or white "form" and African American "content," A. Yẹmisi Jimoh argues that the double consciousness in Brooks's work can be understood as "two conflicting definitions of African American identity: a prevailing and debilitating European American definition as well as a more self-determined African American definition" (167). See also Michelle H. Phil-lips's article "Moving In and Stepping Out: Gwendolyn Brooks's Children at Midcentury," which argues that while for Du Bois the figure of double consciousness "moves from the private to the public," Brooks's sense of the public "is rarely national or universal," her sense of interiority often problematized or doubled in a way Du Bois's is not (150).

47. Du Bois, *The Souls of Black Folk*, 39.

48. Du Bois, 255.

49. "Conversation: Gwendolyn Brooks and B. Denise Hawkins," in *The Furious Flowering of African American Poetry*, ed. Gabbin, 278. In this interview, Brooks suggested that the "arty" style of *Annie Allen* no longer appealed to her poetic practice: "I would never write such a poem again. I wouldn't have the patience and I don't see the point. There are some good things about the expressions I used" (278).

50. Brooks, "March 28, 1969," 151.

51. Brooks, "Summer, 1967," 138 (italics in the original).

52. In her discussion of the Hegelian origins of double consciousness, Jimoh makes the important point that Du Bois does not specify which self or

soul is doing the looking through the eyes of others (174): this means that the experience of double consciousness, or what I have been calling a "dilemma," is itself an artifact of white supremacist culture. Likewise, Kevin Quashie in *The Sovereignty of Quiet* suggests that Du Bois's description of the black subject "over-privileges race as a part of subjectivity and, in this regard, as much as double consciousness is a contemplative idiom, it does not fare well as a concept of interiority" (15).

53. Reed, *Freedom Time*, 16–17 (italics in the original).

54. Natalia Cecire brilliantly clarifies experimental writing as a historical phenomenon in her book *Experimental*, with particular focus on the problem of innovation for literary studies.

55. Nielsen also notes that Brooks's own foreword to the 1964 volume *New Negro Poets U. S. A.* "might serve as a boundary marker between two thematic epochs in black writing, were such things so readily demarcated" (44). In that foreword Brooks writes, "At the present time, poets who happen also to be Negroes are twice-tried," continuing: "Often they wish that they could solve the Negro question once and for all, and go on from such success to the composition of textured sonnets or buoyant villanelles about the transience of a raindrop, or the gold stuff of the sun" (quoted in Nielsen, *Black Chant*, 44).

56. Jeon, *Racial Things, Racial Forms*, xxv.

57. Jeon, xxx.

58. Freud, *Civilization and Its Discontents*, 11, 15.

59. Sound lies at the heart of studies of poetic subjectivity, such as Fred Moten's intricate study of what he calls the "phonic materiality" of resistant subjects in the Black radical tradition. Opening *In the Break* with the scene Frederick Douglass reproduces in his 1845 *Narrative* of his Aunt Hester being beaten, Moten reads Butler's insight that to become a subject is always to become subjected through Marx's critique of commodity speech and argues that the commodity-self comes to know herself "only as a function of having been exchanged" (9)—through slave trade.

60. On the relationship between the sonnet, time, and the "lyric present," see Wright, *Hearing the Measures*, 56.

61. "From Poet to Novelist," in Wright, *On Gwendolyn Brooks*, 15.

62. Brooks, *Maud Martha*, 22.

63. In a chapter devoted to existentialism in *Maud Martha*, Quashie argues that the novel privileges abstraction above identity, Maud Martha's "search not for her identity in social terms, but for her self in human terms" (49).

64. Brooks experimented with apostrophe frequently; Barbara Johnson writes that Brooks's 1945 poem "The Mother" revises the ideology of lyric apos-

trophe by addressing "the lost anthropomorphized other" of an aborted fetus (*A World of Difference*). "The Mother" appears in Brooks's 1945 collection *A Street in Bronzeville* and is generally paired with *Annie Allen* as a modernist-inflected work. Johnson draws from Culler's definition of apostrophe as the emblem of lyric poetry. As Culler puts it, "the figure of apostrophe" can be understood as "a turning aside from supposedly real listeners to address to someone or something that is not an ordinary, empirical listener, such as a nightingale, an urn, or one's own poem" ("Lyric, History, and Genre," 886). Johnson suggests that the self in the poem is represented "as eternally addressed and possessed by the lost, anthropomorphized other" (189), and argues that Brooks "is here rewriting the male lyric tradition"—the apostrophe of Keats, for example—by placing aborted children in the spot addressed by the lyric (189). The poem blurs the distinction between subject and object; "The grammatical I/thou starting point of traditional apostrophe has been replaced" (189).

65. On the cognitive effects of rhyme, see Tsur, "Rhyme and Cognitive Poetics."

66. Brooks, "March 28, 1969," 158. D. H. Melhem suggests that "Hester" recalls both the Hester of Nathaniel Hawthorne's *The Scarlet Letter* (1850) as well as Hestia, the Greek goddess of the hearth, whereas "Annie" derives from the Hebrew name meaning "grace" (*Gwendolyn Brooks*, 56).

Chapter 2

1. H.D., *Helen in Egypt*, 15.

2. For discussions of H.D.'s lyric as anti-epic see, for example, Friedman, "Gender and Genre Anxiety," 214, and Willis, "A Public History of the Dividing Line," 91. Friedman describes the "lyric transgression of narrative" in "Craving Stories: Narrative and Lyric in Contemporary Theory and Women's Long Poems," in *Feminist Measures*, ed. Keller and Miller, 18.

3. Norman Austin writes that Helen's discursive subjectivity is actually anti-epic in the *Iliad*, where Helen "understands that her function is not primarily, or even secondarily, to be a woman but to be first and foremost a story" authored by the gods (*Helen of Troy and Her Shameless Phantom*, 1). Austin characterizes the lyric tradition of Stesichorus and Sappho as a "counter-movement" to "rescue Helen's name from the disrepute that had accrued to it from the epic tradition" (2).

4. H.D., *Paint It Today*, 11.

5. In his famous September 1912 meeting with H.D. in the British Museum tea room, Pound, after affixing edits to the drafts of her poems, signed them "H.D. Imagiste" and deemed them fit to be shipped off to Harriet Monroe's *Poetry*. In her biography of H.D., Barbara Guest summarizes

Pound's maneuver: "For years Pound had been preparing her for this debut. He had found a new name for her, tossing away [her given name, Hilda] 'Doolittle.' She was the first charter member of a new *ism* with which Ezra was preparing to startle London. [. . .] [H]e planned to transform her from a dedicated scribbler into the poet, H.D. He succeeded" (*Herself Defined*, 40–41). In 1956, H.D. told a reporter that the term imagist could not be used to describe the work she produced after the First World War: imagism, she remarked, was "something that was important to any poet learning his craft. But after learning his craft, the poet will find his true direction, as I hope I have" (quoted in Friedman, *Psyche Reborn*, 4).

6. Pound describes the "departments" of epic, lyric, and imagist poetry in *Gaudier-Brzeska*. First identifying lyric as "a sort of poetry where music, sheer melody, seems as if it were just bursting into speech," Pound then posits imagism as "another sort of poetry where painting or sculpture seems as if it were 'just coming over into speech' (95). Pound conceives of imagism, then, as similar to lyric in its relationship to speech, but contrasts lyric's "sheer melody" with imagism's likeness to painting or sculpture ("sheer melody" here anticipating Zukofsky's insistence on melody as the poetic quality that contrasts with historical particulars, as I discuss in chapter 3). As DuPlessis notes, it is in *Gaudier-Brzeska* that Pound "acknowledges his debt to H.D." in his conception of the long poem as structural imagism (*H.D.*, 9).

7. Nielsen, *Reading Race*, 14.

8. Ahmed, *Queer Phenomenology*, 129.

9. Ahmed, 115 (italics in the original).

10. Williams, *Collected Poems*, 2:315. Williams refers literally to the tale of Helen, whose abduction by Paris brought about the Trojan War depicted in *The Iliad*. But Williams also alludes to the idea that Helen's irresistible and destructive beauty is something that all women possess and to which he himself is drawn; "Asphodel" is in large part an apology for infidelity.

11. Williams, *Collected Poems*, 2:316.

12. H.D., "Notes on Euripides," 132–33.

13. Said, *Orientalism*, 3.

14. Gregory, "H.D. and Translation," 145. The unreadable map of Egypt recalls the "writing of the wall" H.D. describes in *Tribute to Freud*.

15. Debo, *The American H.D.*, chapter 4. H.D. writes in *Paint It Today* that her alter ego Midget felt out of touch in her home country because of a certain way of seeing: "It is not an altogether healthy nor wholesome nor sane feeling to feel as Midget did, so thoroughly out of touch with all humanity. [. . .] But that was in America, where the feeling as I have described it was more concentrated" (48).

16. H.D., *Collected Poems*, 38.

17. Collecott, *H.D. and Sapphic Modernism*, 78.

18. Euripides, *Helen*, line 286.

19. Austin argues that Euripides's efforts to write phantom Helen back into the story only serves to confirm her absence from it (192).

20. H.D.'s Victorian uses of Hellenist statuary to explore transgressive desire are discussed extensively by Cassandra Laity, who argues in *H.D. and the Victorian Fin de Siècle* that the speakers of H.D.'s early poems "Pygmalion," "Red Roses for Bronze," and "Charioteer" ought to be understood as "explicitly or implicitly male speakers" who "dwell lovingly on the bodies of their male subjects" (68).

21. Poe, *Poems and Essays on Poetry*, 1.

22. See Friedman, *Psyche Reborn*, 234.

23. Poe makes this remark in "The Philosophy of Composition" (*Poems and Essays on Poetry*, 144), in which he describes how he came to choose the most melancholy lyric for his raven to speak while sitting perched on the bust of Pallas.

24. Friedman equates the silencing of Helen with the aestheticization of woman writ large, arguing that "As statue or symbol, she is safely controlled by the tradition that defines her through its art" (*Psyche Reborn*, 235).

25. See Gregory, "Euripides and H.D.'s Working Notebook for *Helen in Egypt*," 86n7, and *H.D. and Hellenism: Classic Lines*, 226.

26. DuPlessis first identified the palimpsest as the textual enactment of deferred authority in H.D.'s work, a porous, "unauthoritarian, constantly exploratory quality" that "textualises mind, history, [and] reality" (*H.D.*, 56); H.D.'s 1926 novella trilogy *Palimpsest*, like *Helen in Egypt*, draws on US Egyptology. The notion of palimpsest has continued to serve a distinctly argumentative function in feminist readings of H.D.: as Sarah E. Witte notes, "Many critics use 'palimpsest' as a linchpin metaphor to anchor and inform H.D.'s mode and manner of overwriting patriarchal quest myths with matriarchal ones" ("H.D.'s Recension," 122).

27. The syntax in "Helen" anticipates H.D.'s later practice of chiastic patterning. *Chiasmus*, a Greek term literally meaning "diagonal arrangement" or "to place crosswise," is a grammatical figure in which ideas are repeated in inverted order. Diana Collecott cites these lines from H.D.'s "Red Roses for Bronze" as an example of chiasmus: "Yourself in myself, / mirror for a star, / star for a mirror." The star and mirror reverse, crossing over axes of experience (*H.D. and Sapphic Modernism*, 262).

28. Painter, *The History of White People*, 60, 61.

29. Euripides, *Helen*, lines 262–63, trans. A. M. Dale, 1967, quoted in Austin, 203.

30. Euripides, *Helen*, lines 260–66, trans. Burian.

31. Austin notes, "For 'statue,' Helen uses the word *agalma*, the term for a cult idol," and that elsewhere in the play Menelaus refers to Helen's eidolon at Troy as "an *agalma* of cloud" (Euripides, line 705, quoted in Austin, 203n66).

32. Bryant and Eaverly, "Egypto-Modernism." In H.D.'s 1925 novella "Secret Name," published in *Palimpsest*, depicts Helen Fairwood, "high-class secretary" (189) to an Egyptologist. As Meredith Miller points out, "Secret Name" depicts an Egypt that is not only sentimentalized and fantastic but "a British-occupied nation inhabited by Arabs, and this political situation problematizes its redemptive function for Euroamericans" ("Enslaved to Both These Others," 82). In Miller's view, while a "new" version of Egypt functions in the other two novellas of *Palimpsest* as a "countervailing plenitude" to replace a masculine version of Egypt, here "Helen's feminine, sensuous knowledge of Egypt" is both enabled by and opposed to a character named Rafton who stands in for colonial rule (82).

33. H.D. to Pearson, 23 September 1952, in *Between History and Poetry*, 127. To name a few sources on H.D.'s mysticism as alternative knowledge: Albert Gelpi describes *Helen in Egypt* as an "occult version" of Eliot's *Four Quartets* ("H.D.: Hilda in Egypt," 87); Dianne Chisholm writes that H.D. "uncovers a different form of thinking, perceiving, feeling, and communalizing" beneath the metaphysical structure of reasoning (*H.D.'s Freudian Poetics*, 168); and Jeffrey Twitchell-Waas writes that "H.D. is one of the more extreme examples among modernist poets who cultivated disreputable and obsolete 'knowledge': the occult, alchemy, gnosticism, spiritualism, cabala—'sciences' whose utter delegitimization by modernity indicates to H.D. areas of cultural repression" ("Seaward," 469).

34. H.D. to Pearson, 11 May 1953, in *Between History and Poetry*, 140.

35. Gregory, "H.D. and Translation," 145, and *H.D. and Hellenism*, 65–66.

36. Gregory, "H.D. and Translation," 154. Emily Hauser argues that *Helen in Egypt* represents "a deliberate resolution between two modes of epic transmission, the male patrilineage of Homer and the matrilineal epic of H.D.": she takes Euripides out of the equation altogether, arguing that the figure of Helen herself is this unity ("Homer Undone," 168–69).

37. Jaji, "Classic," 60–62.

38. H.D. to Bryher, 2 September 1953, in *Between History and Poetry*, 171n62.

39. H.D., "Notes on Euripides," 132.

40. For the Greeks, as Peter Burian notes, the idea that a person's reputation might belong to a phantom "is of course deeply problematic, especially in terms of heroic culture, where reputation is so essential to identity. [. . .] Thus, Euripides's Helen feels deep shame for what she knows she has not done but nevertheless adheres to her name, so that 'I' and 'name' actually

become synonymous for her at [Euripides, lines] 198–99, though she else-where insists that they are not the same" (introduction to *Helen*, by Eu-ripides, 25). Austin similarly notes that if Helen of Troy is the centerpiece of the epic tradition, Helen the eidolon stands as the anti-myth, a figure whose lyric voice seeks to recuperate Helen from epic: Helen "understands that her function is not primarily, or even secondarily, to be a woman but to be first and foremost a story" (*Helen of Troy and Her Shameless Phan-tom*, 1), and the Greek lyric tradition, beginning with Stesichorus and Sappho, arose as a "counter-movement" to "rescue Helen's name from the disrepute that had accrued to it from the epic tradition" (2).

41. Scholars cite three figures whose parallel actions anticipate the myth of Helen's phantom: Odysseus, Penelope, and Persephone. As Helen waits for Menelaus in Egypt, her tale resembles that of Telemachus and Pe-nelope in the *Odyssey*; as a woman caught in a paradoxical relationship with her beloved and her new king, she must struggle with her reputation, like Penelope; like Persephone, she is abducted by Hermes while gather-ing flowers and requires heroic rescue. Euripides's *Helen*, Austin writes, sought to unite a Helen who had been divided into the three versions found in Homer, Stesichorus, and Herodotus (138). In the *Republic*, Socrates invokes not only phantom Helen but the palinode when he tells Glaucon that false pleasures "impregnate people with an insane lust for the pleasure they offer, and these fools fight over them, as the Trojans in Stesichorus' story, out of ignorance of the truth, fought over the mere apparition of Helen" (*Republic*, line 586c).

42. Plato, *Phaedrus*, lines 243a–b. According to Austin, Socrates then quotes the only known version of Stesichorus's fragmented palinode: "False was the tale [*logos*] I told. / You did not travel on the fair-decked ship, / Nor came to the citadel of Troy" (*Helen of Troy and Her Shameless Phantom*, 95).

43. Twitchell-Waas argues that *Helen in Egypt*'s psychoanalytic lyric revises modernist imagism: whereas Pound used imagism as the fragment for a long poem of infinite diversity, "H.D.'s imagistic practice focuses on the poem as visionary" ("Seaward," 473). The role of trauma in organizing much if not all of H.D.'s work has been explored by many scholars; Donna Krolik Hollenberg writes that the protracted trauma H.D. experienced during the first world war—her stillborn child on May 21, 1915, shortly following the sinking of the *Lusitania* on May 7; her severe illness while giving birth to Perdita in 1919; the breakdown of her marriage to Richard Aldington; and the deaths of her brother and father—"formed the nexus of what she termed her 'personal hieroglyph'" (*H.D.: The Poetics of Child-birth and Creativity*, 5).

44. H.D., *Tribute to Freud*, 6.

45. In different ways, Bryant and Eaverly argue, H.D. and Breasted "constructed an American Nile through which they asserted cultural authority and national identity" (436–37, 448); theirs is an alternative to readings of H.D.'s "Hellenism." See also Renée R. Curry's work on "white authorial imagination" across H.D.'s work, especially her linking of Egypt to the unknowable and of Greece to the knowable as an act of white privilege in *Helen in Egypt* ("H.D., Dove, Glück, and Levin," 174, 189).

46. As Adalaide Morris notes, the "flash," linked also to Helen's meeting with Achilles in Egypt, "has unavoidable resonance in the poem's contemporary matrix, not only as the flash of the atomic bombs dropped by the Allies on Hiroshima and Nagasaki in August 1945 but also as the flash of the hydrogen bombs detonated by the United States on 1 November 1952 at the Eniwetok proving grounds in the Pacific and on 1 March 1954 at the Bikini Atoll in the South Pacific" (*How to Live/What to Do: H.D.'s Cultural Poetics*, 74).

47. H.D., *Collected Poems*, 279.

48. H.D., *Bid Me to Live (A Madrigal)*, 17.

49. H.D., *Collected Poems*, 106.

50. Quoted by Jansen in "Exchange and the Eidolon" (330). Jansen writes that Euripides's play includes a scene in which Helen performs a kind of "self-trafficking": "For indeed, Helen arranges her own marriage, commodifying herself as an object to be given to Theoclymenus, only to be re-abducted by Menelaus" (342).

51. Barbour, "The Origins of the Prose Captions in H.D.'s *Helen in Egypt*," 475, quoting Gregory, *Hellenism*.

52. Friedman writes clarifyingly about the privileging of lyric in an essay that invokes the poststructuralist investment in lyric disruption of narrative: "In spite of a deconstructionist resistance to binaries, a number of poststructuralist theorists have reinstated preexisting and overlapping polarities between narrative and lyric, novel and poem, prose and poetry, representationalism and nonrepresentationalism, realism and surrealism, humanism and modernity. Such binaries are often asserted in ahistorical terms, without regard for the diachronic and synchronic variations in historically produced modes, genres, and discourses. Moreover, there is often an inexact slippage between modes (lyric, narrative) and genres (lyric poem, novel), or between broad discourses (poetry, prose) and specific forms (poem, fiction). What remains relatively constant in these formulations is the inevitability of an oppositional binary in which the lyric/poetic/nonmimetic continuously disrupts the narrative/novelistic/mimetic. In spite of the emphasis on process—the motion of textual

practice—the revolutionary potential of language is statically located at the site of this lyric transgression of narrative" ("Craving Stories," in Keller and Miller, *Feminist Measures*, 18).

53. H.D., *Notes on Thought and Vision*, 32.

Chapter 3

1. Niedecker, *Collected Works*, 194.
2. Pound, *ABC of Reading*, 36, 37.
3. Niedecker to Cox, 10 December 1966, in Dent, *The Full Note*, 36.
4. Niedecker, *Collected Works*, 265.
5. As DuPlessis notes, "We live by the urgent wave / of the verse" can be read as a modification of the following sentence in Robert Duncan's essay "Towards an Open Universe": "Amoebic intelligences, dwelling in the memorial of tidal voice, they arouse in our awake minds a spell, so that we let our awareness go in the urgent wave of the verse" (Duncan, *A Selected Prose*, quoted by DuPlessis in "Lorine Niedecker's 'Paean to Place' and Its Reflective Fusions," in Willis, *Radical Vernacular*, 170).
6. Niedecker to Corman, 2 July 1965, in *Between Your House and Mine*, 64. Echoing the language of "Poet's work," she continues: "But as in all poems everywhere, depth of emotion condensed, I'd say."
7. Niedecker, *Collected Works*, 23.
8. Shelley, "Defence of Poetry," 223. See Milton, *Comus*: "And in the violet-embroider'd vale, / Where the love-lorn nightingale / Nightly to thee her sad song mourneth well" (lines 4–6); or Keats, "Ode to a Nightingale": "Thou wast not born for death, immortal Bird!" (line 61) and "Forlorn! The very word is like a bell / To toll me back from thee to my sole self!" (lines 71–72).
9. Niedecker, 23.
10. Flint, "Imagisme," 199.
11. There is much more to be said about modernism's relationship to meter. Glaser diagnoses Pound's disavowal of meter "as a cover for modern poetry's nostalgia for earlier metrical culture, anxiety about its marginality and limited readership, and dependence on literary criticism" (*Modernism's Metronome*, 1). Glaser identifies meter as a "vestige" that defines the period: "Modernism's 'music,' usually in the form of 'rhythm' and 'cadence,' is a late and defensive consolidation" (2).
12. Adorno, *Essays on Music*, 117.
13. Adorno, *Notes to Literature*, 1:53.
14. Pater continues: "For while in all other works of art it is possible to distinguish the matter from the form, and the understanding can always make this distinction, yet it is the constant effort of art to obliterate it"

(*The Renaissance*, 106). As Brad Bucknell has pointed out, Pater's remarks appear paradoxical when one considers music's association with time. Bucknell argues that Pater's claim that "all art constantly aspires to the condition of music" would seem at first to extend a late Romantic belief in the artist's self as the grounds for epistemological certainty, but it actually anticipates modernism's paradoxical idealization of music, whose association with time undermines the transcendental capability of that ideal. In Bucknell's view, Pater implicates the temporal in the artistic ideal. See *Literary Modernism and Musical Aesthetics*, 37–38 and 49–50. See also Scroggins's discussion of the impact of Pater's remarks on Pound and Zukofsky: for Zukofsky, he writes, Pater's "condition of music" is a horizon for poetry but also is a limit poetry cannot reach (*Louis Zukofsky and the Poetry of Knowledge*, 175–77).

15. Zukofsky, "'Recencies' in Poetry," in *Prepositions+*, 18. In the later version of this essay, published as "An Objective," Zukofsky removes the reference to Pound's *Cantos* and changes "contrasting principles or facts" to "contrasting principles of facts," an edit from "or" to "of" that amplifies the notion of fact as material of the poem. Zukofsky distinguishes music as a form to which poetry can be compared but he also refers to music as, in the colloquial sense, characteristic of the poem. Both meanings are evident in Zukofsky's 1950 essay "A Statement for Poetry," where he suggests musicality enables poetry to cross boundaries of time and space: "And it is possible in imagination to divorce speech of all graphic elements, to let it become a movement of sounds. It is this musical horizon of poetry (which incidentally poems perhaps never reach) that permits anybody who does not know Greek to listen and get something out of the poetry of Homer: to 'tune in' to the human tradition, to its voice that has developed among the sounds of natural things, and thus escape the confines of a time and place, as one hardly ever escapes them in studying Homer's grammar" (Zukofsky, *Prepositions+*, 20).

16. Rancière, *Mute Speech*, 139. Rancière historicizes aesthetic judgment alongside the status of the literary and the poetic in particular, declaring, "antirepresentative art has a name: music" (123–24).

17. Musical, that is, in the sense of engaging directly with music theory. Niedecker does, of course, write poems with ballad and blues structure, closely follows Paul Zukofsky's career as a violinist, and includes myriad musical history references in her work. See *Niedecker and the Correspondence with Zukofsky* for many references to composers and to the performers of her day. See also Patrick Pritchett on her relationship to the blues: "The vernacular, so frequently disparaged by the wardens of official culture, becomes the instrument *par excellence* for a utopian expression

of that most dangerous of emotions, hope" ("How to Do Things with Nothing: Lorine Niedecker Sings the Blues," in Willis, *Radical Vernacular*, 100).

18. Niedecker to Zukofsky, early June 1957, in *Niedecker and the Correspondence with Zukofsky*, 235.

19. Niedecker, *Collected Works*, 128 (italics in the original).

20. Niedecker to Corman, 2 July 1965, in *Between Your House and Mine*, 64.

21. Altieri, "The Objectivist Tradition," in DuPlessis and Quartermain, *The Objectivist Nexus*, 32. Altieri apparently departs from Zukofsky's use of Platonic "measure" in "For My Son When He Can Read": "If number, measure and weighing be taken away from any art, that which remains will not be much" (*Prepositions+*, 6). Zukofsky goes on, however, to differentiate poetry from the other arts: "But poets measure by means of words, whose effect as an offshoot of nature may (or should) be that their strength of suggestion can never be accounted for completely" (7).

22. Rockstro et al., "Cadence."

23. An atonal piece of music can also create its own version of the cadence; as Jonathan D. Kramer describes, without the "a priori" sense of the stable tonic, Arnold Schoenberg's compositions create cadences contextually rather than according to formally explicit goals. Kramer uses the phrase "nondirected linearity" to describe "a sense of continuity and progression" within atonal music ("New Temporalities in Music," 541–42). See also Andrew Timms's point that "whilst equations of musical modernism with atonality project a certain synchronic logic, one which arranges other styles and movements (such as neo-classicism and surrealism) around a self-proclaimed mainstream, they also contain a not-so-secret diachronic scheme, which validates their own position at the vanguard of history": in such a reactionary critical schema, Timms suggests, tonality emerges as a positive formulation ("Modernism's Moment of Plenitude," 15).

24. In his translations of Catullus, Zukofsky aspired to remain faithful to the original cadences of the Latin: "This translation of Catullus," he wrote, "follows the sound, rhythm, and syntax of his Latin—tries, as is said, to breathe the 'literal' meaning with him" (*Complete Short Poetry*, 243). Niedecker alludes to the way the sound of Zukofsky's Latin contrasts with the silence of a poetics not drawn from folk in a 1963 letter to Corman: "Passion in sound, noise (the latin [*sic*] of Catullus) (folk); however, isn't it closer to art when it's still enough (deep enough) to become ice? But of course origins let go the drive without which we could do nothing. I'm a little worried—not really, tho—about my own folk impulse lost—lost? On the way to the ice" (13 January 1963, in *Between Your House and Mine*, 38).

25. Flint, *The Fourth Imagist*, 32. John Wilkinson describes cadence in poetry as a matter of deferred futurity: "The productive points for the writing of a poem lie deep in an inadmissible past," Wilkinson writes, and the poem "becomes felt as cadence, projecting forward to organize the actual and tenderly enveloping day which never will break" (*The Lyric Touch*, 143).

26. As too is the term "rhythm," as Vincent Barletta points out in his book *Rhythm,* which questions the "uncritical insistence on the temporal (even metrical) nature of rhythm" (94) and instead asks what in modernity binds rhythm to human nature.

27. Zukofsky, *"A,"* 38 (italics in the original).

28. Zukofsky, 138 (italics in the original).

29. Zukofsky, *Prepositions+*, 208. For an analysis of both Zukofsky's "purely analogical" (184) relationship to musical form and the analogical relationship between musical and avant-garde poetic form more broadly, see Scroggins, *Louis Zukofsky and the Poetry of Knowledge*. In his introduction to *Upper Limit Music*, Scroggins again categorizes Zukofsky's use of music as analogical, but also argues that the determination of sound values gives Zukofsky's poetics "a redoubtable and even revolutionary formalism, in which structure and shape are the most important elements of the poem. To some degree 'music' in the phrase 'upper limit music' is simply a trope, a figure for the condition of absolute form to which Pater referred in his famous passage on the 'condition of music'" (7). For Scroggins, then, it appears that Zukofsky's music is an analogue for form itself.

30. Scroggins, *Louis Zukofsky and the Poetry of Knowledge*, 194. Zukofsky's musical analogy, as DuPlessis and Quartermain have written, also functions as a symbol: "Objectification was originally formalist because it meant a perception of form, and, since the analogy Zukofsky uses most often is music, the term even had symbolist implications: form as 'the totality of perfect rest'" (introduction to *The Objectivist Nexus*, 8).

31. Scroggins writes: "with her musical training Celia Zukofsky could realize her husband's poetry in a way that he—who never learned to read music or play an instrument—could not" (*The Poem of a Life*, 410).

32. *Poetry* 37 (October–March 1930–31): 288; *Prepositions+*, 200

33. Zukofsky, *"A,"* 24.

34. Woods, *The Poetics of the Limit*, 67. Woods argues that melody here is a "structure" that "seeks to omit any extraneous and 'impure' elements in its concentration on a 'pure music.'"

35. Zukofsky also uses "cadence" as a governing term in *"A"*-12, written 1950–51, to refer to the long poem as a wellspring that lies just outside the poet's full awareness.

36. Zukofsky, *Prepositions+*, 19.

37. Zukofsky, 210.

38. Niedecker to Zukofsky, 12 January 1947, in *Niedecker and the Correspondence with Zukofsky*, 142.

39. Niedecker, "The Poetry of Louis Zukofsky," n.p.

40. Niedecker, "The Poetry of Louis Zukofsky," n.p. See Williams, *Collected Poems*, 2:54: "To make two bald statements: There's nothing sentimental about a machine, and: A poem is a small (or large) machine made of words" (54).

41. Penberthy, introduction to *Niedecker and the Correspondence with Zukofsky*, 9.

42. Zukofsky, *Complete Short Poetry*, 109.

43. Niedecker, *Collected Works*, 125.

44. The "and" could also read as an indication of a coalitional relationship between the people in the room and the people out on the street, a relationship reminiscent again of Zukofsky's own political poetics in a piece such as "Mantis," a poem I discuss in chapter 4. Thanks to Sarah Dowling for this insight.

45. Niedecker's own remarks on the influence of haiku on her work indicate her engagement with a "concentrated" poetics that she eventually found constraining: "I am beginning to worry about the five-line haiku-derived form that dogs me now, it doesn't fit everything" (Niedecker to Zukofsky, 10 March 1958, in *Niedecker and the Correspondence with Zukofsky*, 243). The link Niedecker makes between her stepped lines and haiku rehearses an orientalist appropriation of haiku form by a number of Anglo American poets, and scholarly readings of the "interiority" of her haiku-inflected poetics often resemble readings of the "interiority" of Niedecker's lyric. DuPlessis's discussion of the haiku in Niedecker's work specifies it as a modernist marker of desire for an international style (*Blue Studios*, 152–53).

46. Niedecker to Zukofsky, 10 March 1958, in *Niedecker and the Correspondence with Zukofsky*, 230 (brackets in the original).

47. Incidentally, the year Niedecker writes "Paean to Place" is also the year that cremation becomes the most widespread method of handling the dead in England, according to Ramazani in his study of the modern elegy. In the United States, embalming is on the rise that year (*Poetry of Mourning*, 16).

48. The submerging of Niedecker's own poetics beneath the apparently determinate function of Zukofsky's approval signals how the relationship between the two poets has often been described in scholarship on modernist women poets. One of the first serious treatments of Niedecker comes from Perloff, who suggests in 1990 that Niedecker was left out of feminist recovery projects of women poets because of her affinity for modernist form: "For the male poetry establishment, her work appears to be a foot-

note to an already marginalized 'difficult' poetic movement; for editors of feminist poetry texts, on the other hand, Niedecker's is a lyric that may be perceived as excessively 'male identified'" (*Poetic License*, 43). There is a material aspect to reading Niedecker's relationship to her mentor: Niedecker's archive is stored within Zukofsky's at the Harry Ransom Center in Texas, so that one must literally seek and be granted permission to enter Zukofsky's archive in order to enter Niedecker's. The Zukofsky collection at the Harry Ransom Center at the University of Texas at Austin contains the majority of Niedecker's extant manuscripts and papers, including her posthumous bequest to Zukofsky, which was subsequently transferred to the Ransom Center.

49. In his book *Unending Design*, Conte dates seriality as a specifically postmodern technique, beginning with Oppen's *Discrete Series*, excerpts from which appeared in the 1931 "Objectivists" issue of *Poetry*. Golding has likewise described George Oppen's seriality as moving "fitfully" between fragment and sequence ("George Oppen's Serial Poems," in DuPlessis and Quartermain, *The Objectivist Nexus*, 91).

50. Niedecker, *Collected Works*, 261.

51. Niedecker, 99.

52. Niedecker, 194, 268 (italics in the original).

53. Niedecker, 261–62.

54. Willis, "The Poetics of Affinity: Niedecker, Morris, and the Art of Work," in Willis, *Radical Vernacular*, 223.

55. See, for example, Bucknell, who argues that work by modernist writers embodies an essential tension between the rationality of form and a nineteenth-century invocation of music as the paradigm of transcendent art, and how music in particular raises the question of style versus expression, or between "interiority and artistic form" (*Literary Modernism and Musical Aesthetics*, 4); O'Meally's edited volume *The Jazz Cadence of American Culture*, on the impact of jazz music on US artistic production between 1920 and 1970, which includes discussions of the supposed opposition between form and content in received notions of music for US modernisms such as Harlem Renaissance and Black Arts poetry; Albright's illuminating discussion of consonance and dissonance across the arts in *Untwisting the Serpent*; and Prieto's analysis of representation across music and other genres in *Listening In*. A number of other recent works have linked matters of textual musicality, such as rhythm, with the larger matter of form. For example, in his introduction to *Critical Rhythm*, Ben Glaser writes that efforts to theorize rhythm aid the effort "to articulate conceptions of form, poetry, and the literary," as the notion of rhythm itself is "a term at once suspicious and essential to the discipline

of literary study" (Glaser, "Introduction," in Glaser and Culler, eds., *Critical Rhythm*, 3). The notion that a given term is at once suspicious and essential to the discipline of literary study could be said about lyric.

56. Song, *Climate Lyricism*, 2–3.

57. Keller, *Recomposing Ecopoetics*, 136, 26. Devin Griffiths suggests a precisely ecological formalist theory that recognizes how form "works through wider networks of relation and of the material, energetic, and social interactions that give it life" ("The Ecology of Form," 71).

58. Ronda, *Remainders*, 23.

59. For example, Baker insists that "The new aesthetic that *The Cantos* point to must begin with discarding the notion of 'voice' as it implies an interior monologue, in favor of a model for enunciation by a necessarily 'split subject.' A polyphony of voices—personal, transpersonal, textual, intertextual—speaks through and across the surface of the text" (*Obdurate Brilliance*, 93). And Penberthy writes that when Niedecker, in a letter to Zukofsky, suggests "the polyphonic orchestration she intended for an entire group" to speak in "For Paul and Other Poems," she sets polyphony against lyric: "Such voice-play is possible only in a form more social than the lyric, a form governed not by the solo voice but by conversation" (introduction to *Niedecker and the Correspondence with Zukofsky*, 64).

60. Song, *Climate Lyricism*, 64.

61. John Harley, *William Byrd's Modal Practice*, 42. Harley continues: "A melodic phrase necessarily ends on a note of the chord prevailing at the time (it is, of course, the individual voices that combine to form the chord), yet a cadence in one voice may not coincide with cadences in other voices. A phrase in one voice may end while phrases in other voices continue, or may be extended until other voices have begun new phrases" (42–43).

62. Scroggins, *Louis Zukofsky and the Poetry of Knowledge*, 199. Bernstein summarizes the impact of Bach on *"A"* this way: "intricate pattern of recurrences, recapitulations, and extensions can be compared, at least metaphorically, to the form of a fugue—from the chordal arrangement of syllables to the recurrences both between and within the movements of the work" (introduction to Zukofsky, *Selected Poems*, xxii). In his foreword to Zukofsky's *Prepositions+*, Bernstein notes how Zukofsky uses the fugue to emphasize the relationship between sound and meaning: he writes that Zukofsky's "recourse to music emphasizes the thingness of poetry (its object status), the sound value of poetry (its song), as well as poetry's durational space (its temporality). Unlike music, however, poetry's sound is verbal. For Zukofsky sound, pitch, rhythm, and tone do not accompany meaning, neither are they arbitrary nor conventionally associated with meaning; they *make* meaning" (ix, italics in the original). There have been

attempts to read *"A"* more literally as a fugue; Marvin Bram includes it in an article the aim of which "is to inquire whether a horizontal, 'melodic' univocity and hypotaxis, on the one hand, and a vertical, 'harmonic' polysemy and parataxis, on the other, can be achieved simultaneously in a fugal, natural-language writing system" ("The Art of Fugue," 73).

63. Perelman, *The Trouble with Genius*, 185.

64. Skinner, "Ecopoetics," 94–109.

65. Niedecker, *Collected Works*, 267, 261, 265, 265, 268.

66. Brook Houglum calls attention to the "attunement to precise qualities, durations, rhythms, and materials of sound" across Niedecker's work ("Speech Without Practical Locale," 222), while Beverly Dahlen reads sound in Niedecker's poems as a "thingness" apprehended synaesthetically. Dahlen links Niedecker's description of the "shine (or sombre tone)" of a poem in a letter to Cid Corman with her 1946 poem "There's a better shine / on the pendulum / than is on my hair / and many times / .. .. / I've seen it there" (Niedecker, *Collected Works*, 101, periods in the original). Dahlen suggests that Niedecker describes a synaesthetic process in the poem in which "tone" is, in Dahlen's words, "light perceived as sound" that in turn becomes something "more than sound, always difficult to name," something that "has to do with the substance of the poem, its concrete particular thingness" ("Notes on Reading Lorine Niedecker"). There is more to say about epistemology in Niedecker; I am reminded of the distinction Hejinian, following Jakobson, draws between metonymy and metaphor in describing poetry as a "language of inquiry" that foregrounds the relationships between things ("Strangeness").

67. Robertson, "In Phonographic Deep Song," in Willis, *Radical Vernacular*, 86–87.

68. Robertson, 87.

69. Niedecker uses the variant spelling "pewee" unlike in a different version of these lines in "For Paul and Other Poems."

70. Niedecker to Zukofsky, 1947, in *Niedecker and the Correspondence with Zukofsky*, 146.

71. More historical-political references in Niedecker's later work further clarify her characterization as a "poet of place": as Michael Davidson has argued, a better characterization of Niedecker's relationship to place is "critical regionalism," a term he adapts from architecture to indicate an investment in the local and the vernacular as against globalized modes of social organization. Critical regionalism identifies forms of social production within the local that are in dialogue with the global; it can also, Davidson writes, make possible a class- and gender-inflected survey of a specific locale, a critique that uses tools found both within and without

that locale (Davidson, "Life by Water: Lorine Niedecker and Critical Regionalism," in Willis, *Radical Vernacular*, 4). Davidson notes that in cultural geography, critical regionalism describes "the self-conscious use of vernacular features to critique modernist universalism"; by offering "resistant sites to capitalist production," critical regionalism offers alternative views of universalism. When Niedecker sent a copy of her book *T&G* to the University of Wisconsin at Milwaukee, she was told that it had been placed with "regional materials"; in a letter to Cid Corman, she wondered, "What region—London, Wisconsin, New York?" (*Between Your House and Mine*, 208).

72. Niedecker to Corman, 16 July 1966, in *Between Your House and Mine*, 91 (italics in the original).

Chapter 4

1. Notley, *The Descent of Alette*, 89.
2. Quotation marks and ellipses are retained from Notley's text. Ellipses in brackets indicate omitted text in this and all subsequent quotations throughout this chapter.
3. Notley told an interviewer in 2009: "Inanna shows up, she observes, she dies, in fact, is reborn, but never fights. She makes certain crucial decisions, the most profound one being the decision to confront death by appearing at the door of the underworld. Alette, on the other hand, does fight, but the fight is magical and not bloody. It was very difficult for me to stage her fight with the tyrant, since I am a pacifist. But he is a construct, a symbol; she isn't" ("Evident Being").
4. Cheng, *The Melancholy of Race*, 10.
5. Quoted in Nelson, *Women, the New York School, and Other True Abstractions*, 133. As Nelson notes, Notley's oeuvre would seem to indicate a split between the early New York School style and the later epic work: the back cover blurb to her 2001 collection *Disobedience* refers to Notley's attempts to explore "the despised daily" of the New York School style (134).
6. Fraser, "Alice Notley," 55. Fraser remarks that this pattern seemed to hover behind Notley's visible "discomfort in asserting the personal authority of a mature woman artist" during the residency.
7. Quoted in Nelson, xvi (ellipsis in the original).
8. Perloff writes that "Pound and Williams were consistently excluded from the [modernist] canon, at least until the early seventies, the same period when, as [Alicia] Ostriker observes, women's poetry came into prominence" (*Poetic License*, 32). Perloff's statement would seem to indicate that Williams was being read, not that women were recovering him. Kinnahan seems to suggest that Williams's recovery might actually be attributed to

the contemporaneous recovery of women writers when she describes him as "a bridge between a Poundian modernism and a female counterstrain" in her book *Poetics of the Feminine*, an in-depth study of the "sense of ambiguity, of a simultaneous enabling and disenfranchisement" that characterizes a number of women poets' relationships to Williams (3).

9. Bob Perelman uses the word "saga" to distinguish poetic inheritance from poetic influence, noting that inheritance is a matter of assertion and argument, whereas influence is a "safer" concept: "Exoteric poetic influences are irreducibly democratic, their information available, at least theoretically, to anyone who can read. But poetic inheritance, on the other hand, is esoteric, a matter of luck or grace"—what's more, "the claim of inheritance may provoke respect or envy in the non-inheritor, but it can also be read as a sign of presumption or narcissism." Perelman, "'fucking / me across the decades like we / poets like': Embodied Poetic Transmission," in Kane, *Don't Ever Get Famous*, 201.

10. Notley, "Doctor Williams' Heiresses," n.p. As the pamphlet is unpaginated, further citations from this text do not include page numbers.

11. The "new" of Williams's modernism is, of course, far from empty of inheritance—or history. Williams writes in *Spring and All* both that "the work the two-thousand-year-old poet did and that we do are one piece" (*Imaginations*, 101) and that the "great copying" by modernist "plagiarists" must end (95, 89): his sense of tradition and the individual talent, though not Eliot's, does claim indebtedness.

12. Stein's male-identified self-fashioning is summarized in this remark in a 1906 notebook: "Pablo & Matisse have a maleness that belongs to genius. Moi aussi perhaps" (*Picasso*, 109; also quoted in Joan Retallack's introduction to *Gertrude Stein: Selections*, 25). In Notley's piece, O'Hara, Whalen, and Olson are coded "male-female," but this identification could even refer back to the modernist trope of androgynous decadence that belongs to a sphere of gay male aesthetics (also appropriated by H.D.). One might speculate how such a text as Notley's might characterize Stein were it to take into account the four decades of thinking about gender and sexuality that have transpired since its writing. See Chris Coffman's *Gertrude Stein's Transmasculinity* for a reading of Stein's transmasculinity as "shifting and anti-identitarian" (9).

13. Foucault, "Nietzsche, Genealogy, History," in *Language, Counter-Memory, Practice*, 139.

14. Foucault, 143.

15. Foucault, 160.

16. Williams, *Collected Poems*, 1:86.

17. Foucault, "Nietzsche, Genealogy, History," 146–47.

18. Williams, "Poetry and the Making of Language," 17.

19. Perelman, *Modernism the Morning After*, 179.

20. Adorno, *Aesthetic Theory*, 123, 167.

21. Adorno, 123.

22. Ngai, *Ugly Feelings*, 43.

23. Ngai, 88. In an essay on poetic tone, Anahid Nersessian suggests that a certain kind of tone in contemporary US poetry might "challenge the pedestrian but no less potent conception of lyric poetry as an expressive genre that actively solicits empathy or (minimally) acknowledgment in exchange for intimate revelation"—that tone itself torques what lyric might otherwise mean ("Notes on Tone," 57). See also Fred Moten on tone and the notion of the unthinkable in Cecil Taylor's music: "The unthinkable is a tone" (*In the Break*, 57).

24. Williams, *Collected Poems*, 2:315.

25. Williams, *I Wanted to Write a Poem*, 14.

26. Notley, *Songs for the Unborn Second Baby*, n.p.

27. Nardi, *The Last Word*, 10.

28. Nardi, 195.

29. Nardi, 124.

30. Brown, *Politics Out of History*, 119.

31. Brown, 112.

32. Pound to Henry Swabey, 9 May 1940, in *Selected Letters*, 345.

33. Composed of sustained criticism, imaginative wanderings, and imagistic collage, not unlike "Doctor Williams' Heiresses," *Spring and All* contains both extended prose commentary and Williams's most famous "lyric" poem—"so much depends / upon // a red wheel / barrow" (*Imaginations*, 138).

34. Lacan, *Écrits*, 3.

35. Garber, " " (Quotation Marks)," 660; de Grazia, "Sanctioning Voice," 288.

36. Garber: "In other words, the mark of quotation was an oral, and aural, cue. It was the ear and not the eye that still predominated" (661).

37. Garber, 663.

38. Encyclopaedia Britannica Films, *Arteries of New York City*.

39. Warner, *Publics and Counterpublics*, 8.

40. Saler, "The 'Medieval Modern' Underground," 117.

41. Saler, 114.

42. Saler, 116.

43. Saler, 131.

44. Pound, "In a Station of the Metro," in *Personae*, 251.

45. Pound, *Gaudier-Brzeska*, 100.

46. Pound, 103 (italics in the original).

47. Pound, 103. Pound suggests the imagist long poem would be a contradiction in terms, for "no artist can possibly get a vortex into every poem or picture he does" (109). In fact, Pound would soon abandon the short form for his *Cantos*, after referring to *Mauberley* as a "farewell to London"—he also apparently bid farewell to the Metro and the Underground, as there was no subway in Rapallo. Quoted in Baechler and Litz, "A Note on the Text," in Pound, *Personae*, 271.

48. DeKoven, *Rich and Strange*, 189 (italics in the original).

49. Bush, *Ideographic Modernism*, 32; Ramazani, *A Transnational Poetics*, 114.

50. Pound, *Gaudier-Brzeska*, 95.

51. David Leiwei Li: "In this way, China, whether represented by its language, culture, geography, or any other feature, is detached from its own history and made to conform to American orientalist discourse, ultimately compensating for occidental desires" (*Imagining the Nation*, 47).

52. DeKoven, *Rich and Strange*, 189. Recall Poe: "the death, then, of a beautiful woman is, unquestionably, the most poetical topic in the world" (*Poems and Essays on Poetry*, 144).

53. Zukofsky, "Mantis," in *All*, 73.

54. Zukofsky: "In sincerity shapes appear concomitants of word combinations, precursors of (if there is continuance) completed sound or structure, melody or form. Writing occurs, which is the detail, not mirage, of seeing, of thinking with the things as they exist, and of directing them along a line of melody" (*Prepositions+*, 194).

55. Zukofsky, "'Mantis,' An Interpretation," in *All*, 75 (italics in the original). As many scholars have noted and as he himself alludes in the commentary on "Mantis," Zukofsky most certainly encountered the mantis as a contextual object theorized by surrealist painters and writers of the 1930s who included Salvador Dalí and Roger Caillois and who invested the mantis in a family of so-called "primitive" tropes.

56. Zukofsky, "Mantis," in *All*, 74.

57. Zukofsky, 74.

58. Zukofsky, "'Mantis,' An Interpretation," in *All*, 79.

59. Crane, *The Bridge*, 118 (ellipsis in the original).

60. Quoted in Stalter-Pace, *Underground Movements*, 81.

61. Crane, 55–56.

62. Crane, 57.

63. Williams, *Collected Poems*, 2:330.

64. Williams argued that "A poem is a small (or large) machine made of words" (*Collected Poems*, 2:54), but for the most part his machine of choice was the automobile, which he was frequently driving to visit his patients.

Williams's uses of the car have been referred to as an enactment of the masculine "mobile gaze" central to how the motor car in the United States was conceptualized at the beginning of the twentieth century, and as contrasting female domestic space with male automotive space, traversed by Williams's own roving gaze that has the power to shape what it views (Chatlos, "Automobility and Lyric Poetry"). Williams's mixed feelings about the subway contrast with his own use of underground transit as a conceit for epic descent. In a 1958 letter to Zukofsky, Williams remarked, "when you consider the circumstances, those we meet on the tubes seem to have the faces of the damned" (quoted in Mariani, *William Carlos Williams*, 737).

65. Williams, *Collected Poems*, 2:428.

66. Cheng, *The Melancholy of Race*, 11. Williams's identity as a white anglo is contested.

67. Cheng, 20, 11.

68. Butler, *Bodies That Matter*, 49, 42.

69. Williams, on the deadening recurrence of the old line:

> Without invention nothing is well spaced,
> unless the mind change, unless
> the stars are new measured, according
> to their relative positions, the
> line will not change, the necessity
> will not matriculate: unless there is
> a new mind there cannot be a new
> line, the old will go on
> repeating itself with recurring
> deadliness [. . .] (*Paterson*, 50)

70. Adorno, "On Epic Naiveté," in *Notes to Literature*, 1:24–29.

71. I follow Ngai in identifying the appropriative strategy as a political critique. Ngai cites what she calls the "stuplimity"—a combination of shock and boredom—in Notley's narrative accumulation in *The Descent of Alette*. See Ngai, *Ugly Feelings*, 296–97.

72. Garber, 668.

Chapter 5

1. Kim, *Dura*, 72.

2. Kim, 74.

3. Susan Howe wrote in her long poem "The Liberties" in 1980: "I is the subject of a proposition in logic" (209). Howe continues a few pages later, in perhaps a quite different version of the tracking of the subject in migration:

> Across the Atlantic, I
> inherit myself
> semblance
> of irish susans
> dispersed
> and narrowed to
> home
>
> Namesake
> old Friends,
> on the seashore at Irishtown
> *not in your native land.* (213, italics in the original)

4. Sohn, "*Experiment* Is Each Scroll of White Pages Joined Together," 675n10.

5. Kim, *Dura*, 102 (italics in the original).

6. Kim, *Commons*, 111.

7. Kim, *Civil Bound*, 11.

8. Kim, 30.

9. Kim, *Commons*, 107. Leong writes that Kim's lines contrast "the epistemological confidence" of the micro-narrative documental long poem with "the revisionist suspicion" of the metanarrative documental long poem (*Contested Records*, 27).

10. Dowling, *Translingual Poetics*, 5.

11. Dowling, 6. Dowling calls Kim's confrontations between English and Hangul a poetics of "radically depersonalized autobiography" in which a "refusal to present an adequate self can be read as a demonstration of the scarcity of selfhood" under the conditions of exclusion and linguistic nativism that characterize neoliberalism (119).

12. Kim, *Penury*, 7.

13. Sohn, "*Experiment* Is Each Scroll of White Pages Joined Together," 676n10, 652.

14. Rancière, *The Flesh of Words*, 9.

15. Rancière, 12.

16. Rancière, 19.

17. Rancière, 12–14.

18. Rancière, 18.

19. Chuh, *The Difference Aesthetics Makes*, 22.

20. Chuh, *Imagine Otherwise*, 2.

21. Chuh, 8. Chuh elaborates: "'Asian American' is/names racism and resistance, citizenship and its denial, subjectivity and subjection—at once the becoming and undoing—and, as such, is a designation of *the (im)possibility of justice*, where 'justice' refers to a state as yet unexperienced and

unrepresentable, one that can only connotatively be implied" (8, italics in the original).

22. Chuh, 9.

23. Chuh, 9.

24. Yu, "Form and Identity in Language Poetry and Asian American Poetry," 425.

25. Yu, 436.

26. Yu, *Race and the Avant-Garde*, 147, 17.

27. As Yu puts it at the end of his introduction to *Race and the Avant-Garde*: "At stake are the very terms of contemporary literary value, in which aesthetics are strongly linked with the social" (18).

28. Park, *Cold War Friendships*, 17.

29. Chuh, *Imagine Otherwise*, 10 (italics in the original).

30. Morris, *How to Live/What to Do*, 57.

31. Kim, *Under Flag*, 13.

32. Thoreau, *Thoreau: Political Writings*, 30.

33. Kim, *Under Flag*, 21.

34. Kim, 26.

35. Kim, 27.

36. Dowling reads these fractured moments of romanization of Hangul as "denials of personhood" (*Translingual Poetics*, 95).

37. Kim, *Under Flag*, 29.

38. Dowling, "Interpolation, Coherence, History," 13.

39. Kim, *Under Flag*, 36.

40. See for example Weheliye, *Habeas Viscus*.

41. Kim, "Generosity as Method." Kim also differentiates between "opposition" and the "dialectic" when discussing intertextuality in an interview with Divya Victor in 2013; see "Eight Discourses Between Myung Mi Kim and Divya Victor."

42. Wang, *Thinking Its Presence*, 35.

43. Wang, xxii.

44. "Intersections" doesn't quite connote how the field has tended to approach the relationship between form and the social. DuPlessis uses the phrase "helix" to refer to the interdependence of "a text's social and aesthetic aspects," but Wang's method would question the premise of this schema, perhaps suggesting there is no constant angle within that helix: there is simply no "aesthetic aspect" that is not "social." See DuPlessis, *Blue Studios*, 122.

45. Wang, 57, 297.

46. Kim, "Eight Discourses Between Myung Mi Kim and Divya Victor." Victor and Kim discuss the notion that poetry happens when a "perceiving subject [. . .] converts something into 'experience.'"

47. Kim, "Generosity as Method," answering Morrison's question: "How broad can something be, how much can a form hold before the form is compromised, how inclusive can a poem, a movement, a poetics be before its 'aim' is completely diffused?"

48. A number of discussions of *Citizen* have investigated the important work lyric does for the poem's argument about the political subject, including Walt Hunter in *Forms of a World*, 44–64.

49. Kim, *Civil Bound*, 70.

50. Kim, *Penury*, 111.

51. Kim, *Civil Bound*, 23.

52. Kim, 22.

53. United States Office of Indian Affairs, *Annual Report*, xxiii.

54. United States Office of Indian Affairs, xxiv.

55. Lankford, "The Lesson of Canal Zone Sanitation."

56. Leong, *Contested Records*, 3.

57. Leong, 4.

58. See Leong's brilliant analysis of M. NourbeSe Philip's *Zong!* as a revision of the "shore-lyric" (*Contested Records*, 64).

59. Kim, "Generosity as Method." This political point is similar to one made by Leong: "Twenty-first-century poets of documentation tend not to dwell on the loss of proprietary linguistic ownership; rather, they view preexisting documentation as a shared resource whose manipulation might propose the reconstruction of the social order" (7).

60. At "Boundary Conditions of the Long Poem," a 2017 MLA roundtable, Alan Golding in his discussion of Rachel Blau DuPlessis's uses of the fragment in her long poem project *Drafts* remarked on the long epistemological, cultural, and literary tradition of coding the fragment female (little, incomplete, etc.) and on how DuPlessis has been a key figure in unpacking and problematizing that tradition.

61. Kim, *Commons*, 108 (brackets in the original).

62. Kim, *Civil Bound*, 35. Kim quotes from a *New York Times* article by Jeff Hull ("The Noises of Nature"), who interviewed bioacoustics expert Bernie Krause, who coined the term "biophony" to refer to "that portion of the soundscape contributed by nonhuman creatures." A longer version of this quote from Hull reads: "Many animals, he argues, have evolved to squeeze their vocalizations into available niches of the soundscape in order to be heard by others of their kind. Evolution isn't just about the competition for space or food but also for bandwidth. If a species cannot find a sonic niche of its own, it will not survive."

63. Adorno, *Aesthetic Theory*, 1.

64. Adorno, 2, 3.

65. Adorno, 4–5.

66. Adorno, 5.
67. "I'll Drown My Book" is also a title of a poem by Bernadette Mayer as well as the 2012 anthology of conceptual writing by women, published by Les Figues Press.
68. Adorno, *Aesthetic Theory*, 45.
69. Adorno, 140.
70. Bruns, "On the Conundrum of Form and Material in Adorno's *Aesthetic Theory*," 225. Bruns goes on to point out that for Adorno, the mediation of form happens "by the artist's assorted materials of construction, or by the artist's subjectivity, or for all of that by the modern world in all of its administered, commodified, not to say popular renditions."
71. Kim, *Commons*, 109.
72. Liu, "Making Common the Commons," 255.
73. Kim, *Commons*, 110.
74. Kim, 110.
75. Cha, *Dictée*, 28. In Cheng's reading of this passage in *Dictée*, "Cha reminds us here that classification is also how nations and families organize and mobilize themselves to productive and inhibiting ends. This is why it is insufficient to say that Cha deconstructs social identities such as race and nationhood, for she is painfully aware of the inseparability of construction from deconstruction" (166).

Coda

1. ife, *Maroon Choreography*, ix.
2. ife, 82.
3. Harney and Moten, *The Undercommons*, 31.
4. The title of ife's poem invokes the objectivist poet George Oppen's *Of Being Numerous*.

BIBLIOGRAPHY

Adorno, Theodor W. *Aesthetic Theory.* Translated and edited by Robert Hullot-Kentor. Minneapolis: University of Minnesota Press, 1997.

Adorno, Theodor W. *Essays on Music.* Edited by Richard Leppert. Translated by Susan H. Gillespie. Berkeley: University of California Press, 2002.

Adorno, Theodor W. *Notes to Literature.* Edited by Rolf Tiedemann. Translated by Shierry Weber Nicholsen. 2 vols. New York: Columbia University Press, 1991–1992.

Ahmed, Sara. *Queer Phenomenology: Orientations, Objects, Others.* Durham, NC: Duke University Press, 2006.

Albright, Daniel. *Untwisting the Serpent: Modernism in Music, Literature, and Other Arts.* Chicago: University of Chicago Press, 2000.

Allen, Edward, ed. *Forms of Late Modernist Lyric.* Liverpool: Liverpool University Press, 2021.

Althusser, Louis. "Ideology and Ideological State Apparatuses (Notes Towards an Investigation)." In *Lenin and Philosophy,* trans. Ben Brewster, 127–86. New York: Monthly Review Press, 1971.

Andrews, Kimberly Quiogue. *The Academic Avant-Garde: Poetry and the American University.* Baltimore: Johns Hopkins University Press, 2023.

Ashton, Jennifer. "Lyric, Gender, and Subjectivity in Modern and Contemporary Women's Poetry." In *The Cambridge History of American Women's Literature,* edited by Dale M. Bauer, 515–38. Cambridge: Cambridge University Press, 2012.

Ashton, Jennifer. "Our Bodies, Our Poems." *Modern Philology* 105, no. 1 (August 2007): 160–77.

Austin, Norman. *Helen of Troy and Her Shameless Phantom.* Ithaca: Cornell University Press, 1994.

Awkward-Rich, Cameron. *The Terrible We: Thinking with Trans Maladjustment.* Durham, NC: Duke University Press, 2022.

Baker, Houston A., Jr. *The Journey Back: Issues in Black Literature and Criticism.* Chicago: University of Chicago Press, 1980.

Baker, Peter. *Obdurate Brilliance: Exteriority and the Modern Long Poem.* Gainesville: University of Florida Press, 1991.

Baraka, Amiri. *The LeRoi Jones/Amiri Baraka Reader.* Edited by William J. Harris. New York: Thunder's Mouth Press, 1991.

Barbour, Susan. "The Origins of the Prose Captions in H.D.'s *Helen in Egypt*." *Review of English Studies* 63, no. 260 (June 2012): 466–90.

Barletta, Vincent. *Rhythm: Forms and Dispossession*. Chicago: University of Chicago Press, 2020.

Berlant, Lauren. *The Female Complaint: The Unfinished Business of Sentimentality in American Culture*. Durham, NC: Duke University Press, 2008.

Bernstein, Charles. *Recalculating*. Chicago: University of Chicago Press, 2013.

Bolden, B. J. *Urban Rage in Bronzeville: Social Commentary in the Poetry of Gwendolyn Brooks, 1945–1960*. Chicago: Third World, 1999.

Brady, Andrea. *Poetry and Bondage: A History and Theory of Lyric Constraint*. Cambridge: Cambridge University Press, 2021.

Bram, Marvin. "The Art of Fugue." *Semiotica* 141, nos. 1–4 (2002): 73–97.

Brooks, Gwendolyn. *Blacks*. Chicago: Third World, 1987.

Brooks, Gwendolyn. *Maud Martha: A Novel*. Chicago: Third World, 1953.

Brooks, Gwendolyn. *Primer for Blacks*. Chicago: Third World, 1991.

Brooks, Gwendolyn. *Report from Part One*. Detroit: Broadside, 1972.

Brown, Wendy. *Politics Out of History*. Princeton, NJ: Princeton University Press, 2001.

Bruns, Gerald L. "On the Conundrum of Form and Material in Adorno's *Aesthetic Theory*." *Journal of Aesthetics and Art Criticism* 66, no. 3 (Summer 2008): 225–35.

Bryant, Marsha, and Mary Ann Eaverly. "Egypto-Modernism: James Henry Breasted, H.D., and the New Past." *Modernism/modernity* 14, no. 3 (2007): 435–53.

Bucknell, Brad. *Literary Modernism and Musical Aesthetics: Pater, Pound, Joyce, and Stein*. Cambridge: Cambridge University Press, 2001.

Bush, Christopher. *Ideographic Modernism: China, Writing, Media*. Oxford: Oxford University Press, 2010.

Butler, Judith. *Bodies That Matter: On the Discursive Limits of "Sex."* New York: Routledge, 1993.

Butler, Judith. *Gender Trouble: Feminism and the Subversion of Identity*. New York: Routledge, 1999.

Butler, Judith. *Undoing Gender*. New York: Routledge, 2004.

Carbery, Matthew. *Phenomenology and the Late Twentieth-Century American Long Poem*. Cham, Switzerland: Palgrave Macmillan, 2019.

Cecire, Natalia. *Experimental: American Literature and the Aesthetics of Knowledge*. Baltimore: Johns Hopkins University Press, 2019.

Cha, Theresa Hak Kyung. *Dictée*. Berkeley: University of California Press, 2001.

Chatlos, Jon. "Automobility and Lyric Poetry: The Mobile Gaze in William Carlos Williams's 'The Right of Way.'" *Journal of Modern Literature* 30, no. 1 (Autumn 2006): 140–54.

Cheng, Anne Anlin. *The Melancholy of Race: Psychoanalysis, Assimilation, and Hidden Grief.* Oxford: Oxford University Press, 2001.

Chisholm, Dianne. *H.D.'s Freudian Poetics: Psychoanalysis in Translation.* Ithaca: Cornell University Press, 1992.

Chuh, Kandice. *The Difference Aesthetics Makes: On the Humanities "After Man."* Durham, NC: Duke University Press, 2019.

Chuh, Kandice. *Imagine Otherwise: On Asian Americanist Critique.* Durham, NC: Duke University Press, 2003.

Coffman, Chris. *Gertrude Stein's Transmasculinity.* Edinburgh: Edinburgh University Press, 2018.

Cohen, Ralph. "History and Genre." *New Literary History* 17, no. 2 (1986): 203–18.

Colesworthy, Rebecca. *Returning the Gift: Modernism and the Thought of Exchange.* Oxford: Oxford University Press, 2018.

Collecott, Diana. *H.D. and Sapphic Modernism: 1910–1950.* Cambridge: Cambridge University Press, 1999.

Conte, Joseph M. *Unending Design: The Forms of Postmodern Poetry.* Ithaca: Cornell University Press, 1991.

Crane, Hart. *The Bridge: An Annotated Edition.* Edited by Lawrence Kramer. New York: Fordham University Press, 2011.

Creeley, Robert. "Robert Creeley in Conversation with Leonard Schwartz." *Jacket 25* (February 2004). http://jacketmagazine.com/25/creeley-iv.html.

Culler, Jonathan. "Lyric, History, and Genre." *New Literary History: A Journal of Theory and Interpretation* 40, no. 4 (Autumn 2009): 879–99.

Culler, Jonathan. *Theory of the Lyric.* Cambridge, MA: Harvard University Press, 2015.

Curry, Renée R. "H.D., Dove, Glück, and Levin: The Poetry of Afroasiatic and White Greece." *Sagetrieb* 19, no. 3 (2006): 173–200.

Dahlen, Beverly. "Notes on Reading Lorine Niedecker." *How(ever)* 1, no. 1 (May 1983): 8–9. http://www.asu.edu/pipercwcenter/how2journal/archive /print_archive/niedecker.html.

de Gennaro, Mara. *Modernism after Postcolonialism: Toward a Nonterritorial Comparative Literature.* Baltimore: Johns Hopkins University Press, 2020.

de Grazia, Margreta. "Sanctioning Voice: Quotation Marks, the Abolition of Torture, and the Fifth Amendment." In *The Construction of Authorship: Textual Appropriation in Law and Literature,* edited by Martha Woodmansee and Peter Jaszi, 281–302. Durham, NC: Duke University Press, 1994.

Debo, Annette. *The American H.D.* Iowa City: University of Iowa Press, 2012.

DeKoven, Marianne. *Rich and Strange: Gender, History, Modernism.* Princeton, NJ: Princeton University Press, 1991.

Dent, Peter, ed. *The Full Note: Lorine Niedecker.* Budleigh Salterton, UK: Interim, 1983.

Derrida, Jacques. *Acts of Literature.* Edited by Derek Attridge. Translated by Avital Ronell. New York: Routledge, 1992.

Dickinson, Emily. *The Poems of Emily Dickinson.* Edited by R. W. Franklin. Cambridge, MA: Belknap Press, 1998.

Dowling, Sarah. "Interpolation, Coherence, History: The Works of Myung Mi Kim." In *Nests and Strangers: On Asian American Women Poets,* edited by Timothy Yu, 9–33. Berkeley, CA: Kelsey Street, 2015.

Dowling, Sarah. *Translingual Poetics: Writing Personhood under Settler Colonialism.* Iowa City: University of Iowa Press, 2018.

Du Bois, W. E. B. *The Souls of Black Folk.* Edited by David W. Blight and Robert Gooding-Williams. Boston: Bedford/St. Martin's, 1997.

DuPlessis, Rachel Blau. *Blue Studios: Poetry and Its Cultural Work.* Tuscaloosa: University of Alabama Press, 2006.

DuPlessis, Rachel Blau. *Genders, Races, and Religious Cultures in Modern American Poetry, 1908–1934.* Cambridge: Cambridge University Press, 2001.

DuPlessis, Rachel Blau. *H.D.: The Career of that Struggle.* Bloomington: Indiana University Press, 1986.

DuPlessis, Rachel Blau. "Lyric and Experimental Long Poems: Intersections." In *Time in Time: Short Poems, Long Poems, and the Rhetoric of North American Avant-Gardism, 1963–2008,* edited by J. Mark Smith, 22–50. Montreal and Kingston, Canada: McGill-Queen's University Press, 2013.

DuPlessis, Rachel Blau, and Peter Quartermain, eds. *The Objectivist Nexus: Essays in Cultural Poetics.* Tuscaloosa: University of Alabama Press, 1999.

Eliot, T. S. "London Letter." *The Dial* 71, no. 2 (August 1921): 213–17.

Encyclopaedia Britannica Films. *Arteries of New York City,* 1941. https://youtu.be/UC9U1ILjaOs. Prelinger Archives, https://archive.org/details/Arteries1941.

Euripides. *Helen.* Translated by Peter Burian. Oxford, UK: Oxbow, 2007.

Fanon, Frantz. *Black Skin, White Masks.* Translated by Charles Lam Markmann. New York: Grove Press, 1967.

Felski, Rita. *The Gender of Modernity.* Cambridge, MA: Harvard University Press, 1995.

Ferreira da Silva, Denise. "Hacking the Subject: Black Feminism and Refusal beyond the Limits of Critique." *philoSOPHIA* 8, no. 1 (Winter 2018): 19–41.

Ferreira da Silva, Denise, and Valentina Desideri. "A Conversation between Valentina Desideri and Denise Ferreira da Silva." Amsterdam: Kunstverein, 2015.

Finberg, Keegan Cook. "American Lyric, American Surveillance, and Claudia Rankine's *Citizen.*" *Contemporary Women's Writing* 15, no. 3 (November 2021): 1–19. https://doi.org/10.1093/cww/vpab037.

Fisher, Maisha T. "'I Don't Want Us to Forget the Fire': The Literacy Activism of Gwendolyn Brooks." In *Black Literate Lives: Historical and Contemporary Perspectives*, 27–54. New York: Routledge, 2009.

Flint, F. S. *The Fourth Imagist: Selected Poems of F. S. Flint*. Edited by Michael Copp. Cranbury, NJ: Fairleigh Dickinson University Press, 2007.

Flint, F. S. "Imagisme." *Poetry* 1, no. 6 (March 1913): 198–200.

Flynn, Richard. "'The Kindergarten of New Consciousness': Gwendolyn Brooks and the Social Construction of Childhood." *African American Review*, 34 (2000): 483–99.

Ford, Karen Jackson. "The Last Quatrain: Gwendolyn Brooks and the Ends of Ballads." *Twentieth Century Literature* 56, no. 3 (Fall 2010): 371–95.

Ford, Karen Jackson. "The Sonnets of Satin-Legs Brooks." *Contemporary Literature* 48, no. 3 (Fall 2007): 345–47.

Foucault, Michel. *Language, Counter-Memory, Practice: Selected Essays and Interviews*. Edited by Donald F. Bouchard. Translated by Bouchard and Sherry Simon. Ithaca: Cornell University Press, 1977.

Fraser, Kathleen. "Alice Notley: February 10–13, 1980." In *Artists and Writers in Residence: 80 Langton Street 1980*, edited by Renny Pritikin with Bob Perelman, 54–74. San Francisco: 80 Langton Street, 1980.

Freud, Sigmund. *Civilization and Its Discontents*. London: Penguin, 2004.

Friedlander, Benjamin. *Simulcast: Four Experiments in Criticism*. Tuscaloosa: University of Alabama Press, 2004.

Friedman, Susan Stanford. "Gender and Genre Anxiety: Elizabeth Barrett Browning and H.D. as Epic Poets." *Tulsa Studies in Women's Literature* 5 (1986): 203–28.

Friedman, Susan Stanford. *Psyche Reborn: The Emergence of H.D*. Bloomington: Indiana University Press, 1981.

Frow, John. *Genre*. New York: Routledge, 2015.

Fuss, Diana. "Interior Chambers: The Emily Dickinson Homestead." *Differences* 10, no. 3 (1998): 1–46.

Gabbin, Joanne V., ed. *The Furious Flowering of African American Poetry*. Charlottesville: University Press of Virginia, 1999.

Garber, Marjorie. " " " (Quotation Marks)." *Critical Inquiry* 25, no. 4 (Summer 1999): 653–79.

Gelpi, Albert. "H.D.: Hilda in Egypt." In *Coming to Light: American Women Poets in the Twentieth Century*, edited by Diane Wood Middlebrook and Marilyn Yalom, 74–91. Ann Arbor: University of Michigan Press, 1985.

Genette, Gérard. *The Architext: An Introduction*. Translated by Jane E. Lewin. Berkeley: University of California Press, 1992.

Gery, John. "Subversive Parody in the Early Poems of Gwendolyn Brooks." *South Central Review* 16, no. 1 (1999): 44–56.

Gibson, Mary Ellis. *Epic Reinvented: Ezra Pound and the Victorians*. Ithaca: Cornell University Press, 1995.

Glaser, Ben. *Modernism's Metronome: Meter and Twentieth-Century Poetics.* Baltimore: Johns Hopkins University Press, 2020.

Glaser, Ben, and Jonathan Culler, eds. *Critical Rhythm: The Poetics of a Literary Life Form.* New York: Fordham University Press, 2019.

Gregory, Eileen. "Euripides and H.D.'s Working Notebook for *Helen in Egypt.*" *Sagetrieb* 14, nos. 1–2 (1995): 83–109.

Gregory, Eileen. *H.D. and Hellenism: Classic Lines.* New York: Cambridge University Press, 1997.

Gregory, Eileen. "H.D. and Translation." In *The Cambridge Companion to H.D.*, edited by Nephie J. Christodoulides and Polina Mackay, 143–58. Cambridge: Cambridge University Press, 2012.

Griffiths, Devin. "The Ecology of Form." *Critical Inquiry* 48, no. 1 (Autumn 2021): 68–93.

Guest, Barbara. *Herself Defined: The Poet H.D. and Her World.* Garden City, NY: Doubleday, 1984.

Harley, John. *William Byrd's Modal Practice.* Aldershot, UK: Ashgate, 2005.

Harney, Stefano, and Fred Moten. *The Undercommons: Fugitive Planning and Black Study.* Wivenhoe, UK: Minor Compositions, 2013.

Hauser, Emily. "'Homer Undone': Homeric Scholarship and the Invention of Female Epic." In *Reading Poetry, Writing Genre: English Poetry and Literary Criticism in Dialogue with Classical Scholarship*, edited by Silvio Bär and Emily Hauser, 151–71. London: Bloomsbury, 2019.

H.D. *Between History and Poetry: The Letters of H.D. and Norman Holmes Pearson.* Edited by Donna Krolik Hollenberg. Iowa City: University of Iowa Press, 1997.

H.D. *Bid Me to Live (A Madrigal).* New York: Dial Press, 1960.

H.D. *Collected Poems 1912–1944.* Edited by Louis L. Martz. New York: New Directions, 1983.

H.D. *Helen in Egypt.* New York: New Directions, 1974.

H.D. "Notes on Euripides." In *Ion: A Play After Euripides*, 132–33. Redding Ridge, CT: Black Swan, 1986.

H.D. *Notes on Thought and Vision and The Wise Sappho.* San Francisco: City Lights, 1982.

H.D. *Paint It Today.* Edited by Cassandra Laity. New York: New York University Press, 1992.

H.D. *Palimpsest.* Carbondale: Southern Illinois University Press, 1968.

H.D. *The Sword Went Out to Sea: Synthesis of a Dream.* Edited by Cynthia Hogue and Julie Vandivere. Gainesville: University Press of Florida, 2007.

H.D. *Tribute to Freud.* New York: McGraw-Hill, 1975.

Hejinian, Lyn. *The Language of Inquiry.* Berkeley: University of California Press, 2000.

Hejinian, Lyn. "Strangeness." In *Artifice and Indeterminacy: An Anthology of New Poetics*, edited by Christopher Beach, 140–54. Tuscaloosa: University of Alabama Press, 1998.

Hobson, Suzanne. "'Living up to Her 'Avant-Guardism': H.D. and the Senescence of Classical Modernism." *Humanities* 8, no. 162 (October 2019): 1–13.

Hollenberg, Donna Krolik. *H.D.: The Poetics of Childbirth and Creativity*. Boston: Northeastern University Press, 1991.

Hošek, Chaviva, and Patricia Parker, eds. *Lyric Poetry: Beyond New Criticism*. Ithaca: Cornell University Press, 1985.

Houglum, Brook. "'Speech Without Practical Locale': Radio and Lorine Niedecker's Aurality." In *Broadcasting Modernism*, edited by Debra Rae Cohen, Michael Coyle, and Jane Lewty, 221–37. Gainesville: University Press of Florida, 2009.

Howe, Susan. "The Liberties." In *The Europe of Trusts*, 147–218. Los Angeles: Sun and Moon, 1990.

Hughes, Langston. *The Collected Works of Langston Hughes*. Vol. 9, *Essays on Art, Race, Politics, and World Affairs*, edited by Christopher C. De Santis. Columbia and London: University of Missouri Press, 2002.

Hughes, Langston. *Selected Poems of Langston Hughes*. New York: Vintage, 1990.

Hull, Jeff. "The Noises of Nature." *New York Times*, February 18, 2007. https://www.nytimes.com/2007/02/18/magazine/18wwlnessay.t.html.

Hunter, Walt. *Forms of a World: Contemporary Poetry and the Making of Globalization*. New York: Fordham University Press, 2019.

ife, fahima. *Maroon Choreography*. Durham, NC: Duke University Press, 2021.

Jackson, Virginia. *Before Modernism: Inventing American Lyric*. Princeton, NJ: Princeton University Press, 2023.

Jackson, Virginia. *Dickinson's Misery: A Theory of Lyric Reading*. Princeton, NJ, and Oxford, UK: Princeton University Press, 2005.

Jackson, Virginia. "Who Reads Poetry?" *PMLA* 123, no. 1 (2008): 181–87.

Jackson, Virginia, and Yopie Prins, eds. *The Lyric Theory Reader: A Critical Anthology*. Baltimore: Johns Hopkins University Press, 2014.

Jaji, Tsitsi. "Classic." In *A New Vocabulary for Global Modernism*, edited by Eric Hayot and Rebecca L. Walkowitz, 59–74. New York: Columbia University Press, 2016.

Jansen, Michelle C. "Exchange and the Eidolon: Analyzing Forgiveness in Euripides's *Helen*." *Comparative Literature Studies* 49, no. 3 (2012): 327–47.

Jarvis, Simon. "What Is Historical Poetics?" In *Theory Aside*, edited by Jason Potts and Daniel Stout, 97–116. Durham, NC: Duke University Press, 2014.

Jaussen, Paul. *Writing in Real Time: Emergent Poetics from Whitman to the Digital*. Cambridge: Cambridge University Press, 2017.

Javadizadeh, Kamran. "The Atlantic Ocean Breaking on Our Heads: Claudia Rankine, Robert Lowell, and the Whiteness of the Lyric Subject." *PMLA* 134, no. 3 (2019): 475–90.

Jeon, Joseph Jonghyun. *Racial Things, Racial Forms: Objecthood in Avant-Garde Asian American Poetry*. Iowa City: University of Iowa Press, 2012.

Jimoh, A. Yẹmisi. "Double Consciousness, Modernism, and Womanist Themes in Gwendolyn Brooks's 'The Anniad.'" *MELUS: Journal of the Society for the Study of the Multi-Ethnic Literature of the United States* 23, no. 3 (1998): 167–86.

Johnson, Barbara. *A World of Difference*. Baltimore: Johns Hopkins University Press, 1987.

Kane, Daniel, ed. *Don't Ever Get Famous: Essays on New York Writing after the New York School*. Champaign, IL: Dalkey Archive Press, 2006.

Keene, John. "'White Silences': The Lyric Theory Reader Panel @ ACLA 2014." http://jstheater.blogspot.com/2014/04/white-silences-lyric-theory-reader.html.

Keller, Jim. *Writing Plural Worlds in Contemporary US Poetry: Innovative Identities*. New York: Palgrave Macmillan, 2009.

Keller, Lynn. *Forms of Expansion: Recent Long Poems by Women*. Chicago: University of Chicago Press, 1997.

Keller, Lynn. *Recomposing Ecopoetics: North American Poetry of the Self-Conscious Anthropocene*. Charlottesville and London: University of Virginia Press, 2017.

Keller, Lynn, and Cristanne Miller, eds. *Feminist Measures: Soundings in Poetry and Theory*. Ann Arbor: University of Michigan Press, 1994.

Kim, Myung Mi. *Civil Bound*. Oakland, CA: Omnidawn, 2019.

Kim, Myung Mi. *Commons*. Berkeley: University of California Press, 2002.

Kim, Myung Mi. *Dura*. New York: Nightboat, 2008.

Kim, Myung Mi. "Eight Discourses Between Myung Mi Kim and Divya Victor." *Jacket2*, April 12, 2013. http://jacket2.org/interviews/eight-discourses-between-myung-mi-kim-and-divya-victor.

Kim, Myung Mi. "Generosity as Method: An Interview with Myung Mi Kim." Interview with Yedda Morrison in San Francisco, December 1997. *Electronic Poetry Center*. http://writing.upenn.edu/epc/authors/kim/generosity.html.

Kim, Myung Mi. *Penury*. Richmond, CA: Omnidawn, 2009.

Kim, Myung Mi. *Under Flag*. Berkeley, CA: Kelsey Street, 1991, 1998.

Kinnahan, Linda. *Poetics of the Feminine: Authority and Literary Tradition in William Carlos Williams, Mina Loy, Denise Levertov, and Kathleen Fraser*. Cambridge: Cambridge University Press, 1994.

Kornbluh, Anna. *The Order of Forms: Realism, Formalism, and Social Space*. Chicago: University of Chicago Press, 2019.

Kramer, Jonathan D. "New Temporalities in Music." *Critical Inquiry* 7, no. 3 (Spring 1981): 539–56.

Lacan, Jacques. *Écrits: A Selection.* Translated by Alan Sheridan. New York: Norton, 1977.

LaCapra, Dominick. "History and Genre: Comment." *New Literary History* 17, no. 2 (1986): 219–21.

Laity, Cassandra. *H.D. and the Victorian Fin de Siècle: Gender, Modernism, Decadence.* Cambridge: Cambridge University Press, 1996.

Lankford, J. S. "The Lesson of Canal Zone Sanitation." 1913. Reprinted in "Lessons from the Panama Canal, 100 Years Ago," *Popular Science*, August 19, 2014. https://www.popsci.com/article/technology/lessons-panama -canal-100-years-ago/.

Leong, Michael. *Contested Records: The Turn to Documents in Contemporary North American Poetry.* Iowa City: University of Iowa Press, 2020.

Levine, Caroline. *Forms: Whole, Rhythm, Hierarchy, Network.* Princeton, NJ: Princeton University Press, 2015.

Lewis, Cara L. *Dynamic Form: How Intermediality Made Modernism.* Ithaca: Cornell University Press, 2020.

Li, David Leiwei. *Imagining the Nation: Asian American Literature and Cultural Consent.* Stanford: Stanford University Press, 1998.

Liu, Warren. "Making Common the Commons: Myung Mi Kim's Ideal Subject." In *American Poets in the 21st Century: The New Poetics*, ed. Claudia Rankine and Lisa Sewell, 252–66. Middletown, CT: Wesleyan University Press, 2007.

Lowney, John. *History, Memory, and the Literary Left: Modern American Poetry, 1935–1968.* Iowa City: University of Iowa Press, 2006.

Mackey, Nathaniel. *Blue Fasa.* New York: New Directions, 2015.

Mackey, Nathaniel. "Breath and Precarity." In *Poetics and Precarity*, edited by Myung Mi Kim and Cristanne Miller, 1–30. Albany: SUNY Press, 2018.

Malcolm, Jane. "Hard Women, Hard Modernism: Gendering Modernist Difficulty." PhD diss., University of Pennsylvania, 2009.

Mariani, Paul. *William Carlos Williams: A New World Naked.* New York: McGraw-Hill, 1981.

McCabe, Susan. "Alice Notley's Epic Entry: 'An Ecstasy of Finding Another Way of Being.'" *Antioch Review* 56, no. 3 (Summer 1998): 273–80.

McCaffery, Steve. *North of Intention: Critical Writings 1973–1986.* New York: Roof, 2000.

McGann, Jerome J. *The Romantic Ideology: A Critical Investigation.* Chicago: University of Chicago Press, 1983.

McHale, Brian. *The Obligation Toward the Difficult Whole: Postmodernist Long Poems.* Tuscaloosa: University of Alabama Press, 2004.

McHale, Brian. "Telling Stories Again: On the Replenishment of Narrative in the Postmodernist Long Poem." *The Yearbook of English Studies* 30 (2000): 250–62.

Melhem, D. H. *Gwendolyn Brooks: Poetry and the Heroic Voice.* Lexington: University Press of Kentucky, 1987.

Micir, Melanie. *The Passion Projects: Modernist Women, Intimate Archives, Unfinished Lives.* Princeton, NJ: Princeton University Press, 2019.

Miller, Meredith. "Enslaved to Both These Others: Gender and Inheritance in H.D.'s 'Secret Name: Excavator's Egypt.'" *Tulsa Studies in Women's Literature* 16, no. 1 (Spring 1997): 77–105.

Morris, Adalaide. *How to Live/What to Do: H.D.'s Cultural Poetics.* Chicago: University of Illinois Press, 2003.

Morris, Adalaide, ed. *Sound States: Innovative Poetics and Acoustical Technologies.* Chapel Hill: University of North Carolina Press, 1997.

Moten, Fred. *The Feel Trio.* Tucson, AZ: Letter Machine Editions, 2014.

Moten, Fred. *In the Break: The Aesthetics of the Black Radical Tradition.* Minneapolis: University of Minnesota Press, 2003.

Müller, Timo. *The African American Sonnet: A Literary History.* Jackson: University Press of Mississippi, 2018.

Myrdal, Gunnar. *An American Dilemma: The Negro Problem and American Democracy.* New Brunswick, NJ: Transaction, 2009.

Nardi, Marcia. *The Last Word: Letters between Marcia Nardi and William Carlos Williams.* Edited by Elizabeth Murrie O'Neil. Iowa City: University of Iowa Press, 1994.

Nelson, Maggie. *Women, the New York School, and Other True Abstractions.* Iowa City: University of Iowa Press, 2007.

Nersessian, Anahid. "Notes on Tone: Three American Poets." *New Left Review* 142 (July–August 2023): 55–73.

Ngai, Sianne. *Ugly Feelings.* Cambridge, MA: Harvard University Press, 2005.

Niedecker, Lorine. *"Between Your House and Mine": The Letters of Lorine Niedecker to Cid Corman, 1960 to 1970.* Edited by Lisa Pater Faranda. Durham, NC: Duke University Press, 1986.

Niedecker, Lorine. *Collected Works.* Edited by Jenny Penberthy. Berkeley: University of California Press, 2002.

Niedecker, Lorine. *Niedecker and the Correspondence with Zukofsky 1931–1970.* Edited by Jenny Penberthy. New York: Cambridge University Press, 1993.

Niedecker, Lorine. "The Poetry of Louis Zukofsky." Originally published in *Quarterly Review of Literature* 8, no. 3 (1956): 198–210. Reprinted at Electronic Poetry Center. http://writing.upenn.edu/epc/authors/niedecker/essay1.html.

Nielsen, Aldon L. *Black Chant: Languages of African-American Postmodernism.* Cambridge: Cambridge University Press, 1997.

Nielsen, Aldon L. "Melvin B. Tolson and the Deterritorialization of Modernism." *African American Review* 26, no. 2 (Summer 1992): 241–55.

Nielsen, Aldon L. *Reading Race: White American Poets and the Racial Discourse in the Twentieth Century.* Athens: University of Georgia Press, 1988.

Notley, Alice. *The Descent of Alette.* New York: Penguin, 1996.

Notley, Alice. *Disobedience.* New York: Penguin, 2001.

Notley, Alice. *Doctor Williams' Heiresses.* San Francisco: Tuumba, 1980.

Notley, Alice. "Evident Being: A Conversation with Alice Notley by *KR* poetry editor David Baker." *Kenyon Review*, October 2009. https://kenyonreview.org/conversation/alice-notley.

Notley, Alice. *Songs for the Unborn Second Baby.* New York: United Artists, 1979.

Olson, Charles. "Projective Verse." In *Selected Writings of Charles Olson*, edited by Robert Creeley, 15–26. New York: New Directions, 1966.

O'Meally, Robert G., ed. *The Jazz Cadence of American Culture.* New York: Columbia University Press, 1998.

Painter, Nell Irvin. *The History of White People.* New York: Norton, 2010.

Park, Josephine Nock-Hee. *Apparitions of Asia: Modernist Form and Asian American Poetics.* Oxford: Oxford University Press, 2008.

Park, Josephine Nock-Hee. *Cold War Friendships: Korea, Vietnam, and Asian American Literature.* Oxford: Oxford University Press, 2016.

Pater, Walter. *The Renaissance: Studies in Art and Poetry (The 1893 Text).* Edited by Donald E. Hill. Berkeley: University of California Press, 1980.

Perelman, Bob. *Modernism the Morning After.* Tuscaloosa: University of Alabama Press, 2017.

Perelman, Bob. *The Trouble with Genius: Reading Pound, Joyce, Stein, and Zukofsky.* Berkeley: University of California Press, 1994.

Perloff, Marjorie. "Language Poetry and the Lyric Subject: Ron Silliman's Albany, Susan Howe's Buffalo." *Critical Inquiry* 25, no. 3 (Spring 1999): 405–34.

Perloff, Marjorie. *Poetic License: Essays on Modernist and Postmodernist Lyric.* Evanston: Northwestern University Press, 1990.

Perloff, Marjorie. "Presidential Address 2006: It Must Change." *PMLA* 122, no. 3 (May 2007): 652–62.

Perlow, Seth. *The Poem Electric: Technology and the American Lyric.* Minneapolis: University of Minnesota Press, 2018.

Phillips, Michelle H. "Moving In and Stepping Out: Gwendolyn Brooks's Children at Midcentury." *African American Review* 47, no. 1 (Spring 2014): 145–60.

Plato. *Phaedrus.* Translated by Robin Waterfield. Oxford: Oxford University Press, 2002.

Plato. *Republic.* Translated by Robin Waterfield. Oxford: Oxford University Press, 1998.

Poe, Edgar Allan. *Poems and Essays on Poetry.* Edited by C. H. Sisson. Manchester, UK: Carcanet, 1995.

Ponce de León, Jennifer. *Another Aesthetics Is Possible: Arts of Rebellion in the Fourth World War.* Durham, NC: Duke University Press, 2021.

Posmentier, Sonya. *Cultivation and Catastrophe: The Lyric Ecology of Modern Black Literature.* Baltimore: Johns Hopkins University Press, 2017.

Pound, Ezra. *ABC of Reading.* New York: New Directions, 1960.

Pound, Ezra. *The Cantos of Ezra Pound.* New York: New Directions, 1972.

Pound, Ezra. *Gaudier-Brzeska: A Memoir by Ezra Pound.* London and New York: John Lane, 1916.

Pound, Ezra. *The Literary Essays of Ezra Pound.* Edited by T. S. Eliot. New York: New Directions, 1968.

Pound, Ezra. *Personae: The Shorter Poems.* Edited by Lea Baechler and A. Walton Litz. New York: New Directions, 1990.

Pound, Ezra. *The Pisan Cantos.* Edited by Richard Sieburth. New York: New Directions, 2003.

Pound, Ezra. *The Selected Letters of Ezra Pound 1907–1941.* Edited by D. D. Paige. New York: New Directions, 1971.

Prieto, Eric. *Listening In: Music, Mind, and the Modernist Narrative.* Lincoln and London: University of Nebraska Press, 2002.

Quashie, Kevin. *The Sovereignty of Quiet: Beyond Resistance in Black Culture.* New Brunswick, NJ: Rutgers University Press, 2012.

Ramazani, Jahan. "Poetry and Race: An Introduction." *New Literary History* 50, no. 4 (Autumn 2019): vii–xxxvii.

Ramazani, Jahan. *Poetry of Mourning: The Modern Elegy from Hardy to Heaney.* Chicago: University of Chicago Press, 1994.

Ramazani, Jahan. *A Transnational Poetics.* Chicago: University of Chicago Press, 2009.

Rancière, Jacques. *The Flesh of Words: The Politics of Writing.* Stanford, CA: Stanford University Press, 1998.

Rancière, Jacques. *Mute Speech: Literature, Critical Theory, and Politics.* New York: Columbia University Press, 1998/2011.

Rankine, Claudia. *Citizen: An American Lyric.* Minneapolis: Graywolf, 2014.

Rankine, Claudia. "On Lyric," in "Reading for the New Writing Series, UC San Diego, February 8, 2012." https://writing.upenn.edu/pennsound/x/Rankine.php.

Reed, Anthony. *Freedom Time: The Poetics and Politics of Black Experimental Writing.* Baltimore: Johns Hopkins University Press, 2014.

Rich, Adrienne. *The School Among the Ruins: Poems 2000–2004.* New York: Norton, 2004.

Riley, Denise. *The Words of Selves: Identification, Solidarity, Irony.* Stanford, CA: Stanford University Press, 2000.

Rockstro, William S., George Dyson, William Drabkin, Harold S. Powers, and Julian Rushton. "Cadence." *Grove Music Online*, January 20, 2001. https://doi.org/10.1093/gmo/9781561592630.article.04523.

Ronda, Margaret. *Remainders: American Poetry at Nature's End.* Stanford, CA: Stanford University Press, 2018.

Ronda, Margaret. "'Work and Wait Unwearying': Dunbar's Georgics." *PMLA* 127, no. 4 (October 2012): 863–78.

Rooney, Ellen. "Symptomatic Reading Is a Problem of Form." In *Critique and Postcritique*, edited by Elizabeth S. Anker and Rita Felski, 127–52. Durham, NC: Duke University Press, 2017.

Said, Edward. *Orientalism.* New York: Vintage, 1979.

Saler, Michael. "The 'Medieval Modern' Underground: Terminus of the Avant-Garde." *Modernism/Modernity* 2, no. 1 (1995): 113–44.

Scappettone, Jennifer. "Response to Jennifer Ashton, Bachelorettes, Even: Strategic Embodiment in Contemporary Experimentalism by Women." *Modern Philology* 105, no. 1 (August 2007): 178–84.

Schultz, Kathy Lou. *The Afro-Modernist Epic and Literary History: Tolson, Hughes, Baraka.* New York: Palgrave Macmillan, 2013.

Scott, Chris. "Beyond Theory of the Lyric." *Critical Quarterly* 64, no. 3 (October 2022): 80–106.

Scroggins, Mark. *Louis Zukofsky and the Poetry of Knowledge.* Tuscaloosa: University of Alabama Press, 1998.

Scroggins, Mark. *The Poem of a Life: A Biography of Louis Zukofsky.* Emeryville, CA: Shoemaker Hoard, 2007.

Scroggins, Mark, ed. *Upper Limit Music: The Writing of Louis Zukofsky.* Tuscaloosa: University of Alabama Press, 1997.

Shaw, Lytle. "Framing the Lyric." *American Literary History* 28, no. 2 (Summer 2016): 403–13.

Shelley, Percy Bysshe. "Defence of Poetry." In *Romantic Critical Essays*, edited by David Bromwich, 216–43. Cambridge: Cambridge University Press, 1987.

Shockley, Evie. *Renegade Poetics: Black Aesthetics and Formal Innovation in African American Poetry.* Iowa City: University of Iowa Press, 2011.

Shockley, Evie. *Semiautomatic.* Middletown, CT: Wesleyan University Press, 2017.

Silliman, Ron. "Poetry and the Politics of the Subject: A Bay Area Sampler." *Socialist Review* 88, no. 3 (July–September 1988): 61–81.

Silliman, Ron, Carla Harryman, Lyn Hejinian, Steve Benson, Bob Perelman, and Barrett Watten. "Aesthetic Tendency and the Politics of Poetry: A Manifesto." *Social Text* no. 19/20 (Autumn 1988): 261–75.

Skinner, Jonathan. "Ecopoetics: Outsider Poetries of the Twentieth Century." PhD diss., State University of New York at Buffalo, 2005.

Smethurst, James. *The Black Arts Movement: Literary Nationalism in the 1960s and 1970s*. Chapel Hill: University of North Carolina Press, 2005.

Sohn, Stephen Hong. "'*Experiment* Is Each Scroll of White Pages Joined Together': Reading Punctuation, Mathematics, and Science in Myung Mi Kim's *Dura*." *College Literature* 42, no. 4 (Fall 2015): 648–82.

Song, Min Hyoung. *Climate Lyricism*. Durham, NC: Duke University Press, 2022.

Stalter-Pace, Sunny. *Underground Movements: Modern Culture on the New York Subway*. Amherst: University of Massachusetts Press, 2013.

Stein, Gertrude. *Gertrude Stein: Selections*. Edited by Joan Retallack. Berkeley: University of California Press, 2008.

Stein, Gertrude. *Picasso: The Complete Writings*. Edited by Edward Burns. Boston: Beacon Press, 1970.

Sullivan, James D. "Killing John Cabot and Publishing Black: Gwendolyn Brooks's 'Riot.'" *African American Review*, 36 (2002): 557–69.

Terada, Rei. "After the Critique of Lyric." *PMLA* 123, no. 1 (January 2008): 195–200.

Thomas, Lorenzo. *Extraordinary Measures: Afrocentric Modernism and Twentieth-Century American Poetry*. Tuscaloosa: University of Alabama Press, 2000.

Thoreau, Henry David. *Thoreau: Political Writings*. Edited by Nancy L. Rosenblum. Cambridge: Cambridge University Press, 1996.

Timms, Andrew. "Modernism's Moment of Plenitude." In *The Modernist Legacy: Essays on New Music*, edited by Björn Heile, 13–24. Farnham, UK: Ashgate, 2009.

Tolson, Melvin B. *Harlem Gallery: Book One, The Curator*. New York: Twayne, 1965.

Tolson, Melvin B. *"Harlem Gallery" and Other Poems of Melvin B. Tolson*. Edited by Raymond Nelson. Charlottesville and London: University Press of Virginia, 1999.

Tsur, Reuven. "Rhyme and Cognitive Poetics." *Poetics Today* 17 (1996): 55–87.

Twitchell-Waas, Jeffrey. "Seaward: H.D.'s *Helen in Egypt* as a Response to Pound's *Cantos*." *Twentieth Century Literature* 44, no. 4 (Winter 1998): 464–83.

Tyson, Timothy B. *The Blood of Emmett Till*. New York: Simon and Schuster, 2017.

United States Office of Indian Affairs. *Annual Report of the Commissioner of Indian Affairs, for the Year 1886*. Washington, D.C.: G.P.O., [1886]. http://digital.library.wisc.edu/1711.dl/History.AnnRep86.

Wang, Dorothy. "Response to [Julia] Bloch." In "Symposium: *Thinking Its Presence*, by Dorothy Wang." Edited by Michael Leong. *Syndicate*, August 19, 2020. https://syndicate.network/symposia/literature/thinking-its -presence.

Wang, Dorothy. *Thinking Its Presence: Form, Race, and Subjectivity in Contemporary Asian American Poetry*. Stanford, CA: Stanford University Press, 2014.

Warner, Michael. *Publics and Counterpublics*. New York: Zone, 2002.

Weheliye, Alex G. *Habeas Viscus: Racializing Assemblages, Biopolitics, and Black Feminist Theories of the Human*. Durham, NC: Duke University Press, 2014.

Wellek, René. "Genre Theory, the Lyric, and *Erlebnis*." In Jackson and Prins, *The Lyric Theory Reader*, 40–52.

White, Gillian. *Lyric Shame: The "Lyric" Subject of Contemporary American Poetry*. Cambridge, MA: Harvard University Press, 2014.

Wilkinson, John. *The Lyric Touch: Essays on the Poetry of Excess*. Cambridge: Salt, 2007.

Williams, William Carlos. *The Collected Poems of William Carlos Williams*. Edited by Christopher MacGowan. 2 vols. New York: New Directions, 1991.

Williams, William Carlos. *I Wanted to Write a Poem: The Autobiography of the Works of a Poet*. Edited by Edith Heal. Boston: Beacon Press, 1958.

Williams, William Carlos. *Imaginations*. Edited by Webster Schott. New York: New Directions, 1971.

Williams, William Carlos. *Paterson*. Edited by Christopher MacGowan. New York: New Directions, 1995.

Williams, William Carlos. "Poetry and the Making of Language." *The New Republic* 133, no. 18 (October 31, 1955): 16–17.

Williams, William Carlos. *Something to Say: William Carlos Williams on Younger Poets*. Edited by James E. B. Breslin. New York: New Directions, 1985.

Willis, Elizabeth. "A Public History of the Dividing Line: H.D., the Bomb, and the Roots of the Postmodern." *Arizona Quarterly* 63, no. 1 (2007): 81–108.

Willis, Elizabeth, ed. *Radical Vernacular: Lorine Niedecker and the Poetics of Place*. Iowa City: University of Iowa Press, 2008.

Willis, Elizabeth. "Work This Thing." *Boston Review*, July 15, 2015. http:// bostonreview.net/poetry/elizabeth-willis-fred-moten-little-edges-feel-trio.

Witte, Sarah E. "H.D.'s Recension of *The Egyptian Book of the Dead* in *Palimpsest*." *Sagetrieb* 8, nos. 1–2 (Spring and Fall 1989): 121–47.

Woods, Tim. *The Poetics of the Limit: Ethics and Politics in Modern and Contemporary American Poetry*. New York: Palgrave Macmillan, 2002.

Wright, George T. *Hearing the Measures: Shakespearean and Other Inflections.* Madison: University of Wisconsin Press, 2001.

Wright, Stephen Caldwell, ed. *On Gwendolyn Brooks: Reliant Contemplation.* Ann Arbor: University of Michigan Press, 1996.

Wynter, Sylvia. "The Ceremony Found: Towards the Autopoetic Turn/ Overturn, Its Autonomy of Human Agency and Extraterritoriality of (Self-)Cognition." In *Black Knowledges/Black Struggles: Essays in Critical Epistemologies,* edited by Jason R. Ambroise and Sabine Broeck, 184–252. Liverpool, UK: Liverpool University Press, 2015.

Wynter, Sylvia. "On Disenchanting Discourse: 'Minority' Literary Criticism and Beyond." *Cultural Critique* no. 7 (Autumn 1987): 207–44.

Yu, Timothy. "Form and Identity in Language Poetry and Asian American Poetry." *Contemporary Literature* 41, no. 3 (Autumn 2000): 422–61.

Yu, Timothy. *Race and the Avant-Garde: Experimental and Asian American Poetry Since 1965.* Stanford, CA: Stanford University Press, 2007.

Zukofsky, Louis. *"A."* Berkeley: University of California Press, 1978.

Zukofsky, Louis. *All: The Collected Short Poems, 1923–1964.* New York: Norton, 1965.

Zukofsky, Louis. *Complete Short Poetry.* Baltimore: Johns Hopkins University Press, 1991.

Zukofsky, Louis. *Prepositions+: The Collected Critical Essays.* Hanover, NH: University Press of New England, 2000.

Zukofsky, Louis. *Selected Poems.* Edited by Charles Bernstein. New York: Library of America, 2006.

INDEX

Bodies on the Line:
Performance and the
Sixties Poetry Reading
by Raphael Allison

Industrial Poetics:
Demo Tracks for a Mobile Culture
by Joe Amato

Lyric Trade:
Reading the Subject in the
Postwar Long Poem
by Julia Bloch

What Are Poets For?:
An Anthropology of Contemporary
Poetry and Poetics
by Gerald L. Bruns

Reading Duncan Reading:
Robert Duncan and the
Poetics of Derivation
edited by Stephen Collis
and Graham Lyons

Postliterary America:
From Bagel Shop Jazz
to Micropoetries
by Maria Damon

Among Friends:
Engendering the Social Site of Poetry
edited by Anne Dewey
and Libbie Rifkin

Translingual Poetics:
Writing Personhood Under
Settler Colonialism
by Sarah Dowling

Purple Passages:
Pound, Eliot, Zukofsky, Olson, Creeley,
and the Ends of Patriarchal Poetry
by Rachel Blau DuPlessis

On Mount Vision:
Forms of the Sacred in
Contemporary American Poetry
by Norman Finkelstein

Writing Not Writing:
Poetry, Crisis, and Responsibility
by Tom Fisher

Form, Power, and Person
in Robert Creeley's Life and Work
edited by Stephen Fredman
and Steve McCaffery

Redstart:
An Ecological Poetics
by Forrest Gander
and John Kinsella

Jorie Graham:
Essays on the Poetry
edited by Thomas Gardner
University of Wisconsin Press,
2005

The Collaborative Artist's Book:
Evolving Ideas in Contemporary
Poetry and Art
by Alexandra J. Gold

Gary Snyder and the Pacific Rim:
Creating Countercultural
Community
by Timothy Gray